**David Craig** has spent most of his career as a management consultant working for and competing against some of the world's best and worst management and IT systems consultancies. He has helped to sell consulting to almost 100 organizations in 15 countries across Europe, Asia and the US, as well as the British public sector. He is the author of the controversial bestsellers *Rip-Off! The Scandalous Inside Story of the Management Consulting Money Machine* and *Plundering the Public Sector* (Constable, 2006). He has an MA from Cambridge and an MBA from Warwick Business School.

**Praise for *Plundering the Public Sector***

'A gripping and important book, one that is impossible to read without becoming angry.'

*New Statesman*

'If I were Sir Gus O'Donnell or Gordon Brown, or indeed Tony Blair, I would invite Craig into Whitehall to reveal the many and ingenious ways in which taxpayers have been compelled to provide welfare for the wealthy.'

Nick Cohen, *Observer*

'Craig writes with ... passionate disgust and with rich detail.'

*Management Today*

# SQUANDERED

How Gordon Brown is wasting over
one trillion pounds of our money

David Craig

CONSTABLE • LONDON

Constable & Robinson Ltd
3 The Lanchesters
162 Fulham Palace Road
London W6 9ER
www.constablerobinson.com

First published in the UK by Constable,
an imprint of Constable & Robinson Ltd, 2008

A copy of the British Library Cataloguing in
Publication Data is available from the British Library.

ISBN 978-1-84529-832-6

Printed and bound in the EU

1 3 5 7 9 10 8 6 4 2

This book is dedicated to the memory of Paul Steane.
Unfortunately, I never had the chance to meet you.
Nevertheless it was the story of how appallingly you were
treated by NHS hospitals, bureaucrats and regulators that
gave me the idea of writing *Squandered*.
I hope some good comes from my book.

# CONTENTS

# PART I

# SQUANDERING OUR MONEY

Health........................ £269,200,000,000

Education................... £185,700,000,000

Welfare...................... £343,300,000,000

Police/Public Order... £80,200,000,000

Others........................ £350,700,000,000

Total......................... £1,229,100,000,000

# CHAPTER I

# HOW TO SPEND OVER A TRILLION POUNDS

## BACK WHERE WE STARTED?

If you had left the UK just after the 1997 election which swept New Labour to power and then returned in Autumn 2007 to hear Gordon Brown's first speech as party leader to a Labour conference, you would have been struck by a certain familiarity in what was being said.

In 1997, Tony Blair pledged he would be 'tough on crime, tough on the causes of crime'. A decade later, Prime Minister Brown promised to 'punish crime and prevent it by dealing with the root causes'. In 1997 we were told that education would be the Government's 'number one priority' and that we would be given schools 'which identify the distinct abilities of individual pupils'. In 2007, Brown told us that 'education is my passion' as he promised schools where 'not one size fits all but responding to individual needs'. Blair's education system would, he said, ensure 'every 16- and 17-year-old on the road to a proper qualification by the year 2000'. A decade on, Brown announced that it was his ambition for 'every teenager to have a good qualification'. Blair said the UK should 'develop the potential of all our people'; in 2007, Brown told us 'we must unlock the talents of all of the people'. In 1997, New Labour pledged 'we will relieve the police of unnecessary bureaucratic burdens to get more officers back on the beat'. In 2007, Brown committed to 'cutting paperwork so that officers stay on the beat and do not waste time returning to the station to fill out forms'. Blair told us, 'we will tackle the unacceptable level of anti-social behaviour on our streets', while Brown insisted he would 'take action against anti-social behaviour'. In 1997 Blair pledged 'we will get the unemployed from welfare to work'. In 2007 we were told by Brown that we would 'advance to a Britain of full employment in our generation'. In 1997, before he surrendered both our money and sovereignty to the European Union (EU), Blair had assured us 'we will stand up for Britain's interests in Europe'. As Brown prepared to push through the shabby EU 'Constitution by another name', he echoed Blair's tough talk: 'at all times we will stand up for the British national interest'. In 1997 Blair had promised pensioners 'everyone is entitled to dignity in retirement'. Brown was still singing from the same song-sheet in 2007: 'I want to ensure respect, dignity and security in old age'. In 1997 Blair promised us 'a Government that seeks to restore trust in politics in this country' because 'I want to renew faith in politics'. Ten years on Brown vowed to give us 'a new kind of politics … in order to rebuild trust in the British people in our democracy' (see Figure 1).

However, Brown's 2007 speech was not all just a 'cut-and-paste' job of what had been promised ten years before. There were differences between what these two leaders said – some topics had changed during the intervening ten years. In 2007, Brown pledged a 'deep clean of all our wards' to deal with MRSA (Methicillin Resistant Staphylococcus Aureus) and C Diff (Clostridium Difficile). In 1997 there had been no need for New Labour to mention hospital-acquired infections as they were not such a problem back then. By 2007, due to growing public anxiety about New Labour's ten years of almost uncontrolled immigration, Brown had to announce the introduction of immigration controls. Moreover, following the fiasco of the Home Office allowing dangerous foreign criminals to stay in the UK, a stern-jawed Brown now sombrely threatened, 'but let me be clear any newcomer to Britain who is caught selling drugs or using guns

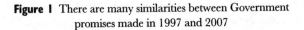

**Figure 1** There are many similarities between Government
promises made in 1997 and 2007

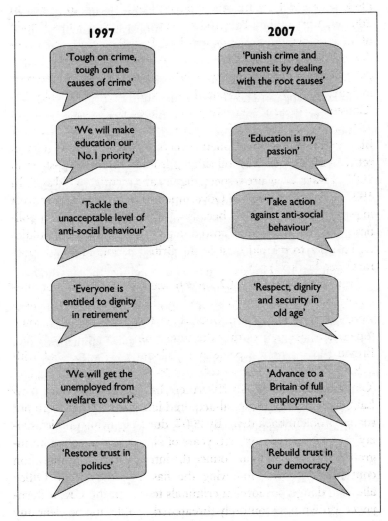

will be thrown out'. In making this statement, it possibly slipped the Prime Minister's mind that the European Treaty/Constitution that he was pantingly eager to sign would make it almost impossible to deport any European criminals as they would have a right to freedom of movement within the EU, and almost equally as difficult to chuck out non-EU criminals as they would be largely protected by EU Human Rights legislation.

There were other differences too. In 2007, after New Labour had set up the Scottish Parliament and Welsh Assembly, Brown had to keep repeating how he was 'proud to be British' and how we all shared 'British values'. In 2007 Brown expressed sympathy for those being killed in New Labour's new wars: 'we mourn those who have been lost and we honour all those who in distant places of danger give so much to our country'. There was no need to do that in 1997 as we were not at war with anybody. Also, amusingly, in 2007 Brown paid special tribute to those who had fought the recent outbreak of foot and mouth disease: 'During the outbreak this summer, our vets, scientists and public officials in DEFRA cancelled their holidays'. The only problem was that it was the Government's own bungling officials who had contributed to the outbreak in the first place.

However, perhaps the most important difference between 1997 and 2007 is that during the last decade, this Government has used over £1 trillion of our money (approximately £1,229,100,000,000) implementing its 1997 promises to transform our hospitals, schools, police, pensions and social services. Yet by late 2007, after this vast, almost unimaginable sum had been spent, the Government seemed to be giving us pretty much the same commitments that it had made over ten years earlier.

## THE NEW DAWN

There has seldom been a General Election victory that has been as welcome as New Labour's May 1997 landslide which ended

18 years of Conservative rule. This was not just a change of government; it felt more like the beginning of a new age. In their early years, the Tories had some admirable successes. On the home front, they managed to break trade-union power and encourage a new spirit of entrepreneurialism. Abroad, Mrs Thatcher bludgeoned the EU into agreeing the British budget rebate, she was widely respected as an international stateswoman and the Falklands victory rekindled a sense of national pride. However, the Tories also gave us two of the worst recessions of the last half century, with unemployment going over three million. Many of our traditional industries, particularly car manufacturing, coal mining and steel, were decimated. Billions of pounds were made by a few fortunate, well-connected insiders from the privatization of the railways and utilities like water, gas and electricity. Although the Tories did actually increase public-sector spending during their last few years in power, many people had the impression that our public services were being underfunded – for example, waiting lists for hospital operations appeared to get ever longer and almost every winter there would be hospital bed shortages. Black Wednesday all but destroyed the Tories' reputation for economic competence and, by the final years of the Major administration, the Tories seemed to have lost all sense of direction and had descended into almost weekly outbreaks of infighting and sleaze. In 1997 the British people wanted change and this aspiration seemed to be embodied by the young, charismatic Blair with his New Labour and their promises to revolutionize our neglected public services and restore our faith in our political processes and our government.

## WISE SPENDERS, NOT BIG SPENDERS

When it put itself up for election in 1997, New Labour was keen to portray itself as being a future government that we could trust with our money. Its 1997 manifesto poured scorn on the

Conservative administration's wastefulness: 'The myth that the solution to every problem is increased spending has been comprehensively dispelled under the Conservatives. Spending has risen. But more spending has brought neither fairness nor less poverty.'

For New Labour, what was important was not how much money it spent, but rather ensuring that it was well spent: 'The level of public spending is no longer the best measure of the effectiveness of government action in the public interest. It is what the money is actually spent on that counts more than how much money is spent.' New Labour politicians promised a new approach where they would be 'wise spenders, not big spenders'. Nevertheless, in the 11 years between May 1997 and April 2008, the amount of money that this Government will have taken from us in taxes and spent on public services will have increased by over 80 per cent (equal to about 55 per cent when inflation is taken into account) (see Figure 2).

In health, it will have spent around £269 billion more than if spending had been kept at 1997 levels. In education, the figure is over £185 billion. In policing and justice, there is another £80 billion, while in social security benefits there is a further massive

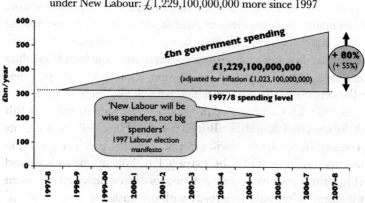

**Figure 2** Government spending has increased by over 80% under New Labour: £1,229,100,000,000 more since 1997

£343 billion, in spite of sustained economic growth and falling unemployment. Then with defence, housing, the EU and other services, we can add on about £350 billion more. All in all, New Labour will have spent comfortably over £1 trillion – £1,229,100,000,000 extra on public services (equivalent to about £1,023,100,000,000 after inflation is taken into account): around £50,000 per household. If New Labour stays in power for its current full five-year term until 2010, this figure of extra spending will be moving effortlessly upwards past £1.5 trillion towards £1,700,000,000,000.

So what have we got for the extra trillion or so of our money that the Government has spent on our behalf? Have the politicians and civil service bosses selflessly burnt the midnight oil labouring to bring us schools and hospitals that are the best in the world; a safe society with dynamic effective policing and a falling crime rate; a simplified and equitable tax system; contented pensioners whiling out their twilight years in financially secure contentment; increased social mobility through greater opportunities for the less well-off; and balanced and stable immigration that benefits both our country and the new arrivals?

Or has the Government overseen a situation where the politicians and the bureaucrats have just squandered most of our hard-earned cash in a sorry spectacle of ever-shifting policies, apparent stupidity and inveterate incompetence that is probably unequalled in British history? And in doing so, have they created a political and managerial culture where mistakes are never admitted, failings are always covered up and mind-boggling bungling is rewarded by promotion, honours and generous inflation-proof pensions for which we will also have to pay?

In 1997 this Government promised, 'New Labour will establish a new trust on tax with the British people'. How well has it kept its promise? In *Squandered*, I will examine how the politicians and the bureaucrats have spent the extra £1 trillion of our money and what British taxpayers have got, or more often have not got, from our rulers' admirable generosity with our cash.

# CHAPTER 2

# THE NHS CAN DAMAGE YOUR HEALTH

With a budget of over £95 billion in 2007–8, the National Health Service (NHS) has the largest budget of any government department. Over the last 11 years, the Government has more than doubled spending on the NHS (equivalent to a rise of around 87 per cent once inflation is taken into account) – a significantly greater increase than in any other area. So it is in the NHS that we can best judge the success or otherwise of the money the politicians and the bureaucrats have spent on our behalf.

When New Labour came to power, it embarked on an ambitious programme of reforms aimed at improving standards in the NHS and making it more responsive to patients. This was based on the Government's 1998 White Paper with the ambitious title 'A First Class Service – Quality in the New NHS'. New Labour has had some successes – spending on health has been brought up to 7.3 per cent of national income, closer to the European average; around 200,000 extra staff have been employed; the Government claims waiting lists have been reduced by 25 per cent from 1,158,000 to 857,000; we no longer have winter bed shortages or patients lying in A&E for eight hours or more; and many new hospitals have been built. However, useful as these may be, the primary job of the NHS is not to employ as many people as possible or to build large numbers of hospitals: it is to improve health and to save lives. So we should judge the Government's management of our health service on whether its

11 years of hugely increased spending have made it safer for us ordinary taxpayers to go into our hospitals and whether we are now more likely to be cured or harmed by our hospitals.

## THE UNSEEN SLAUGHTERHOUSE

According to the NHS's own estimates, 34,000 people a year now die unnecessarily in today's NHS hospitals.[1] Other calculations come up with over 40,000 unnecessary deaths a year.[2] However, even taking the NHS's 'low' number, this means that about 100 people are now dying unnecessarily in our hospitals every single day of the year. This is an awful lot of wasted lives and devastated families. Compare this to Iraq where the United Nations estimated 35,000 people were killed in violence in 2006, and that was called a 'civil war'. Moreover, the NHS admits that in its hospitals another 25,000 people are unnecessarily permanently disabled every year.

For cancer and strokes, the UK now has some of the worst survival rates in Europe. Cancer survival rates are around 20 per cent higher in countries like France, Spain, Germany and Italy than they are in the UK. The Government would claim that its NHS Cancer Plan, published in 2000, is improving UK survival rates. However, the UK rates are only increasing at around the same speed as those of other countries as new treatments become available, so there is still a large gap between our survival rates and those of comparable countries. Many British cancer sufferers have to wait months for scans and treatments that are provided in Europe and the US within two to three days, and the UK is now around 14th out of 17 European countries in terms of survival five years after cancer is diagnosed. Moreover, the UK's rate of deaths from strokes is over 30 per cent higher than that of most other EU countries. In an international study of 'mortality amenable to healthcare'[3] the UK came last out of the 19 countries studied, and reasonably reliable estimates suggest that at least 30,000 (over 80 a day) of the over 200,000 people who die from cancer or strokes each year would survive if they were treated in any other Northern European country rather than by our NHS.

The differences between the rates of hospital-acquired infections in our health service compared to those of some of our European neighbours are even more striking. We have about 300,000 cases of hospital-acquired infections each year – about 50 times higher than some other European countries. Two of these infections, MRSA and C Diff, have been particularly prominent in the news. Although the NHS has increased the effort to document cases, it is difficult to find reliable figures as recording methods have changed and many cases are not reported at all. However, from the information that is available, it seems that cases of MRSA more than doubled from 1997 to 2004 to over 7,200 a year.[4] Faced with public concern about rising MRSA infection rates, in November 2004 Health Secretary John Reid pledged to drastically reduce MRSA rates by 2008: 'I have made it clear that lowering rates of healthcare-acquired infections is a top priority. I expect MRSA bloodstream infection rates to be halved by 2008.'[5]

Following numerous NHS campaigns, MRSA rates did start to level off and then fall slightly. After a slight decrease (a drop of around 2 per cent) by the end of 2006, Health Minister Lord Hunt announced, 'We are now starting to see significant reductions in rates of MRSA infections'.[6] The level then fell again, possibly by up to 10 per cent by the end of 2007. Given the more than 100 per cent increase since New Labour started reforming the NHS, this 10 to 12 per cent drop could seem quite modest in comparison. Moreover, while playing up its MRSA 'success' the Government has tended to be less loquacious about the explosion in the number of cases of the much more unpleasant and deadly C Diff (see Figure 3).[7]

Even more serious than hospital-acquired infection rates are the resultant numbers of deaths. In the UK today, someone in an

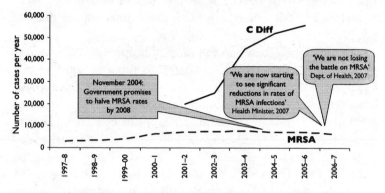

**Figure 3** The Government has talked up its 'success' against MRSA, but the more dangerous C Diff is rising rapidly

NHS hospital catches MRSA or C Diff every 10 minutes and someone dies from one of them every 80 minutes. The number of deaths from both MRSA and C Diff seems to have gone up massively under this Government (see Figure 4) and now many more people in the UK die unnecessarily from these two hospital-acquired infections (6,500) than are killed on our roads (around 3,000).

While we now have over 6,500 people a year (about 120 a week) dying from hospital-acquired infections, we would only have 100 deaths a year (just two a week) if we could match the levels of some other Northern European countries. The Government claims that the rise in deaths is just a result of better reporting; however, many experts believe that the reported numbers are significantly less than the real figures because, partially due to pressure from the Department of Health to show that infection rates are under control, hospital managers are encouraging doctors not to mention either MRSA or C Diff as a cause of death even when they are major contributory factors. Many people, when questioning why relatives died in hospital, have discovered that the real cause was a hospital-acquired infection even though this was not stated on the death certificate. This was one of the major reasons for bereaved families contacting the Patients'

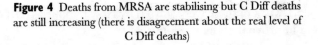

**Figure 4** Deaths from MRSA are stabilising but C Diff deaths are still increasing (there is disagreement about the real level of C Diff deaths)

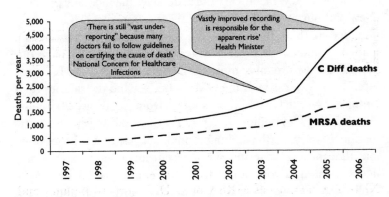

Association: 'Inaccurate reporting on death certificates is a constant feature of calls to our helpline. Bereaved relatives should not have to fight for accuracy, doctors have a duty to provide it.'[8]

Given that C Diff kills over twice as many people as MRSA, a cynic might be tempted to suggest that the rates of MRSA have started to fall, not because of the Government's brilliant management of the NHS, but because thousands of patients are catching and dying from the more serious and more deadly C Diff before they even get the chance to become infected by MRSA. To make matters even worse, the UK is now being invaded by a new and more virulent strain of MRSA, called PVL MRSA. This destroys white blood cells, leaving the immune system too weak to fight the infection. Victims usually get pneumonia, high temperatures and start coughing up blood. If PVL MRSA spreads to the lungs, about three-quarters of people who catch it die.

## BRING ON THE BUREAUCRATS

Hundreds of millions of pounds a year of our money goes to various bureaucracies to ensure that we receive quality care from the NHS. Most of these were started by New Labour as part of its plan to improve the UK's healthcare.

One of the few healthcare bureaucracies that actually predates New Labour is the General Medical Council (GMC). It was founded in 1858. Its motto is the very fine-sounding 'protecting patients, guiding doctors'. As rates of unnecessary deaths in our hospitals have probably more than tripled during New Labour's decade in power, so has the GMC's budget and the salaries of its employees – the GMC's costs shot up from just over £20 million in 1997 to £72.6 million by 2007. Yet the rapidly rising numbers of unnecessary deaths in our hospitals suggest that it is not obvious that this eye-watering 300 per cent increase in bureaucracy has benefited anyone apart from the employees of the GMC. Following Doctor Harold Shipman's murder of about 215 patients, the 2004 enquiry into the GMC accused it of being self-serving, overly-secretive and all too ready to look after its own at the expense of patients.[9] The president of the GMC insisted that there was no need for him to resign and said, 'We need to learn the lessons from the past. Perhaps we were once like an old boy's club but that is absolutely not the case now.'[10] The Health Secretary promised, 'We will consider carefully the recommendations Dame Janet [Smith] makes for further reform, and the implications of her recommendations for other regulatory bodies.'[11] However, over three years later, anybody who tries to make a complaint to the GMC about a doctor's performance or a relative's death will still find themselves deluged by delays, bureaucratic hurdles, unnecessary paperwork and blocked by continuous stonewalling and excuses for inaction. In spite of its claims that it has implemented reforms, little to nothing seems to have changed in the way the GMC manages to avoid taking action on most patient complaints.

We also have the Health Protection Agency (HPA) to look after our well-being. This was set up by New Labour in 2003 'to provide an integrated approach to protecting UK public health'. The HPA has certainly been effective at spending our money. Its total costs increased by 40 per cent, from £180 million in 2004 to £252 million in 2007, and the number of staff went up from 2,518 to 3,042. The HPA produces a vast amount of presumably valuable literature about almost any medical topic, including Athlete's Foot, Cosmic Rays and Dengue Fever. It has also produced an awful lot of guidance about reducing hospital-acquired infections such as MRSA and C Diff. In the meantime, these infections have claimed over 20,000 British lives. During this time, the death toll would have been less than 400 had these victims been living in countries like Holland, Denmark or Sweden, even though they do not have the benefit of the HPA's vaunted 'integrated approach to protecting UK public health'.

The Healthcare Commission (HC), set up in 2004, is another of New Labour's big ideas for improving our healthcare. Perhaps someone envisaged the organization's likely effect on healthcare when it was decided that the HC would come into being on 1 April. The HC has been slightly more prudent than the HPA – between 2004 and 2007, it increased its spending of our money by about 30 per cent to a mere £80.3 million a year. The HC's motto is 'Inspecting, improving, informing' and it has an inspiring mission statement for its 500 plus staff: 'The Healthcare Commission is committed to driving improvement in the quality of both the NHS and independent healthcare services and to making sure that patients are at the centre of everything we do.'[12] One of the key focuses of the HC's work since its inception has been getting to grips with hospital-acquired infections, whose incidence and mortality rates have hugely and relentlessly increased since the HC started producing documents about how to go about tackling them. No doubt, over the next few years the HC will demand ever greater amounts of our money to continue its demonstrably ineffectual inspecting and report-writing on our behalf.

Monitor also seems to like inspecting things for the benefit of patients. Set up by New Labour in January 2004, its mission is 'To operate a transparent and effective regulatory framework that incentivises NHS foundation trusts to be professionally managed and financially strong and capable of delivering innovative services that respond to patients and commissioners.'[13] Its chairman earned over £205,000 in 2006–7 (around £20,000 more than the Prime Minister) and it spends about £13 million of our money a year supposedly regulating NHS foundation trusts so they will provide better healthcare to us.

Then there is the Nursing and Midwifery Council (NMC). Yet another New Labour invention, the NMC was set up by Parliament in 2002 in order 'to protect the public by ensuring that nurses and midwives provide high standards of care'. Its motto is also inspiring: 'protecting the public through professional standards'. The NMC has been comparatively restrained in its use of our money. It has increased its own budgets by about 16 per cent to £23.7 million in the first four years of its existence and it employs about 242 staff. Perhaps a little worrying for people in hospital is the fact that the NMC, which is responsible for ensuring we receive quality nursing, takes no disciplinary action against nurses in around 90 per cent of the complaints it receives – most are rejected as 'trivial'.

The NHS Confederation, also founded in 2002, calls itself 'The voice of NHS Leadership' and tends to focus more on the managerial rather than the medical aspects of running the NHS. Its aim is to 'help members improve health and patient care'. It, too, seems to be in the business of destroying innumerable forests to produce mountains of reports. Some could be useful, such as *Managing Excellence in the NHS* and *Bringing Leaders into the NHS*. Some, like *Why We Need Fewer Hospital Beds*, might seem a little worrying to those of us who believe that hospital over-crowding is one of the major causes of hospital-acquired infections. Like most of the other healthcare bureaucracies, the NHS Confederation also tries to tackle the horror of MRSA with reports like *Reducing MRSA – Improving Quality and Safety*. Though it does not spend too much of our money, the NHS Confederation has been a true leader in the way it has increased its own budget. This rose by a factor of five from a tiny £5.3 million in its first year of operation to a much more impressive £26.5 million in 2007.

The organization that is most directly tasked with ensuring our safety in hospital is the National Patient Safety Agency (NPSA). This was established in 2001, again by New Labour, to 'improve patient safety in the NHS' and by 2007 it had amassed 309 staff and an annual budget of over £30 million. The NPSA seems like quite a fine place to work. Ten of its senior managers earn between £75,000 and £130,000 a year and the average salary cost of each staff member is a cool £55,200 a year.[14] Nevertheless, after the NPSA had spent over £100 million of our money, a 2006 report by the Public Accounts Committee found that it had made 'insufficient progress'; that there had been too many delays and cost over-runs; that it had failed to provide and promulgate solutions to improve patient safety; and that it was questionable as to whether it had provided 'value for money'.[15] However, the Chief Medical Officer declared 'over the last five or six years we have put in place a comprehensive patient safety framework for this country which is admired internationally'.[16]

Finally, there are over 3,000 more administrators at the Department of Health (DoH), costing us around £225 million a year and bringing the total cost of the bureaucrats most directly employed to ensure we receive good healthcare to over £722 million a year. In its 1997 election manifesto, New Labour promised to reduce administrative costs in the NHS: 'The key is to root out unnecessary administrative cost and to spend money on the right things – frontline care'.[17] As about £425 million of the £722 million goes to regulators set up by New Labour, so that we now pay more than twice as much for bureaucrats as we did in 1997, it is far from obvious that the Government has delivered on its pre-election promise. Yet in reaction to rising public concern over the filthy state of many hospitals and in particular the C Diff scandal at the Maidstone and Tunbridge Wells NHS Trust, in the autumn 2007 Queen's Speech the Government announced that it was adding yet another organization to this costly and confused cacophony of inspectors, regulators and administrators: 'Legislation will be introduced to create a stronger health and social care regulator with a remit to ensure clean and safe services and high-quality care'.[18] Had any of the other bureaucracies done their job properly, this new regulator would not have been necessary. Moreover, there is only one certainty in today's NHS – this new body will be as expensive and ineffectual as all the others.

## WHO CARES?

Cold statistics of ever-rising, avoidable injuries and deaths and the hundreds of millions being wasted on ineffective, self-serving bureaucracies give little real insight into the tens of thousands of family tragedies being caused by the Government's mismanagement of the NHS. In her 2007 book, *Who cares?*, Midlands housewife Amanda Steane was probably one of the first people to describe how thousands of ordinary families experience today's NHS. Her 40-year-old husband Paul was admitted to hospital with stomach pains. Over the next year, he suffered kidney failure three times in two different hospitals as a result of not being given enough water to drink. The third time he went into hospital was just to have his little toe amputated. Two days after his operation, he was mistakenly discharged while suffering kidney failure and that night went into a coma. He survived, but only after losing both legs, his eyesight and having a tracheotomy (his throat was cut open and a pipe inserted to enable him to breathe). Under pressure to free up Paul's bed for another patient, doctors had not looked at the blood tests done that day, which showed that Paul would probably die if sent home. Finally, months later, in increasing pain and unable to walk, talk, see or breathe properly, Paul Steane spared his family the burden of looking after him by committing suicide.

Unfortunately, Paul Steane's story is not just an isolated aberration. Thousands of people are dying every year in today's NHS because of a lack of basic care. A few months before Paul was discharged in kidney failure, an eight-year-old boy was also discharged from the same hospital while in kidney failure – tragically he died when he got home. Moreover, two years after Paul Steane's death, a nationwide study showed that the hospital where he suffered most of his injuries had the highest rate of preventable deaths in the country. The hospital rejected the results of the study and claimed that its high mortality rate had been caused by 'deficiencies in the hospital's recording of information regarding a patient's diagnosis and is not reflective of the quality of patient care'.[19] While visiting her husband in this hospital, Amanda Steane saw several patients a week dying from hospital-acquired infections, dehydration and neglect. The nurses called this 'hospital syndrome' and would often say to her, 'Mandy, last night we lost another one from hospital syndrome'. However, relatives were always told by the doctors that the patients had died of natural causes. This widespread neglect seemed to be confirmed at a coroner's inquest in July 2006, when a consultant physician giving evidence into the death of a patient at another hospital said that he saw two to three patients dying from dehydration every week.[20] Moreover, since the publication of her book, Amanda Steane has been contacted by people with over 800 similar stories – of their relatives dying in NHS hospitals from poor care. One distressed relative, a pharmacist, wrote:

> Dad died through neglect at what the Government label as a 'top hospital' with Foundation Trust status in a ward where not even the basics were followed. He got C Diff and rampant diarrhoea and was left without IV fluids first for 16 hours and then for the 27 hours just before he died. No matter what we said, and I am a healthcare professional as is my wife, it made no difference to the care. We were treated with contempt for daring to question nursing and medical practice.[21]

One nurse wrote to Amanda about how, in order to meet the Government's target of patients being treated within four hours by Accident & Emergency (A&E), she was forced by hospital management to put patients with MRSA and C Diff into wards with patients who were infection-free:

> I have to nurse patients with infectious conditions such as diarrhoea, MRSA and C Diff in a main ward area simply because I do not have enough side-rooms to isolate patients. I am prevented by confidentiality from telling the other patients that they are now at risk. If I complain about things then I am told that it is tough luck on me and the patient has to go into that bed because they cannot breach the 4-hour trolley wait target in A&E.[22]

Several other people who had read Amanda's book contacted her to describe how their relatives died painful deaths, often in pools of their own excrement, due to neglect. This scandal of shameful neglect finally hit the headlines in 2007 when patients with diarrhoea at one hospital, where filthy conditions led to an outbreak of C Diff killing around 90 people, were told to 'go in their beds' because staff did not have enough time to get them to the toilets.

It seems incredible that such situations can occur in an advanced country like the UK. However, not only is this happening, a large majority of medical staff surveyed say it is getting worse. Due to the Government's mismanagement, we are suffering from a breakdown in care in many of our hospitals. There are obviously many reasons why this is happening. One over-simplified but still meaningful explanation is to say that there are five groups of people that must work together to keep hospital patients alive – managers, doctors, nurses, cleaners and caterers. As part of the trend towards privatizing healthcare, cutting costs and outsourcing activities that are not considered 'core', it was decided that cleaning and catering should be handed over to whichever private company was judged to offer 'best value' (usually the cheapest). For thousands of patients, this has proved to be a fatal misjudgement.

A cleaner employed by a hospital will get to know the nurses, become familiar with the wards and often become friendly with the patients. Even though they are 'just a cleaner', they will see themselves as part of a team responsible for patients' welfare and will tend to take pride in doing as good a job as possible. However, a cleaner employed on minimum wages by a low-cost, outsourced cleaning company might be cleaning the toilets at a football ground one week, it could be a factory the next week and the week after it might be a hospital. They will not be so familiar with hospital procedures, will probably not get to know either nurses or patients and will be under pressure from their managers to get the job done quickly in order to maximize that company's profits. Moreover, the number of hospital cleaners has halved since outsourcing was introduced.[23] As the massive rise in superbug deaths has shown, proper cleaning is actually core to patients' health and the decision to outsource it, which was taken under the last Tory Government and maintained by New Labour, has been a disaster.

Outsourcing catering, a policy also started by the Conservatives, has had similar, unexpectedly dreadful effects. The people distributing the meals must get the meals out and then collected again within fixed times so that their employers can make good profits on their contracts. However, the caterers have no responsibility for ensuring that any food is actually eaten, so they do not consider that some patients cannot actually reach the food trays, that others might have conditions like arthritis which prevent them even opening some of the food or that some may be so sedated that their food has come and gone without them even being aware that it was ever served. When patients do not eat, for whatever reason, the nurses just mark 'food refused' on their papers, even if the patient had no chance of eating the food in the first place. The number of people leaving hospital suffering from malnutrition has almost doubled from around 74,000 a year in 1997 to over 139,000 in 2007.[24] A quote from just one of the hundreds of people who contacted Amanda Steane graphically describes how we are often failing to give such basics as food and water to vulnerable patients:

> I experienced at first hand shocking examples of dreadful care of the elderly in a hospital ward. Women in their 80s, 90s, often after a stroke or fall, some blind, some in plaster, many immobile needing help to get about – the food was placed on trays on their bed tables and just left whilst the staff went to the staff room for a chatter. We could hear laughter and raised jolly voices as all the elderly women sat unable to eat without help. Some were placed too far from their food and could not reach. Some, being blind, could not see it to eat. Some were unable to eat due to stroke symptoms. Some were without appetite and needed encouragement. All were failed by the staff. After about 30 minutes, staff would reappear and very quickly whisk away all the trays so many were left not having touched a thing! Those that got to eat something only did so because a family member (usually a daughter) came in to feed them.[25]

As nurses are in constant attendance on the wards, it is theoretically their job to coordinate patient care. However, nurses complain that they are being drowned in a flood of new paperwork which is distracting them from the job they want to do. And when nurses do get the chance to see to their patients, they face time-wasting obstacles – for example, if nurses see cleaners using dirty, possibly infected water, they are not allowed to say anything directly to the cleaner, or if a vulnerable patient is moved into a bed where there are blood and faeces on the curtains around the bed, the nurse is not allowed to take action. Instead, they have to phone the manager responsible for cleaning who then has to contact the outside cleaning company to sort out the problem. This can sometimes take more than a day – plenty of time for a newly operated-upon patient to catch a life-threatening infection.

## MANAGEMENT MADNESS IN THE NHS

The area of the NHS that appears to have received the greatest benefit from the Government's massive increase in NHS spending is NHS management. While overall numbers of NHS staff went up by just 20 per cent between 1997 and 2007, the number of managers doubled from about 20,000 to about 40,000. Over the same period, the number of hospital beds that this growing army of managers had to manage fell from around 250,000 to less than 180,000. So, in ten years the NHS went from having 12 beds per manager to less than five beds per manager – a quite extraordinary decrease in managerial efficiency and one that is probably unequalled anywhere else in the public services. This is in spite of New Labour's 1997 manifesto promise to control NHS administrative costs. However, this huge managerial population explosion was apparently not enough for hospital managers. In 2007 the NHS Confederation claimed that NHS managers offered 'value for money' as the NHS actually needed 195,000 managers.[26] Had anybody been stupid enough to take this claim seriously, we would have ended up with more managers than there were hospital beds. In 2007 the Health Secretary at the time, Patricia Hewitt, claimed that the reduction in the number of hospital beds was a sign of the success of her policies: 'fewer beds are a sign of success – not of failure'.[27] However, not everybody agreed and the Health Secretary was accused of 'living on a fantasy planet, far removed from the reality of the frontline cuts that are having a daily adverse impact on NHS staff and patients'.[28] Moreover, the more managers there are in the NHS, the more they seem to need management consultants to tell them how to do their jobs. As the number of NHS managers has doubled, the NHS's spending on management consultants seems to have increased about ten times to over £600 million a year – around £15,000 of management consultancy a year for each manager in the NHS – so the NHS now spends more on management consultants than the whole of the British manufacturing industry.[29] When criticized by the British Medical Association for spending so much on management consultants, a spokesman for the Department of Health said, 'We only bring in consultants where they add to management expertise, not duplicate it. Overall we are reducing management costs in the NHS.'[30]

At first sight, it is not obvious what benefit all these extra managers and their management consultants have been to NHS patients. There is strong evidence that the decline in the number of hospital beds has had a catastrophic influence on the number of patients who have been disabled or killed by hospital-acquired infections. We now have about half the number of hospital beds per 100,000 of population that they have in France, Holland or Germany, giving the UK bed occupancy rates of over 85 per cent compared to around 60 per cent in some other European countries. This reduction in the number of UK hospital beds has led to a practice that NHS staff call 'hot-bedding' – getting a patient into a hospital bed when it is still hot from the previous occupant who has either been discharged or died. Naturally, hot-bedding is not exactly conducive to good hygiene as the pressure to get the next patient into the bed can take precedence over thorough cleaning. The UK's huge rise in hospital-acquired infections has time and again been directly linked to a lack of beds available to isolate patients with infections, though the Government keeps denying this. Even a government report commissioned in 2001, but never published, concluded that patients in a hospital where bed occupancy rates were over 90 per cent were 42 per cent more likely to contract an infection like MRSA than in hospitals where occupancy rates were below 85 per cent.[31]

It would be extremely politically sensitive to admit that the causes of hospital-acquired infections are so simple, as this would concede that the Government's policies and NHS mismanagement have caused close to 40,000 people to die unnecessarily. The Government has chosen to ignore the issue of overcrowding and instead has given a wide variety of creative explanations as to how the epidemic of hospital-acquired infections could be halted: staff and visitors should wash their hands a bit more often; doctors should not wear ties as these can transmit infections; flowers given to patients may be passing on infections; hospital staff should not have sleeves that go down lower than their elbows, and so on and so forth. By the start of 2008, the Government finally promised to screen all non-emergency hospital patients for MRSA and C Diff – a practice that has been common in many other European countries for more than a decade. There are strong arguments for prosecuting senior NHS managers for corporate manslaughter. Moreover, if a private hospital killed patients because of filthy conditions over several years, an army from our over £722 million worth of healthcare regulators and health-and-safety inspectors would be crawling all over the place, busily investigating and writing reports. Yet when top NHS managers, spurred on by short-termist, results-hungry politicians, appear to be guilty of massive malpractice, leading to tens of thousands of unnecessary deaths, there is complete silence from the regulators who spend so much of our money failing to protect us.

One might have thought that this ever-increasing multitude of managers would at least ensure that the NHS's finances were kept in order. In fact, given the huge rise in NHS spending under this Government, it should have been almost impossible not to have been able to balance the books. However, the NHS managers seemed to have failed even here and achieved the almost impossible when the NHS reported a financial deficit of about £50 million in 2003–4. This rose to £251 million in 2004–5 and rose again to £547 million in 2005–6. Under pressure to get costs under control, Health Secretary Patricia Hewitt announced that she would resign if there was a financial deficit in 2006–7. When the numbers were crunched and the 2006–7 results were reported, the NHS miraculously claimed it now had a surplus of about £500 million. However, the effect on services and patients had been brutal. While the number of managers remained largely intact, over 20,000 healthcare jobs were cut, recruitment of medical staff was put on hold, training budgets for medical staff were slashed by about £450 million and many hospitals set minimum waiting times of six months for what they considered 'non-urgent' operations. Worrying for many ordinary people was the fact that scores of A&E units were downgraded or shut altogether, though perhaps they had no reason to be concerned because, as Patricia Hewitt explained, 'increasing sophistication of ambulances' meant that it was safer for patients involved in emergencies to travel longer distances to get to hospital.

Perhaps the worst consequence of the NHS's incompetent financial management was the squeeze put on budgets for medicines. One study found that NHS managers were wasting up to £500 million by paying far too much for drugs.[32] However, because of budget shortages, the NHS began delaying the introduction of, or even refusing to fund, new life-saving treatments. Several cancer sufferers successfully used the courts to force their local health trusts to provide treatment that had previously been refused. One elderly couple both started going blind from wet age-related macular degeneration (AMD). When the NHS refused treatment, they had to make the agonizing choice of deciding which one of them would receive the treatment privately – they could not afford to pay for two treatments. Hearing of their case, the Royal National Institute for the Blind supported them in a campaign to get the NHS to treat the couple and after months of pressure their health authority relented and reversed its previous refusal. Not everyone is so fortunate – about 50 people a day lose their sight to AMD because their health authorities refuse to treat them, and in 2007 over 100,000 sufferers of Alzheimer's disease found that the NHS could not afford the £2.50 a day required for drugs to alleviate their dementia. The problem is particularly severe in England where patients are unable to obtain 12 key drugs that are available on NHS prescription in Scotland for treating conditions like AMD, Alzheimer's and several cancers.

There have been other indicators of gross management failure in addition to the spiralling rates of unnecessary deaths, budget deficits and drug-rationing. The number of operations cancelled for non-medical reasons rose over 30 per cent in the first six years of New Labour's NHS reforms. The key factor for these cancellations was found to be 'poor bed management' in spite of the massive increase in the number of managers. The Government claimed large reductions in waiting lists, but subsequent investigations found that many hospitals had fraudulently fiddled the figures to make it look as if they were meeting their targets. Meanwhile, the level of patient complaints rose by about 45 per cent from around 95,000 per year in 2004 to about 138,000 in 2006, and the number of complaints that were passed on to the Healthcare Commission, because NHS managers did not deal with them effectively, went up 2.5 times from about 3,200 a year in 2004 to over 8,000 a year by 2007.

There are many other examples of breathtaking incompetence. NHS managers negotiated a pay deal with GPs which gave the GPs a 63 per cent increase in salary whilst allowing many of them to stop working out of normal surgery hours. Billions of pounds were lost on Private Finance Initiative hospital-building programmes that gave massive profits to the private companies and tied the NHS into paying huge annual fees, sometimes for as long as 125 years. In the year that New Labour was elected, around 3,400 nurses and midwives emigrated. By 2007 this figure had virtually doubled to 7,772. Many reportedly left because of low morale in the NHS and because staff cuts meant they could not find jobs in the UK.[33] Yet, as all these nurses were emigrating, the NHS was spending around £800 million a year on agency nurses, and it faces a shortfall of about 14,000 nurses by 2010, and more after that, as 18,000 nurses are expected to retire each year up to 2010 and beyond.

The one area where the new army of NHS managers was most definitely effective was in looking after its own welfare. As over 20,000 healthcare jobs were cut to rein in the NHS's financial deficit, most managers emerged from the butchery unscathed. The pitifully few that did lose their positions, in what the NHS called its 'reconfiguration' of health services, were well looked after. In one reorganization aimed at saving around £250 million in administration costs, the NHS was thought to have spent close to £320 million on redundancy packages for those managers who lost their jobs – one 50-year-old former head of a regional strategic health authority received a package worth £899,810 in what an MP described as 'a lottery win rather than a payout'. The MP went on to say, 'How do I explain these payouts to people who can't get their Azheimer's disease drugs or they can't get drugs for conditions causing blindness?'[34]

Though NHS managers seldom get disciplined or fired for incompetence, one who did manage to get the boot got a £243,000 pay-off and kept his full pension after only two-and-a-half years as director of an NHS trust that was £5 million in debt. When another manager resigned from her £150,000 job as a result of years of squalor at her hospital, leading to a C Diff outbreak that killed about 90 patients, the NHS tried to slip her about £250,000 of our money in severance pay.[35] In comparison, the parents of an 18-month-old child that died as a result of poor treatment in an NHS hospital were offered £12,000 in compensation. Meanwhile, as a reward for their work in managing the NHS, 231 senior civil servants at the Department of Health received a 29 per cent increase in their 'performance-related' bonuses in 2006–7.

## IT'S A TOTAL DISASTER

The area where health service managers have most clearly and most unambiguously revealed their arrogance, incompetence, disregard for the welfare of patients and automatic tendency to present abject failures as successes is probably in the way they have gone about squandering billions of pounds of NHS money on poorly planned and hopelessly managed computer systems.

In 2003 NHS managers launched their programme to transform healthcare through the effective use of modern IT systems.[36] Originally rather boringly called the 'National Programme for IT' (NPfIT), this was sexily renamed 'Connecting for Health' (CfH). The head of the programme, Sir John Pattison, described Prime Minister Tony Blair's impatience to make this great leap forward:

> There was only one question which I thought was rather tricky and that was 'how long will this take?' I swallowed hard because I knew I had to get the answer right ... and I said three years. The answer was that is too long, how about two years. But in the end we got two years and nine months starting in April 2003.[37]

Due to a lack of anyone in the NHS capable of running the programme, an outsider, Deloitte consultant Richard Granger, was brought in on a salary of well over £200,000 a year. As Sir John Pattison explained to a Parliamentary committee, 'I cannot exaggerate the value of Richard Granger to this programme and the likelihood of its success'.[38] There was optimism in the air as the programme was launched. Sir John Pattison again: 'We have introduced somewhere in the NHS everything that we want to install'. Richard Granger seemed to share Sir John's confidence at how easy the whole thing would be:

> It is misleading to say the scale is bigger than has ever been done before, the extra spending of £2.3 billion over three years is not such a terrifyingly large project – it is comparable to other mid-size projects in industry and government that are regularly completed on time.[39]

By 2006, the year in which the programme should have been completed, the outlook had changed somewhat. After a series of apparently bad decisions, the cost had jumped from £2.3 billion to £6 billion, then to £9 billion and then to £12.4 billion. Moreover, the planned time to implement the system had extended from a mere two years and nine months to at least ten years, with no guarantee that even this would be long enough. The key players also seemed to have changed their minds. Sir Ian Carruthers, who replaced Sir John Pattison as Senior Responsible Owner, explained how difficult and risky the programme actually was: 'the programme is the largest in the world – it is extremely ambitious. With a programme of this scale there is bound to be risk, there is bound to be delay.'[40] Richard Granger now claimed, 'It is a very ambitious programme. I thought it would be a big risk from day one,' a statement that appeared to contradict some of his earlier pronouncements. In spite of the obvious delays and budget over-runs, the Health Minister declared that the whole project was 'broadly on time and within budget'.[41]

By 2007 the whole programme was, predictably, in melt-down.[42] Accenture, one of the largest and most experienced systems suppliers in the world, had walked away; Richard Granger had announced his resignation; about £2 billion had been spent and there was hardly any evidence of anything having been achieved except for enormous disruption at the few hospitals where CfH had tried to install its almost worthless systems. Meanwhile, the politicians and bureaucrats responsible for wasting so many billions on this disaster went into a state of denial and hired one of the country's most expensive PR firms, while the Health Minister insisted 'we are not going to be deflected by naysayers from any quarter'.[43]

## THE 'COVER-UP' CULTURE

Despite everything detailed above, perhaps the most dangerous consequence of the Government's healthcare reforms is that the public service ethos of the NHS has been replaced by a kind of corporate 'cover-up culture'. When an oil company has a spillage that pollutes huge stretches of coastline or there is an explosion in a chemical works that kills hundreds of people or a car-manufacturer sells a car that tends to burst into flames when involved in an accident, we expect these corporations to deny, cover up and generally do all they can to avoid responsibility for their actions. That is how the business world works. However, this is not what we expect from a public service organization like the NHS.

When Paul Steane was discharged in kidney failure and went into a coma, the hospital tried to avoid any admission of responsibility. The hospital's directors claimed that there were no blood tests done on Paul showing he was not well enough to have been discharged. However, a nurse was so outraged at the way management were treating Paul and Amanda Steane that she sent them a copy of blood tests done on the day of Paul Steane's discharge – tests that hospital directors had insisted, both in a meeting with the Steanes and in a letter to them, did not exist. These blood test results proved that the hospital had negligently discharged Paul Steane in kidney failure. The hospital bosses then claimed that they had never seen these blood tests. Again, the nurse sent incriminating evidence to the Steanes confirming that, six days before meeting Paul and Amanda Steane to deny the blood tests existed, hospital directors received an internal memo from the hospital records manager confirming that she had carried out the directors' instruction to reprint all of Paul's blood tests. These included the ones done on the day he left hospital, proving he had been negligently discharged in kidney failure. Even when they were confronted by all this documentation the NHS lawyers continued to try every trick and delaying

tactic they could to avoid admission of responsibility and payment of damages. When the NHS did finally make Paul Steane
an offer of compensation for his horrific injuries, this was withdrawn by the NHS lawyers within an hour of his suicide on the
basis that, as he was dead, he was not likely to need the compensation money any more. Moreover, when presented with all the
evidence of possible malpractice and possible cover-up from the
Steanes' case (including hospital memos showing which doctors
and nurses attended the meetings where the hospital decided to
deny responsibility), the Healthcare Commission and the
General Medical Council concluded that nobody had been at
fault for anything. The Nursing and Midwifery Council is still
considering the case.

Paul's case is not an isolated incident. In the 800 or so cases
that have been sent to Amanda Steane, there are numerous
examples of key medical records going 'missing', of bereaved
families being threatened by NHS lawyers and of hospital managers throwing legal actions at the media to stop stories about
NHS negligence.

In today's NHS, patients are dying from neglect, cover-ups are
widespread and figures are fudged so that managers can further
their own careers by appearing to meet targets dreamt up by
their bosses at the Department of Health. Rather than seeing
patients as their responsibility, these managers refer to them dis-
paragingly as 'bed-blockers' when they stay in hospital longer
than the managers have planned and as 'frequent flyers' when
patients have serious conditions that require them to keep going
back to hospital. This is definitely not the NHS that this
Government inherited.

## WHERE HAS ALL THE MONEY GONE?

As taxpayers and potential users of the NHS, we are entitled to
ask where all our money has gone. During his time at the

Treasury, the Chancellor spent over £269 billion more on the NHS than would have been spent had expenditure been kept at the 1997 level. In a 2007 poll of 3,000 doctors, about three-quarters (72 per cent) did not believe the extra money had been well spent and the same percentage felt there had been no improvement in care.[44] Today, about 55 per cent of senior doctors have medical insurance because they do not want to be treated by the NHS should they fall ill. The sorry spectacle of rising rates of unnecessary deaths, poorer GP service and billions squandered on ever-increasing numbers of managers, greater privatization and failing computer systems suggests that we ordinary taxpayers have not received much in return for the 11 years of reforms and the extra hundreds of billions of pounds of our money that have gone into building New Labour's 'new' NHS.

# CHAPTER 3

# LAW AND DISORDER

## A LOT MORE MONEY – A FEW MORE POLICE

True to Tony Blair's 1997 pre-election pledge that New Labour would be 'tough on crime, tough on the causes of crime', his Government significantly increased spending on the police – from around £8.5 billion a year in 1996–7 to over £12 billion a year by 2007–8. This is a very healthy rise of over 40 per cent, which over the course of 11 years means a total of £19.8 billion more was spent on policing than would have been the case if expenditure had remained at the 1997 level.

This £19.8 billion increase in taxpayers' money has enabled the Government, amongst other things, to increase the total number of police staff between 1997 and 2006 from 180,000 to 227,000 – a rise of 47,000, equal to about 26 per cent. Unfortunately, not all these extra staff were actual police officers. In fact, only 14,000 were real police and the other 33,000 were extra civilian staff. So, a rise in the police budget of over 40 per cent only resulted in 11 per cent more police (up from 127,000 to 141,000) but a much more impressive 62 per cent rise in administrative and support staff (up from 53,000 to 86,000).[1] At first sight this might seem slightly worrying to ordinary members of the public, as it possibly reflects what happened in the NHS where the massive increase in its budget resulted in only around 15 per cent more frontline medical staff, but a doubling in the number of managers and administrative staff. However, the police claim that the £19.8 billion has been put to good use as increasing the numbers of administrative and support staff has freed up trained police to get on with the job of reducing crime. The Chairman of the Association of Police Authorities explained:

> Obviously some people would suggest this is additional bureaucracy. I do feel it enables us to release police officers for frontline duties ... We have had some extremely impressive outputs in terms of the return of the investment that has been put in both nationally and locally.[2]

Even more reassuringly, this conviction that our money has been spent intelligently was also supported by the Association of Chief Police Officers who claimed that the additional investment had not been 'blindly spent on additional officers but has been wisely spent across a range of initiatives so as to maximise the return in relation to service performance'.[3]

## EFFICIENT AND EFFECTIVE?

Not only do the police claim to have been careful custodians of all the extra cash we have given them, they also believe they have been super-effective in improving their own efficiency. As the Chairman of the Association of Police Authorities said in 2007, 'We have introduced a whole series of initiatives and clearly the big headline figure, of course, is in terms of the efficiency gain. The efficiency gain since 1999–2000 to date represents £1.76 billion, 4.1 per cent of budgets.'[4]

A 4.1 per cent efficiency gain in seven years equates to just about 0.6 per cent a year. Most private-sector businesses running an efficiency programme would expect at least 10 per cent a year and so should achieve in just one year what it would take our police almost 17 years to accomplish. Nevertheless, the police appeared uniquely proud of their rather modest efficiency improvement: 'So we believe we are at the forefront of both the public sector but, arguably the private sector, in terms of driving out that sort of efficiency'.[5]

When the Government spends so much more of our money on the police, what we, the public, want are not just obscure efficiency measures, but for the threat of crime to fall so that our communities are safer places in which to live. Here again, the police are proud of what they have achieved in apparently almost halving the number of crimes committed: 'The risk of being a victim (of crime) has fallen from 40 per cent to 24 per cent'.[6] The Government's pride in its successful reduction of crime has understandably been trumpeted by both the police and the politicians. In his letter to John Reid, who briefly took over the running of the Home Office, Prime Minister Tony Blair wrote on 15 May 2006, 'you should build on and seek to accelerate your predecessor's success in reducing overall crime'.[7] This view of significant reductions in crime was echoed by Home Office Minister Tony McNulty in 2007 when he commented on the latest crime figures:

> We have already seen massive reductions in crime in this country – 8.4 million fewer crimes committed last year than in 1995 – and I am encouraged by the latest police and British Crime Survey figures.[8]

However, not everybody has been convinced by the Government and police bosses' constant assertions that they are winning the war on crime, so I propose to examine what is really happening with crime levels, whether it is more or less safe for us to venture out of our homes and if the top cops' claims that our money has been 'wisely spent' are justified or not.

## THE CRIME FIGURES CONUNDRUM

Confusingly for the public, but conveniently for the politicians, there are actually two sets of annual statistics of crime levels. Often these are contradictory so that when one shows crime is going up, the other suggests it is going down and vice versa. This means that whichever party is in power can triumphantly brandish its set of statistics supposedly proving that it is driving crime levels ever further down, while whichever party is in opposition can brandish the other set of statistics as it furiously denounces the Government for allegedly allowing crime to spiral out of control. For example, in 2005 the Labour manifesto stated, 'Overall crime is down by 30 per cent on 1997 … violent crime down by 26 per cent'. At the same time the Conservative Party manifesto demanded action on crime by claiming, 'Overall crime is up by 16 per cent. Violent crime is up by over 80 per cent.' One expert explained:

> You can use crime statistics to 'prove' just about anything you want about crime. The overall trend seems to me to be certainly up, but you will find statisticians who will question that claim.[9]

Very occasionally, both sets of figures do move in the same direction. When this happens, the Government and Opposition each choose small parts of the overall statistics to 'prove' either that crime is going down (the Government) or that it is going up (the Opposition).

By 2006 the Government realized that there was a credibility problem with the crime figures and Charles Clarke, Home Secretary at the time, set up a group of experts to suggest more reliable ways of recording crime. As he explained:

> I have been concerned for some time that Home Office statistics have been questioned and challenged. This has got

to the point where most people seem confused about what is happening to crime in this country.[10]

The two sets of crime figures are the Police Reported Crime (PRC) and the British Crime Survey (BCS). We need to briefly look at the strengths and flaws of each of these before moving on to consider how well the Government and police have used our billions. The police have been reporting crime statistics for almost 200 years with their PRC numbers. Recently, the Government improved the PRC figures. In 1998 they added some new offences and in 2002 the National Crime Recording Standard was introduced to standardize the way different police forces compiled their crime statistics. The effect of these two changes was to cause an apparent 10 per cent increase in crime and so the PRC figures are really only useful for tracking trends in crime from 2002 onwards. One major weakness with the PRC figures is that somewhere between a half and two-thirds of crimes are not reported to the police and therefore never show up in the figures.

To get a better idea of crime rates, in 1981 the Conservative Government set up a new way of measuring crime – the BCS. This was a survey of around 40,000 people. It questioned them about whether they had been victims of crime over the previous year. The idea was that this survey would provide a more accurate picture of crime levels as it would pick up crimes that were not reported to the police. However, there were some gaps in the BCS figures. They did not include murder and rape as these crimes were too rare to be statistically reliable given the small sample size. There was also the obvious difficulty that it would have been impossible to contact and interview murder victims and there was a feeling that many rape victims might not have wanted to talk about their experiences with a total stranger from a government-sponsored research company. Similarly, the BCS does not include drug-taking and drug-dealing, as again those involved might not be keen on discussing their crimes. Also, as the BCS only interviewed adults, it did not pick up the rapidly increasing spate of crimes against children and, as it only interviewed private individuals, it excluded crimes against business like shoplifting and fraud. In spite of these shortcomings, and possibly because the BCS provided the picture that best suited New Labour, the Home Office has consistently claimed, 'The BCS is generally accepted as the most authoritative and reliable indicator of crime trends and has measured people's experience of crime in the same way for over twenty years'.[11]

A further difficulty with both sets of figures is that this Government has been almost hyperactive in creating new criminal offences. According to some estimates, around 3,023 offences have been created or revised between May 1997 and the end of 2007, compared with about 500 during the last decade of Conservative rule.[12] So, if you are caught doing something dastardly like entering the hull of the *Titanic* without permission from the Secretary of State, selling a grey squirrel or failing to nominate a key-holder where an audible intruder alarm is present, you would now be committing a criminal offence, whereas previously such actions were not deemed criminal. This profusion of new offences will tend to push crime figures upwards.

## MORE POLICE, MORE CRIME?

The BCS figures, the statistics that most solidly support the Government's claim to be successfully driving down crime levels, indicate that since New Labour has been in power the annual numbers of crimes have fallen from just under 17 million a year (16,712,000) to just under 11 million a year (10,912,000) – a fairly impressive drop of over a third (34.7 per cent). This would suggest that the Government's investment of extra billions of our money in policing has been phenomenally successful. However, the reality is not quite as the Government would have us believe. According to the BCS, crime peaked at over 19 million crimes a year in 1995, dropped rapidly between 1995 and 2001 and since then has levelled off. Unfortunately, the Government's big investment in extra resources for the police did not really begin to filter through until 2002, by which time most of the fall in crime had already happened. This lack of correlation between the Government's favourite crime statistics and the Government's investment in more policing is fairly clear (see Figure 5). This prompted the Home Affairs Committee (HAC) to note: 'It is striking that much of the decrease in overall crime rates over the past ten years occurred before the major increase in investment during that period'.[13]

Although the BCS comfortably reports that crime is falling each year, this may be only partly true. To find out what is really happening, we have to look in a bit more detail at which types of crime are actually falling and which are increasing.

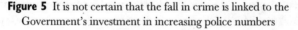

**Figure 5** It is not certain that the fall in crime is linked to the Government's investment in increasing police numbers

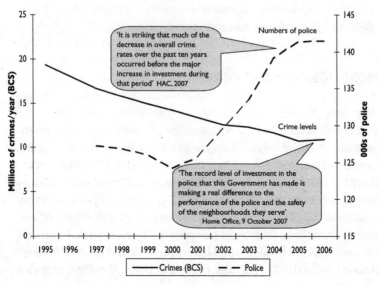

Since 1995, there has been a massive fall in what is called 'volume crime' – mainly vehicle crime and burglary – with both reducing by around 60 per cent. However, most (two-thirds) of these impressive reductions happened between 1995 and 2001, before the Government started increasing investment in policing. One study indicated that these huge reductions happened because of improvements in security technology: car alarms, immobilizers, better locks, home security systems and so on.[14] Moreover, a leaked report from the Prime Minister's Strategy Unit (PMSU) wrote that increases in spending on the police 'appear unrelated to productivity' and that it was the improving economy with the resultant falling unemployment and increasing wealth, rather than police work, which was contributing to much of the fall in these volume crimes. The PMSU concluded that '80 per cent of the reduction in the official crime rate since 1997 was the result of economic, not criminal justice, factors'.[15]

Both the BCS and the PRC seem to reflect this marked drop in volume crime. However, while the Government's favoured statistics (the BCS) also show violent crime falling year after year, the PRC figures indicate that the number of violent crimes is increasing relentlessly – more than doubling since 1998. Figure 6 shows the completely contrasting trends according to the PRC.

This means that if you stay barricaded in your home, protected by good security devices, you are less likely to be a victim of crime than you would have been when New Labour first came to power. However, if you dare to venture out of your home, you are much more likely to be a victim. One issue that should concern us is that Government research suggests that while about half of all volume crimes are reported to the police, only one in every three violent crimes is ever reported.[16] So, the actual number of thefts and burglaries (volume crimes) is probably twice that shown in Figure 6, whereas the number of violent crimes is likely to be three times higher than depicted.

Incidentally, by 2007 even the Government's cherished BCS figures indicated that violent crime was on the rise from 2.32

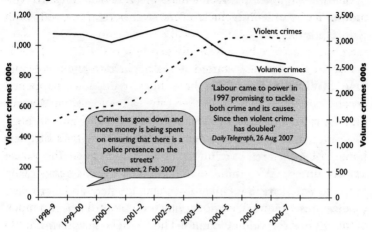

**Figure 6** Volume crime has fallen but violent crime has doubled

million cases in 2004–5 to 2.35 million cases in 2005–6 and to 2.47 million cases in 2006–7. The Home Office immediately claimed that the 6.5 per cent rise in violent crime in two years was 'not statistically significant'. However, it might have been statistically significant to the 180,000 extra people who were victims. Moreover, one suspects that had the BCS statistics suggested that violent crime had fallen by even a fraction of a per cent, our newspapers and TV screens would have been awash with government ministers and top policemen crowing about how 'statistically significant' this was and how effective their policies had been.

Within this apparent overall rise in violent crime, certain types of crimes have exploded. Street robberies increased from around 255,000 in the year 2004–5 to 320,000 by 2006–7 – up over 25 per cent in just two years. Worryingly, within these figures, muggings using a knife shot up from 25,500 in 2004–5 to about 64,000 in 2006–7 – a rise of 151 per cent. This means that there is a street robbery every two minutes and a mugging with a knife every ten minutes, making the UK the most violent crime-ridden country in Europe.[17] However, nothing quite matches the rise in gun crime, up from 864 offences (over two a day) in New Labour's first year in power to 3,296 (nine a day) by 2005–6, a rise of four times.

## THE GOVERNMENT ACTS

Our Government has not been idle in confronting the problem of rising crime. We have probably had more new laws and new initiatives in the area of criminal justice than in any other aspect of government. With more than 3,000 new criminal offences in just over ten years, the Government has created a new criminal offence for every working day it has been in power. In addition, there has been a flood of initiatives aimed at tackling crime.

Anti-social behaviour was one of the Government's major targets. In 2003 the Home Office set up the Anti-Social Behaviour Unit with an annual budget of £25 million to draw up and implement an effective policy for dealing with anti-social behaviour. This was followed in 2005 by the creation of the Respect Task Force and then in 2006 the Government published the Respect Action Plan. We now have at least ten different types of intervention available to police and the courts for dealing with anti-social behaviour – Acceptable Behaviour Contracts, Anti-Social Behaviour Orders (ASBOs), Crack House Closure Orders, Demoted Tenancies, Dispersal Power, Housing Act Injunctions, Penalty Notices for Disorder (PNDs), Individual Support Orders, Parenting Contracts and Parenting Orders. Many of these were introduced by New Labour. One of the best-known is probably the Anti-Social Behaviour Order. For some people, ASBOs may have acted as a deterrent; however, for many young people getting an ASBO has almost become a rite of passage – not a mark of shame, but rather a sign of achievement, a bit like getting A-Levels used to be in a long-lost pre-New Labour era. Ten years after the introduction of ASBOs, there had been no proper research into the effectiveness of either ASBOs or the other anti-social behaviour measures apart from some research done in 2005. The results of this were inconclusive and the Home Office chose not to publish them.

Another somewhat questionable Government brainwave was the introduction of electronic tagging by the then Home Secretary, David Blunkett, in 2004. At the time these 'jails without bars' seemed like the perfect solution to the two problems of rising crime and prison overcrowding. Theoretically, tagged prisoners could not commit new crimes as the authorities would always know where they were at any time. Of course, reality was quite different with many criminals appearing to be somewhat smarter than the highly paid Home Office officials responsible for ensuring our safety. Many simply removed their tags, others left their tracking devices at home and others found they could do pretty much what they liked as the electronic tracking did not work inside some buildings and even in the shadow of tall buildings. One in four criminals re-offended within weeks of being tagged – many of these were serious offenders like robbers, sex-attackers and violent thugs – and six out of ten breached their conditions. In 2005–6 there were 11,435 breaches, primarily ignoring night-time curfews. By 2006–7 this had risen almost four times to 43,843. In 2007 a professor of criminal justice wrote a report questioning the effectiveness of tagging. The Government commented, 'The Ministry of Justice is considering the evaluation report and the recommendations of a National Offender Management Service Working Group on the future of satellite tracking of offenders'.[18]

David Blunkett also gave us Police Community Support Officers (PCSOs). First introduced in 2003, there were close to 16,000 PCSOs by 2007.[19] Critics of PCSOs have called them 'Blunkett's bobbies', 'plastic bobbies' and 'a cheap alternative to police officers'. However, PCSOs are not actually that cheap. In 2007 a PCSO could earn up to £24,500 a year while a police officer started at about £21,000, which could rise to £33,000. Several senior policemen have complained that for the cost of every ten PCSOs, they could have, and would rather have, six to eight fully trained police officers. However, as the Government has separated the budgets for police officers and PCSOs, police forces cannot transfer the money from hiring PCSOs to paying for trained police. Therefore, they either have to employ PCSOs or else lose that money. As one senior policeman explained, 'The point is police forces can have them (PCSOs) and it does not cost any extra money'.[20]

On average, a PCSO gets about five weeks' training compared to six months for a regular police officer. Moreover, PCSOs' powers are limited to handing out fines for anti-social behaviour, public disorder or motoring offences. Our PCSOs seem to have used their powers somewhat sparingly – a study of 2,454 PCSOs in 2006–7 showed that they dealt with a mere 384 crimes, meaning that the average PCSO issues some form of penalty once every six years. In comparison, the average police officer deals with 11 crimes a year – 66 times more than the average PCSO. Curiously for a government often accused of being obsessed with targets, when asked about the apparent ineffectiveness of PCSOs, the Home Office said:

> to attempt to measure their success solely by looking at the number of penalty notices and crimes they detect is to miss the point. Their primary role is to provide high visibility reassurance, build confidence in communities and support police officers.[21]

PCSOs came under heavy criticism in 2007 when two of them refused to jump into a pond to try to save a drowning boy because they had not received the appropriate training. By the time a real police officer arrived and did dare to enter the water, the boy was dead.

The Government has also given us the Street Crime Initiative, the 101 Service, the Victims' Code, the Quality of Service Commitment, Neighbourhood Policing, the Police Bureaucracy

Taskforce (2002) and the Bureaucracy Minimisation Programme (2007). The latter was presumably introduced when its predecessor, the Police Bureaucracy Taskforce, got confused by its title and increased rather than reduced bureaucracy. By 2007, following extensive and quite unnecessary research over many years, the Government discovered the 80/20 rule, namely that 80 per cent of crimes are committed by 20 per cent of criminals. On the basis of this new insight, the Government launched yet another initiative, this time targeted at persistent offenders. With what appears to be great pride, the Home Office explained its rather obvious new idea:

> Tackling the offender and not just the offence is at the heart of a visionary strategy issued today which outlines ambitious policies for meeting the ever-changing challenge of protecting the public.[22]

Perhaps this latest initiative will be successful whereas all the others have so patently failed.

## HITTING TARGETS AND MISSING CRIME

Given that we pay our taxes on the understanding that the Government will use some of our money to protect us, one might be forgiven for wondering what has happened to all the extra money that has been given to the police and why this extra cash has not resulted in a safer society.

One of the Government's key indicators for judging police performance is the number of what are called Offences Brought to Justice (OBTJ). An OBTJ is pretty much any crime where a police officer has taken action and can vary from an on-the-spot fine to arresting a serial rapist or mass-murderer. The Government and police bosses claim that the fact that the number of OBTJs has increased by 6 per cent per police officer in the last seven years proves we are getting improved performance from the police. One of the problems with measuring OBTJs is there is no distinction between a police officer issuing a PND for a trivial offence like littering and a police officer solving a serious crime like violent assault or terrorism. So a police officer who fines two litter louts in one day can be seen to be twice as effective as a colleague who catches a murderer. The Chairman of the Police Federation for England and Wales explained the issue:

> What gets counted gets done and there is no relevance at the moment for the quality of what is getting counted and one theft is the same as one serious assault on paper.[23]

This means that to meet their targets, there will be pressure on the police to act on trivial cases as this easily allows them to make their numbers. Moreover, if a police officer catches two people involved in a crime, say having a violent argument, and then issues a warning to both, he gets credited with two OBTJs. Another top cop agreed that 'the offences-brought-to-justice-targets do lack a lot of subtlety'.[24] The rising number of PNDs (many for quite minor offences) enabled the Government and police to claim that they had achieved 1.43 million OBTJs in 2006–7, comfortably beating their target of 1.25 million. One thing that particularly worried the Home Affairs Committee, which was assessing the performance of the police, was that while serious OBTJs stayed fairly stable, the number of trivial OBTJs had hugely increased, suggesting that many police were tending to focus more on achieving targets rather than dealing with serious crime:

> If we look at the number of offences brought to justice, the increase is almost entirely explained by fixed penalty notices, cannabis cautions and other cautions for presumably minor offences. There has not been what we in the

public might have expected, a significant increase in the number of offences brought to court, indicating they are more serious. Have we really got real value for money out of the resources that the Police Service just had over the last four or five years?[25]

An answer to this question could be found in a report written by the Prime Minister's Strategy Unit: 'there is still little chance that a crime will be detected and result in a caution or conviction'.[26]

One theory the police have come up with to explain their inability to get to grips with crime was to apply Darwinism and claim that the police have been so successful in catching and locking up all the stupid criminals that the only ones left at large are the very clever ones who are understandably more difficult to apprehend. A Chief Constable from the Association of Police Officers explained the problem: 'Through a process of natural selection those offenders still active tend to be smarter than their convicted contemporaries and consequently harder to successfully convict'.[27]

In fact, the risk of arrest and conviction is currently probably less than 3 per cent, so most criminals are probably sleeping a lot more soundly than their past, present and future victims.[28] Perhaps the most telling indictment of the Government and the police's apparent failure to protect innocent citizens comes from the victims of crime who increasingly feel that we are in a society with plenty of crime but far too little punishment. The girlfriend of one victim of violence said:

> A mob can attack an innocent family, hurl bricks through their windows, then smash in a man's head with a brick and ruin his life – and get six months in prison. They must be laughing their heads off. All it will do is enhance their reputation. Then they'll be back out free to do the same to someone else in no time.[29]

Many members of the public are also convinced that the only people to have benefited from the European Human Rights laws, introduced by the then Home Secretary Jack Straw (who later became Justice Minister) in 1998, are criminals egged on by their lawyers who contrive to use millions of pounds in legal aid to avoid the consequences of their actions. The widower of a woman who was stabbed to death by a violent criminal, who should have been subject to supervision, expressed what many people now believe:

> It is just cover-up after cover-up. People don't do their job and they get away with it. They feel they have to protect the prisoner's human rights all the time. The victims are just not considered and are not important. Somebody some-where has not done their job but they will keep their job and their pension and their sick pay and all their perks while the victims are just fobbed off.

A Ministry of Justice spokesman commenting on the case said, 'public protection is our top priority'.[30]

## WHAT DO THE POLICE ACTUALLY DO?

There has been much heat and noise from the police about how targets and increased bureaucracy are preventing them getting on with the job they want to do. There is some evidence to back this up. Recently, the Government claimed that the average police officer was spending 63.5 per cent of their time on what was called 'frontline work'.[31] However, this definition of 'front-line' policing included 10.8 per cent spent doing paperwork, so at most the average police officer was only spending about half their time on frontline work. One chief constable complained about the 'phenomenal' amount of paperwork:

in case anything goes wrong you have to have a record of it. I can see the logic in it, but it means police officers are spending 45 per cent to 50 per cent of their time in the station.[32]

In fact, the situation may be much worse. Some Home Office figures reportedly showed that 'just 14 per cent of all police officer time is spent on patrol and that only one in fifty-eight officers is on the beat at any given time'.[33] Another top cop complained of a lack of clear direction from the Government:

We in the police – and this is going to sound defensive – are sometimes on the end of mixed messages as well. Is it that we need to send more people to prison or is it we send less people to prison? It changes every week.[34]

However, for senior police officers to blame Government targets and bureaucracy can sometimes seem a little disingenuous. Police bosses have good salaries, generous pensions and attractive early retirement packages. Moreover, they have recently received close to £20 billion in extra funding from us. For them to keep blaming government interference for their own failure to do the job we pay them to do could appear to look rather like an abdication of responsibility. In a rare moment of honesty a senior police officer admitted, 'Many of my colleagues feel they are failing the public and some of it is down to poor supervision and some of it is down to leadership'.[35] The Home Affairs Committee also seemed almost dismayed at what it saw as the wasting of our money. 'We consider it unacceptable that the significant recent investment in the police is not being used to maximum effect'.[36] Even the usually subservient Treasury was worried about how our police were spending our taxes: 'forces are typically short of people with the experience or appetite to ask the most incisive questions about where resource is deployed and what productivity it is delivering'.[37]

New York has about 37,000 police, while London has around 31,000, yet New York has about twice as many police on the streets as London. Crime has fallen significantly in New York and increased just as significantly in London. However, when the leader of Liverpool city council called on the police there to show 'zero tolerance', his request was rejected by the President of the Police Superintendents Association as being 'Unachievable. While it sounds very good and New York-ish, it's just not on the agenda.'[38] Another big difference between the US and the UK is that many police chiefs in the US are elected and so have to be seen to perform. In the UK, being a police chief is a secure job for life, sitting behind a desk with great pay and an even better pension, however poorly you perform, providing of course you do not upset your bosses by being too outspoken.

Over the last ten years or so, about 700 British police stations have closed. These have tended to be smaller, local stations close to the neighbourhoods where crime is highest. When new police stations have opened, they have usually been on pleasant greenfield, out-of-town sites, like fortresses of calm far away from the crime-ridden areas where they are most needed. Faced with rising serous crime, our police do not seem to have tried to take back the streets. Instead, they have retreated to their usually well-appointed offices and have left us largely at the mercy of a tsunami of lawlessness.

Increasing crime is clearly a result of deep and growing social problems, but it is far from obvious that either our Government or our police have risen to the new challenges in spite of spending billions of pounds more of our money. The police like to quote such shocking 'facts' as a 'file for a simple assault case contained 128 bits of paper and had been handled by about 56 different people before it went to court'.[39] In this way, they prefer to portray themselves as victims of circumstances who would willingly and enthusiastically rush off and solve the problem of rising crime if only the over-interfering Government would allow them. Some politicians, on the other hand, have suggested that it is the police who are responsible for their own failures: one of the members of the Home Affairs Committee said, 'I find that police forces up and down the country are bureaucratic, risk averse and technologically illiterate. Do you not have yourselves to blame?'[40] However, while the police and the politicians play 'pass the parcel' with who is responsible for increasing lawlessness, billions of pounds seem to be spent without any visible results.

# CHAPTER 4

# A MILITARY DISASTER

## THE TRIPLE BETRAYAL

The Government spends about £34 billion a year on defence. However, while spending on areas like health, education and the police has been increased in the ten years up to 2007 by a very generous 40 per cent to 100 per cent, spending on our military has only gone up by a worryingly modest 23.2 per cent, only slightly above the rate of inflation. Even worse, defence is probably the only major area of government spending that has actually gone down as a percentage of our national income (Gross Domestic Product – GDP) since this Government came to power. This is in spite of the fact that this Government has used the military more than any other since 1945 – in Kosovo (1999), Sierra Leone (2000), Afghanistan (2001–8) and Iraq (2003–8).

Not only has the Government strictly controlled spending on the military, but it has also imposed a programme of cutbacks on the armed services, while giving them ever more to do. In spite of Government claims that it has given its support to the military, whole regiments and squadrons have been scrapped and many of our ships have been mothballed or sold off. The decline in the amount of fighting equipment under New Labour has been dramatic – the number of tanks dropped from 415 in 1997 to 280 by 2007, major ships have dropped from 38 in 1997 to 22 ten years later and combat aircraft have fallen from 264 in 1997 to 156 by 2007 (see Figure 7).[1]

Moreover, the number of people in the armed services has also been deliberately reduced. In the latest Ministry of Defence (MoD) annual report, the top brass were able to proudly confirm that they were on course with their Spending Review Efficiency Target by reducing manpower costs by £86 million in the year 2005–6, a further £344 million in 2006–7 and an eye-watering £557 million in 2007–8.[2] In 1998 there were 212,200 armed forces personnel. By 2007 this had fallen almost 8 per cent to 195,730. In fact, almost the only clear increase the military has had under this Government is in the number of casualties it has suffered trying to do ever more tasks with ever-decreasing resources. The casualty rate has gone up from 78 persons per 100,000 in 1998 to 96 persons per 100,000 in 2006 – a rise of 23 per cent. It is likely that final figures for 2007 will probably be significantly higher and so we will most likely see an overall increase in casualty rates of around 30 per cent. In 2007, when monthly casualty rates seemed to be spiralling ever higher, Tory and Liberal Democrat (Lib Dem) MPs started to express their concern at the increasing loss of life. However, an MoD spokesman

**Figure 7** There has been a large reduction in military equipment between 1997 and 2007

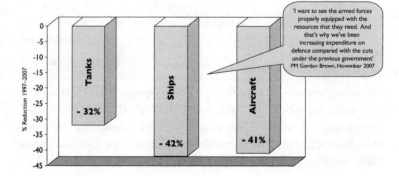

said that it was 'oversimplistic' to draw conclusions from a monthly death toll and that 'fatalities over a short period of time do not provide an accurate reflection of the overall death rates of British troops in Iraq and Afghanistan'.[3] This leads to the one other area where there has been constant uninterrupted growth in the military: the number of people employed in 'communications', basically PR. This reached about 1,000 by 2007 – one communications person for every 200 service personnel, giving an indication of the priorities of the Government and military chiefs.[4]

Looking at how our money has been spent on defence under New Labour, one gets the feeling that we, the taxpayers, and more importantly our service personnel have been betrayed in three ways by the Government and the military establishment: there has been a managerial betrayal, a military one and a moral one. Firstly, there has been a management failure as much of the extra money given to defence has been wasted by military bosses. This has led to a military betrayal as our soldiers have been sent into action with inadequate equipment, incomplete training and insufficient support. And there has been a moral betrayal as those in power, both in Government and at the top of the military, have used our military for questionable foreign adventures, and when things have gone wrong, those who were to blame have tried to avoid their responsibilities and cover up their mistakes.

## THE MANAGEMENT BETRAYAL

### Wasting Billions

Of the £34 billion or so that we now spend on defence each year, around £6 billion goes on developing and buying new equipment – Astute Class submarines, Typhoon jet fighters, aircraft carriers, Panther armoured vehicles, Type 45 Destroyers, Nimrod reconnaisance planes and so on. As most of these projects last several years, at least £30 billion of projects will be ongoing at any one time. Clearly, it is important that these projects are completed on budget so that money is not wasted and also on time so that our service personnel are provided with the weapons they need to carry out the tasks they are given.

Over the last ten years there have been very few large defence projects that have actually been completed on time and on budget. One that has was the refurbishment of the MoD HQ in Whitehall, home to military chiefs and about 3,300 other staff. The project was launched in 1997 because the Secretary of State for Defence at the time, George Robertson, felt:

> The MoD's main London headquarters badly needs modernisation. The accommodation is of poor quality and not up to the standard I would expect my staff to have to work in. It is also inefficient and expensive to run.[5]

This rebuilding and running of the MoD HQ will cost an estimated £2.347 billion over 30 years – about £78 million a year.[6] This is equivalent to office costs of £23,636 per person per year, a fairly interesting amount considering that the starting wages of a basic infantry soldier are only just over £15,000 per year and that office costs in main cities outside London can be as low as £4,000 per person per year. The building was reported to be equipped with large plasma-screen televisions, a gym, oak doors, marble floors, expensive paintings, high-quality furniture and many excellent facilities for the staff.[7]

At a time of military cutbacks and when private-sector companies have used modern communications to reduce the numbers of their headquarters staff, it is odd that the MoD felt it necessary to provide such excellent premises for so many administrative staff right in the centre of London. The MoD appeared proud of its achievement. An MoD spokesman explained, 'The modernisation of the UK's top level defence headquarters – home to 3,300 military and civilian staff – was completed early and on budget'.[8]

A spokeswoman added, 'The modernisation of Main Building has been a huge success'.[9] They also seemed pretty pleased over at the Office of Government Commerce (OGC). The OGC had helped the MoD draw up the £2.347 billion contract with the suppliers and appeared delighted by the results of their work:

> In one of the busiest periods for defence in modern history, the MoD managed to provide a new HQ, renewing pride in the undeniably and recognisably better workplace … Details of the MoD Main Building redevelopment programme make pretty exciting reading, not only for professionals and MoD personnel, but also for the average lay-person.[10]

One might be forgiven for speculating that this splurging of our money on fancy offices for the MoD pen-pushers would not have been 'pretty exciting reading' for the average squaddie, crouching in a ditch in Afghanistan and trying to avoid being killed by the Taliban.

In 2007 the MoD announced that it was moving around 1,000 staff out of its new HQ as part of its reduction of administrative costs. We do not know the exact terms of the MoD's £2.347 billion contract for running its HQ. However, we should not be surprised if, because of its commercial naivety, the MoD will still have to pay almost the same level of costs for its HQ even though it is reducing the staff there by almost a third. Meanwhile, accommodation for ordinary soldiers was described by some officers as 'cramped, decaying and frankly shaming', to which an MoD spokesman replied from the comfort of his new offices that soldiers' accommodation was 'not perfect'.[11]

It is unfortunate that the MoD bureaucrats' 'success' in providing comfortable accommodation for themselves in one of the most pleasant and expensive locations in Central London was not repeated on their projects to provide vital new equipment for our troops to help them deal with those the Government chose to make our enemies. Every year the now discredited National

Audit Office (NAO) examines how well or badly the MoD is running the top 20 military equipment procurement projects and then, using the NAO report, the Public Accounts Committee (PAC) summons a couple of defence bosses to explain where all our money is going. Sadly, the MoD's management capabilities are so dismal that even the normally submissive NAO could not avoid cataloguing the horror stories staring it in the face. In 2004 the PAC lambasted the MoD bosses: 'This report once again records the woeful performance of the Department in procuring defence equipment'.[12] In 2005 the MoD's performance was the worst the PAC had ever seen. Then, in 2006, the MoD's results were even worse. Currently, the MoD's 20 largest projects are around £2.6 billion over their original budgets and hideously late. In 2005 the top 20 projects were delayed by a total of almost 19 years. In 2006 this went up to close to 22 years. The MoD claimed that it had been successful because, whereas in 2003–4 the delays on the top 20 projects had increased by 62 months, in 2004–5 the delays only increased by 45 months and then in 2005–6 by a mere 33 months – the idea being that it was an achievement that the MoD's rate of getting worse had slowed down. The Defence Procurement Minister commended the MoD's success: 'Defence procurement is complex but I am glad that we have continued to make progress in bringing costs and delays under control'.[13] When the 2006–7 results came out, delays on the top 20 projects had increased by another 38 months, so the MoD's performance was once again getting worse.

As regards doing something to sort out the mess, the MoD does not seem to be in a great hurry. When a member of the PAC asked, 'In relation to the procurement of weapons, as far as the MoD is concerned, there have always been problems in relation to delays and overspend. Is that a fair summary or is that unfair?', one MoD boss replied, 'It has been the case for as long as most of us can remember and we have repeatedly looked at the causes and what we would need to do to improve'.[14] Unfortunately for us taxpayers and for ordinary soldiers, all this 'looking at the causes' does not seem to have produced much meaningful action. In 2007, as it does almost every year, the PAC expressed its concern that the seemingly endless delays were putting our soldiers' lives at risk. One key project – acquiring armoured vehicles to protect our forces – was described by the Commons Defence Committee as 'a sorry story of indecision, changing requirements and delay'.[15] However, as usual the MoD bigwigs patted themselves on the back for their achievements:

> I am pleased the NAO has recognised the work we have done to tighten our control of costs and live better within our means while continuing to deliver top class equipment to our troops.[16]

There is also a wider question about the relevance and usefulness of all the expensive kit that MoD bosses have set their hearts on acquiring, however high the cost and however long it takes. Some military analysts have predicted that in the future most conflicts involving British troops will be 'fourth generation wars' (4GW) like Iraq and Afghanistan. In these wars there is no clear enemy as they will be largely indistinguishable from the civilian population and will use a wide range of weapons, ranging from AK47s, RPGs (rocket-propelled grenades), roadside bombs and suicide bombers. Against such an enemy, expensive Type 45 Destroyers and even more expensive Astute Class Submarines will be useless. What our troops will need are guns that work in harsh environments (unlike the army's oft-redesigned but still inadequate SA80 rifle), decent amounts of body armour and medical supplies (too often lacking), vehicles that protect our troops against RPGs and roadside bombs (unlike those we have at the moment) and a large force of modern helicopters (not a tiny fleet with an average age of over 15 years).[17] If it is the case that military chiefs are wasting billions on military hardware that was only relevant for past wars, while failing to spend the few hundred million required to adequately equip the troops currently doing the real fighting, this more than anything will reduce our forces' effectiveness and lead to unnecessary loss of life.

## Cooking the Books

Every year the MoD claims to have made huge cost savings in some areas of its operations. In one year it announced that it had reduced its stock of military equipment by over £2 billion. Subsequent investigation by the NAO showed that the £2 billion figure was largely fictitious, achieved only by fiddling around with the figures rather than by any concrete actions.[18] For the year up to the end of 2006, defence bosses yet again proclaimed a cost-reduction success. This time they announced that they had managed to reduce the £2.6 billion plus budget over-run on the major projects by an impressive £781 million. However, as so often happens with MoD pronouncements, a closer look revealed these 'savings' to involve even more cooking of the books. About £91 million of the 'savings' came from a tax rebate, another £448 million was from reclassifying expenditure (just shoving it on to some other part of the budget) and £139 million from reducing the quantity of weapons they were buying (thus risking our soldiers having insufficient supplies). Most of the rest was a result of changing accounting treatments and reducing safety features. When their tricks were exposed, the MoD said that it had never claimed that the £781 million were actual savings at all, evidently forgetting what it had said to the PAC[19] and what was written on page 23 of its own annual report, signed off by the Secretary of State for Defence. Reviewing the MoD's next attempt at book-cooking in late 2007, the PAC seemed less than impressed by the project management capabilities of our military chiefs. The PAC chairman said:

We need to be clear: these are not savings. This juggling act must not happen again next year. The MoD should focus its creative efforts more on effective project management and less on shuffling figures around on balance sheets.[20]

It is interesting to note that in the year that New Labour was elected, one of the PR agencies used by the MoD stated on its official MoD press releases that the agency 'does not warrant or make any representations regarding the correctness, accuracy or reliability of the contents of the press release … All facts should be independently checked.'[21] This is a lesson that still seems relevant today.

## Paper Generals

The MoD's £34 billion seems to provide a lucrative source of income to quite a few people whose contribution towards the defence of our country may not be absolutely obvious to the uninitiated. No less than four MPs are getting many tens of thousands of pounds a year, plus satisfyingly large contributions to their pensions, for their part in defending our freedoms.[22] There is a Secretary of State for Defence, a Minister of State for the Armed Forces, a Minister of State for Defence Equipment and Support and a politician who is both Parliamentary Under Secretary of State for Defence and Minister for Veterans.

Then there is the MoD top brass. Being an MoD boss looks like quite a cushy number. Firstly, they have salaries of somewhere between £175,000 and £215,000. There are also lots of perks – chauffeur-driven cars, living allowances and foreign travel (for many this is usually to attend international conferences and not to visit anywhere dangerous like a war zone). Several senior military figures also spend about £20,000 each on entertainment. Best of all, perhaps, is the pension – a lump sum of £200,000 to £300,000 plus about £100,000 a year, index-linked to protect it from inflation.[23] However, if the pension that we taxpayers so generously provide is not enough, when they retire they can usually earn an extra six-figure sum a year by getting a job as an adviser to one of the many weapons suppliers and consultancies whose products and services they bought with our money while we taxpayers were paying their salaries.

Moreover, it seems as if the job of an MoD big shot may not always be too stressful, unlike the conditions faced by our soldiers fighting to survive in the deserts of Iraq and Afghanistan. We have many more admirals than we have ships, more air marshals than we have squadrons and more brigadiers and generals than we have regiments.

It is not only the top bosses in the MoD who have an admirably comfortable lifestyle. In his revealing book, *Lions, Donkeys and Dinosaurs*, author Lewis Page entertainingly describes the tens of thousands of military personnel who have administrative duties and never have to leave the safety of their offices.[24] Even in 2006, at one of their busiest times since the Second World War, less than 15 per cent of the 89,170 members of the navy and air force and less than 25 per cent of the army were 'undertaking operations and other military tasks'.[25] This means that of the 201,000 service-people in 2006, while around 41,300 military personnel were on active assignment, there were about 159,700 doing other, presumably useful things back in Blighty. Thousands of these will have been resting after active service and getting trained to go back into action. However, many tens of thousands are administrators – 'shiny-arses' who spend their whole lives pushing paper and avoiding anything that looks remotely like active service as they wait patiently for promotion and retirement. Lewis Page eloquently describes how during the 2003 firemen's strike, when 19,000 military personnel had to take over running the fire service, it was so difficult to shift the shiny-arses from behind their desks, that ordinary soldiers had to be taken off their training for the Iraq invasion to drive fire engines: 'Throughout all this, through the fires and the invasion, thousands upon thousands of majors and colonels and commanders and group captains stayed right where they were: behind desks in Britain'.[26] One study indicated that while the number of ships in the Royal Navy fell by over 40 per cent between 1997 and 2006 and the number of sailors by 37 per cent, the number of administrators increased by 5 per cent.[27] Every 1,000 unnecessary pen-pushers costs us over £50 million a year. If there are 10,000 too many of these desk-drivers (and that is probably well short of the real figure), then that is burning up over £500 million a year. This is money that could probably be put to better use buying decent equipment for our frontline troops.

In the UK we probably have one of the best-trained, most professional military forces in the world. However, that should not be allowed to mask the fact that our military also contains tens of thousands of apparatchiks, desk-commanders and other creatures of the corridor who are a drain on the money we pay for defence and an insult to those who actually do risk life and limb in the service of their country.

## THE MILITARY BETRAYAL

With so many billions being wasted on apparently incompetent procurement of new military equipment, excess top brass, luxury headquarters buildings and tens of thousands of administrators, it is not surprising that there are limited resources available for those who actually have to do some fighting. It was reported that paratroopers preparing to go to Afghanistan had to train with less than ten Land Rovers instead of the 110 they should have had, that there were only six Challenger 2 tanks available for training because others had been cannibalized for spares to be used in Iraq and that one fighting unit in Afghanistan had to borrow machine-gun and mortar rounds from the Americans and Canadians because the MoD had not ordered enough. Moreover, an MoD report found that almost half of British forces were unfit to be sent on operations because of shortages of key equipment.[28]

This lack of effective equipment has led to avoidable casualties. Some soldiers were injured and killed because there was not sufficient body armour.[29] Others died because they had to drive around the most dangerous parts of Iraq and Afghanistan in 20-year-old 'snatch' Land Rovers that had been originally used in Northern Ireland and gave no protection against heavy machine-gun fire or rocket-propelled grenades. There was a shortage of Rover terminals, which soldiers use to help direct air attacks and avoid being killed by 'friendly fire'. In one case, troops who had been ambushed by the Taliban had to wait 45 minutes before a US F15 fighter pilot called to destroy an enemy position could begin his bombing run because he was afraid of bombing and strafing the wrong position. In another incident under investigation, three soldiers were killed by a US bomb probably because either they did not have a Rover terminal or because it was not working properly. And, although a wounded soldier's survival chances depend mainly on how he is treated in the first hour after being injured, there were rumours of inadequate medical supplies. One soldier, a medic, summed up the medical equipment crisis when he wrote to his aunt:

> I think if the public knew what was happening out here then they would demand an end to it instantly. For every soldier that dies, about ten lose a limb or similar. And what do we have to treat them? Well I have nothing, despite being a team medic. My medic pouch was taken off me and given to people in more hostile areas. There's simply no excuse for that, it's just lack of funding and it could easily lead to someone dying from it. I have a single bandage for myself, not great considering a bullet causes two holes and I'm meant to treat the eight guys in my section as I'm their first medic. I bought two chest seals before I came out here from the Internet. They cost me £10 each and I bought them

because I knew what the army is like. I mean £10 for Christ's sake.[30]

At times the situation was so serious that even the MoD admitted there were problems. One MoD report confirmed that a decorated soldier died unnecessarily in a minefield in Afghanistan because there were no aircraft available with a suitable winch to help him (all the winches had been returned to the UK for inspection).

Other disturbing examples of the conditions faced by our soldiers also began to reach the British press. When a Hercules transport aircraft was shot down in Iraq with the loss of ten lives, we found out that all the American Hercules had been fitted with anti-explosive foam. Although this had been standard equipment on US planes since the Vietnam War, the MoD had decided not to fit this safety device to British planes because 'it was judged that there was a low risk of a fuel tank explosion'.[31] Over two years later, only two of the RAF's over 40 Hercules had been fitted with the foam. When 14 servicemen died after a Nimrod reconnaissance plane exploded over Afghanistan following a mid-air refuelling, it emerged that the MoD had been warned many times about Nimrod fuel leaks but had done nothing to deal with the problem. Moreover, questions were asked as to why the programme to upgrade all Nimrod planes had been delayed ten years from 2000 to 2010. There was also some horror at the news that in order to save money, the MoD Nimrod upgrade would involve using airframes that were on average 35 years old rather than buying completely new planes.

Perhaps the biggest scandal concerned the lack of helicopters to support our almost 8,000 troops in Afghanistan. According to some reports, there were only eight troop-carrying Chinooks and 12 Apache attack helicopters. Moreover, keeping more than half of them serviceable was difficult due to the heat and fine dust. In October 2006, Tony Blair visited the troops in Afghanistan and made a very clear promise: 'If commanders on the ground want more equipment – armoured vehicles for example, more helicopters – that will be provided. Whatever package they want, we will do'. Returning to the UK, Blair reiterated his promise in a newspaper article stating that British forces 'will get, I promise, whatever frontline commanders tell us they need to complete the job'.[32] A year later, only 16 out of 96 new armoured vehicles had been delivered and, although the MoD was spending £230 million on new helicopters, because of a procurement bungle these would not be ready until about 2009 at the earliest. One officer said:

> These guys are ready to give their lives for the job, but all we are talking about is a little protection. The constraint on equipment is increasing the dangers faced by our soldiers. This is not right.[33]

However, this view was not shared by the MoD spokesman back in the safety of his new £2.347 billion London headquarters: 'As far as helicopter provision in Helmand is concerned, we keep force levels and commanders' requirements under constant review. The appropriate number of platforms is currently available for operational needs.'[34]

There has also been concern at how our troops have been treated. Some people have criticized the low pay levels of soldiers considering the dangerous conditions they are expected to face – while a police officer's starting salary is about £22,000 and a firefighter's is around £25,000, a combat soldier starts on just over £15,000.[35] Another issue is a shortage of trained people. In 2007 the army needed another 2,520 (up 45 per cent in two years), the air force 1,470 more (up 200 per cent in two years) and the navy another 1,860 (up 4 per cent in two years). However, more worrying was the fact that there were shortages of many key skills – flying instructors, radiologists, surgeons, ammunition technicians, bomb disposal experts and combat signallers. Many troops, particularly from the Territorial Army, were hastily deployed for fighting in Iraq and Afghanistan without completing their training and so had to learn on the job – all this despite the fact that there were over 150,000 military personnel stationed back in the UK.

While soldiers in Iraq and Afghanistan struggled to survive, MoD staff back in London did not seem to be sharing the cost constraints of their colleagues on the battlefield. In the last four years about £141 million in bonuses has been paid to MoD civil servants and, in the last ten years, the MoD has spent around £2.3 billion of our money on management consultants to help the military sort out such things as equipment supply. At an average of £230 million a year, this would have been sufficient to pay and equip close to 5,000 extra infantry soldiers.

## THE MORAL BETRAYAL

However, perhaps the most contentious aspect of how our money is being spent by the Government and military bosses concerns the various quite dubious justifications that the powers-that-be have given for exposing our soldiers to danger in the first place. The Government's reasons for keeping our troops in Afghanistan seemed to change by the week. We were there to aid reconstruction, then it was to win hearts and minds so the Taliban could not come back, then it was to spread the power of an incompetent and corrupt government in Kabul. One British government minister claimed our soldiers were there 'to defeat the drugs trade', but another one insisted, 'Our forces are not a narcotics police and never have been'.[36] Anyway, despite British soldiers losing their lives to reduce the opium trade, in the years after the invasion opium production more than doubled so that by 2007 Afghanistan was successfully supplying around 93 per cent of the world demand – much more than when the Taliban was in power. It was estimated that in 2007 about 14 per cent of the population (including many senior politicians, governors, judges and police) were involved in the drugs business, with a hectare yielding £2,300 compared to just £264 for wheat. So bad was the corruption that one analyst commented:

> The British public would be up in arms if they knew that the district appointments in the south for which British soldiers are dying are there just to protect drug routes.[37]

Yet, while our soldiers created new enemies by trying to disrupt the opium trade in Afghanistan, in the UK a British company was trying to recruit farmers in Britain to grow opium to meet our hospitals' growing demand for diamorphine. If the British Government had really wanted to stop the opium trade, it could just have bought up most of the Afghanistan opium crop. Then it could have sold part of the opium to pharmaceutical companies and either destroyed the rest or else even made heroin legally available to addicts in the UK on NHS prescription. This would have largely wiped out the illegal drugs trade, significantly reduced crime in the UK and made us rather more friends than enemies.

The task given to our few thousand poorly equipped and poorly supported soldiers had always been impossible. When one looks at how Afghanis have successfully fought off foreign invaders, including the Russians in the twentieth century and the British in the nineteenth century, it seems more than incredible that our Government and military bosses ever thought they could successfully control the country. The Russians sent 120,000 troops to Afghanistan and had to retreat after horrendous losses. We had fewer than 8,000 personnel as part of a so-called NATO force of 80,000, many of whom hid in the safety of their barracks while the UK, US and Canada bore the brunt of the action. There were several reported incidents where British and Afghan fighting troops had to retreat from the Taliban because German pilots assigned to support them went back to their bases mid-afternoon because they felt it was too dangerous to fly after dark.

By 2007 the battle for hearts and minds had been lost; the battle to disrupt the opium trade had been lost; the battle to impose the authority of the Kabul government had been lost; most construction activity had been abandoned; and the battle to prevent the Taliban returning was being lost. Faced with humiliation, our politicians and military top brass tried to find some way out of the mess without losing face and without having to admit they had ever made a mistake. While they dithered and blustered and made excuses, our soldiers died in ever-increasing numbers.

When things did go horribly wrong and our troops were possibly involved in injuries and deaths of civilian prisoners, the politicians and the military big noises were quick to haul our soldiers before what our leaders self-righteously called 'justice' for their supposed 'crimes'. Some of our servicemen were imprisoned, others had their careers destroyed. However, when our troops were killed by friendly fire or left to die because of equipment shortages, they found that their senior commanders were slow to investigate and their families usually had to wait years before coroners could extract even the most basic information out of a recalcitrant and obstructive military establishment. In one case the logs of critical communications went 'missing' so it was impossible to establish what really happened, and in another it took almost three years for the coroner to obtain cockpit recordings that the Government and military leaders initially claimed did not exist.

As the public lost confidence in the Iraq operation and little progress seemed to be made in Afghanistan, the Government decided to turn up the propaganda machine. A Director General of Media Communications (DGMC) was appointed, supported by his 1,000 communications staff. Renamed 'Team Defence', this army of PR specialists aims to deliver the 'Defence Vision': 'enhance the reputation of the Department (MoD) and Armed Forces both internally and externally through influencing the understanding, activity and perceptions on internal, domestic and international audiences'.[38] Team Defence has apparently realized there is a major perception problem to be overcome:

> Operations in Iraq are not supported by a majority of the public ... There is a growing perception that – particularly on operations – our Armed Forces are not as well-equipped as they should be and that we do not look after our people as well as we should.

Team Defence does not suggest that our troops should get the benefit of all the money we spend by being provided with better support, equipment or accommodation. Instead, the DGMC believes it will meet its objectives by 'creating a steady stream of positive stories which directly promote MoD and the Forces' reputation but also helps to offset the inevitable bad stories' and by 'ensuring that all key stakeholders convey messages on key personnel issues (e.g. Manning, Accommodation and Allowances) which are consistent with a single core script'.

## CONCLUSION – THE POISONED LEGACY

In late 2007, a group of retired military chiefs attacked the Government for underfunding the armed forces. However, their credibility was somewhat undermined when it was revealed that some of them were now working for defence equipment suppliers who would be the first to benefit from more of our money going on weaponry.

In the short term, our Government and defence chiefs' management and military betrayals are having the most serious consequences as they are leading to injury and loss of life for hundreds of our troops and for tens of thousands of innocent civilians in wars that are increasingly difficult to justify. However, in the longer term, our troops have seen how they have been abandoned and betrayed by their leaders, and this will have a devastating effect on the morale of the armed forces and their ability to attract quality recruits in the future. For example, the numbers of officers leaving the forces more than doubled between 2006 and 2007. One of these officers, who was awarded a Distinguished Service Order for leading his troops in heavy fighting in Afghanistan, was reported to have resigned because of concerns over his soldiers' training, equipment, welfare and housing.[39] The longer term risk is that when we do need a strong, professional military to genuinely protect our interests, we may find that we no longer have what we need. That is the poisoned legacy that we will inherit from this Government and its obedient military chiefs' triple betrayal of our troops.

# CHAPTER 5

# EDUCATION AND IGNORANCE

Education provided the opportunity for one of Tony Blair's most memorable soundbites: 'Education, education, education'. The ambitions that New Labour had for improving education and thus reducing social failure were clearly expressed in their 1997 manifesto: 'Education will be our number one priority, and we will increase the share of national income on education as we decrease it on the bills of economic and social failure'.[1] Curiously, over ten years later the next Labour Prime Minister, Gordon Brown, was still promising us 'world class education'. Labour certainly kept the first part of its promise – it has hugely increased the amounts of our money being spent on education. What is less than clear is whether it has actually improved our education and thus decreased 'the bills of social and economic failure'.

Spending on education and training has gone up from £38 billion in 1997–8 to over £73 billion by 2007–8 – an increase of over 90 per cent (equal to around 68 per cent in real terms after inflation is taken into account). It has also gone up from just 4.6 per cent of GDP at the 1997 election to 5.7 per cent in 2007–8, so the Government has spent around £186 billion more on education than it would have done had it kept spending at the 1997 level.

For our money, we have got about another 40,000 teachers and 100,000 classroom assistants. Teachers' salaries have also moved comfortably upwards, with more than 220 head teachers earning over £100,000 (one being paid £180,000) and a third of secondary school leaders (about 1,100) getting £78,500 or more. Thanks to this Government, the era of teachers accepting a smaller salary than other workers in return for longer holidays seems to be a thing of the past. The Government is also planning to spend about £45 billion of our money on its Building Schools for the Future programme, although as many of these will be paid for under 30-year Private Finance Initiative (PFI) schemes, we have hardly begun to see the effect of these on education budgets and on our taxes.

A 2007 report by the Office for National Statistics (ONS) seemed to question whether we taxpayers had got value for money for our extra £186 billion. Educational productivity, as measured by the ONS, rose significantly between 1996 and 1999 – the years when spending was kept under tight control – and then was fairly level as the Government invested huge amounts of money in staff, equipment and buildings at a time of falling pupil numbers. The Director for Social and Public Services at the ONS explained, 'This is a broadly flat productivity performance. Why is productivity important? It is value for money.'[2] The Government naturally rejected the ONS's suggestion that our money had not been spent as well as it could have been. The Schools Minister put forward its position:

> The crucial point for us parents and teachers is to improve the education of every child and, thanks to us consistently prioritising education spending, we now have more teachers, better buildings, better teachers' pay and the highest exam results.[3]

There is validity to the Government's position that putting more teachers and more teaching assistants in the classroom when there are fewer pupils to teach will lead to a theoretical decline in a blunt measure like productivity, but that improving the quality of education is probably more important than increasing productivity. So, to judge our Government's success we need to review whether the massive extra investment of our money is leading to a generation of more highly educated schoolchildren.

## A NATION OF YOUNG GENIUSES

In the new world economy, a country's ability to increase the knowledge of its citizens will be key to its economic success or failure. New Labour's 1997 manifesto made clear this link between educational achievement and economic success: 'It [education] is not just good for the individual. It is an economic necessity for the nation. And quality comes from developing the potential of all our people'. A frisson of fear should have gone through our international competitors in August 2007 when the exam results of the UK's schoolchildren were announced. There should have been headlines around the world warning of the coming threat of the UK's incomparably well-educated youth. Foreign politicians should have been rushing on to television to exhort their idle children to follow the shining example of their British counterparts. Strangely, the British exam results do not seem to have been noticed by our competitors. Either our competitors are so stupid that they do not understand how our educational success will threaten their well-being or else they do not really believe what our Government's numbers appear to be showing.

The 2007 exam results were stunningly good. Around 98 per cent of the 750,000 GCSE pupils passed and about 97 per cent of the 310,000 A-Level candidates passed. When many readers of this book took their GCSEs or O-Levels and A-Levels, some would probably have been genuinely afraid that they might not pass their exams. Today's students are evidently so intelligent and so hard-working that they do not have to share previous generations' real fear of possible failure. Not only did 2007's children pass their exams, but they also passed with flying colours. Just over 63 per cent achieved A* to C grades in GCSEs and 25 per cent got A grades in their A-Levels. The Schools Minister attributed the results to 'high quality teaching and strong investment in schools'.[4] When some observers dared suggest that a dumbing-down of exams and grade inflation, rather than academic brilliance, might be behind some of the results, they were dismissed by those responsible for our children's education: 'Whatever the usual grumpy old persons want to say about how it used to be much harder in their day, what we want to say is congratulations to the students'.[5]

Those in the educational establishment were not slow to take credit for our children's results. The director general of AQA, England's biggest exam board, commended these extraordinary educational achievements: 'They reflect the hard work and skill of teachers and the motivation and energy of young people'.[6] Unfortunately, these excellent A-Level results posed a problem for universities' admissions bodies as it was now difficult to distinguish the best students when so many were achieving such high grades. The director general of AQA recognized this and called it a 'problem of success': 'You can see why a small number of universities at the moment have a problem differentiating between the very, very, very best and the very best'.[7]

Those paid to deliver our children's education are gratifyingly quick to claim credit for every figure that goes up, showing improving results. However, they do not appear to be quite so keen to take responsibility when the figures go the wrong way and indicate that our children's academic performance is actually getting worse in spite of the gargantuan investments to improve it. When the results for the Foundation Stage Profile tests were published in 2007, they showed a decline from 48 per cent of children achieving a satisfactory level in 2005–6 to 44 per cent for 2006–7. Rather than admitting that this was a statistically significant fall, showing a serious problem of underachievement for tens of thousands of children, the Department for Education and Skills chose instead to apply the 'heads I win, tails you lose' scientific method and attributed this worrying decline in standards to improvements in their methods of assessment: 'Analysis of the data suggests that improvements to assessment and moderation continue to be the most significant factor in the apparent decline in results'. Another Government tactic has been to pin the blame for educational failure on someone else. When a review of the Government's £500 million literacy programme indicated that standards had hardly improved since the 1950s, and when an international study of children's literacy levels showed that England had fallen from 3rd to 15th place and Scotland had slumped from 14th to 26th since 2001 in spite of increased spending, the Government blamed parents for failing to encourage their children to read.[8] Similarly, when the Government's huge investments in improving education failed to increase the number of children from poorer backgrounds who went to university, the Government accused universities of missing out on a 'huge amount of talent' by recruiting the 'vast majority of students from a small minority of society'.[9] A third common reaction to declining educational performance has been outright denial of reality. When the 2007 results for seven-year-olds' mastery of reading, writing and maths showed they had fallen back to the 2000 level, the Schools Minister expressed his satisfaction with the Government's achievements: 'I am pleased that we are maintaining high standards at this crucial stage in education'.[10]

## EDUCATIONAL APARTHEID

One clue as to whether we should believe the Government and the educational bureaucrats' claims of almost superhuman success is in the way they report their results. They do not use a 'neutral' word and just call them 'results' any more; they now refer to them as 'School Achievement and Attainment Tables'. This rebranding to make schools' results sound more positive is something that seems to pervade this Government's attempts to dress up its efforts in the most positive way possible.

There are several ways of viewing how well the educationalists have spent our money. One is to note that over ten years the amount spent on each pupil has almost doubled (up 87 per cent in real terms). At the same time, the number of children achieving Government targets at ages 11, 14 and at GCSE has gone up by less than 30 per cent.[11] Even if we believe the Government's assertion that exams have not got easier, getting pupils' results up is clearly an expensive business.

One could look at the other side of the coin. If 58 per cent of pupils are getting five GCSEs at grade A* to C, this means that after over ten years of school and probably more than 10,000 hours spent in a classroom, over 40 per cent of our children are failing to get the absolute minimum qualifications they will need to have any reasonable chances in life. Within this 40 per cent there are some truly shocking figures: at 14, 20 per cent of boys have a reading age of seven and around 63 per cent of working-class boys and 43 per cent of working-class girls cannot read or write properly; at 16, 60 per cent of children fail to get a grade C or above in the two basic GCSE subjects of Maths and English and about 90,000 boys (one in four) have no GCSEs at all at grade C or above. By 17 and 18, 64 per cent of boys and 56 per cent of girls will not sit one single A-Level.[12] Seemingly unaware of this educational apartheid, a Government spokesman claimed, 'The state school system is continuing to deliver for parents, regardless of their wealth or background, with record results across the board'.[13] So, while some children may actually be performing well, even better than past generations, there is a mass – about half of our schoolchildren – who can spend many thousands of hours being taught just a few basic subjects by more teachers and teaching assistants than we have ever had, in better-equipped schools than we have ever had, yet apparently hardly learn anything of substance.

## WHEN IS A QUALIFICATION A QUALIFICATION?

There is probably nothing in education quite as sensitive as the question of whether exams are becoming easier. To suggest that it is simpler to get better grades now than it was 10 or 15 years ago is usually branded as an 'insult' to teachers and children. Yet the evidence that the standard required to succeed in exams has been falling is becoming overwhelming. This is not a phenom-enon unique to this Government. GCSE results have improved almost continuously for 15 years and A-Level results for 25 years. However, this Government has perhaps done more to claim the credit for these improvements than any other before it. There seem to be two things happening simultaneously – grade inflation and simplification of questions.

A report for the Office for National Statistics suggested that between 1988 and 2006 there has been grade inflation of two grades for most subjects and over three grades in Maths. So at A-Level, a person who would have got an E grade in exams like Geography or Biology in 1988 would get a C in 2005 and some-one getting an F in Maths in 1988 would on average have got a C in 2005. One teacher who had been marking Maths exams for over 20 years explained in a Radio Four interview why and how the lowering of standards worked. People setting and marking Maths papers were told that fewer students were taking Maths because the children (and their parents) felt that their chances of getting good results were less than on other possibly easier subjects. The only way the Maths teachers could increase the number of students taking their subject (and in the process pre-serve their jobs) was to both remove some of the more complex theoretical questions and to mark more leniently than they had done in the past. An examiner for the French Oral admitted in an interview that she was powerless to prevent the same thing happening in her subject, especially after the number of students taking French declined rapidly when modern languages were no longer compulsory subjects: 'We complain at examiners' meetings but our hands are tied. I, for one, will not be renewing my order for red biros in 2008.'[14]

Naturally, ministers denied any dumbing down: 'If more young people are making the top grade, and aiming higher, we should cheer, not carp'.[15] However, the educational establishment got caught with its pants well and truly down around its ankles in 2007 when a newspaper obtained a document prepared by the Joint Council for Qualifications (JCQ). The JCQ, which represents examining bodies across the UK, recommended that on GCSE science papers from 2008 the percentage of 'low-demand questions' requiring simpler or multiple-choice answers should rise from 55 per cent to 70 per cent. When faced with proof of deliberately lowering standards, those involved denied it would be easier to get a higher grade and explained that they were trying to avoid students being 'turned off' by science:

> Part of the desire is that the student can come out of the exam with a feeling of success that they have actually tackled a significant proportion of the questions … They can only have that by being allowed to tackle questions which are at their level … It is about making exams accessible to candidates.[16]

Old-fashioned, grumpy, out-of-touch people were probably under the misapprehension that the purpose of education was to raise students' knowledge and abilities so that they could easily cope with challenges like exams, not to lower exams to the level of the worst-performing pupils' knowledge.

Other concerns expressed by the few teachers who dared to rock the boat were that children were flocking to newer subjects that were academically less stretching. By 2008, some universities were so concerned at the number of pupils taking 'easier' subjects that they drew up a list of A-Level subjects which would not be accepted as a basis for gaining a university place. Some 'off-message' teachers also worried that the opportunities for repeated resits allowed children to improve their grades and that splitting exam questions into smaller bite-sized pieces made them less difficult. When the record-breaking 2007 GCSE results were announced, the Schools Minister vigorously defended them: 'GCSEs are robust, rigorous and respected. The steady improvement over the last ten years is unarguable evidence of rising achievement and the benefits of sustained investment in teaching and resources.'[17] However, shortly after the controversy surrounding the results, although the Schools Minister denied there was a problem, the Government announced that it was splitting the Qualifications and Curriculum Authority (QCA) in order to restore public confidence in the exams system. The Children, Schools and Families Secretary explained the reasons for this apparent change of mind: 'We have not managed to persuade the public, parents and employers about the standards of exams'.[18]

## NO NEET ANSWERS

A key aim of this Government's drive to improve education was 'to decrease the bills of economic and social failure'. Yet perhaps the most glaring and most unarguable demonstration of the Government's failure to really improve the education of all our children is in the inexorable rise in the number of NEETs. A NEET is someone (normally between 16 and 24) who is not in employment, education or training. The Government has recognized the social consequences of the NEETs: 'Being NEET between the ages of 16 and 18 is a major predictor of later unemployment, low income, teenage motherhood and depression and poor health'.[19] In his first budget speech, the then Chancellor Gordon Brown made it clear that hanging around doing nothing except collecting state benefits would not be an option for young people. Announcing the New Deal for Young People programme in 1997, he described the bright productive future for the UK's youth:

Tomorrow the Secretary for Education and Employment will detail the four options, all involve training leading to qualifications: a job with an employer; work with a voluntary organization; work on the environmental task force; and, for those without basic qualifications, full time education or training. With these new opportunities for young people come new responsibilities. There will be no fifth option – to stay at home on full benefit.[20]

The New Deal for Young People has cost us around £2 billion since its full introduction in 1998. It was designed to be a mandatory programme for 18–24-year-olds. After claiming Jobseeker's Allowance for six months, they had to apply for jobs while committing to the New Deal programme. They were then given a personal adviser who would work with them to improve their skills and help them find employment or put them in temporary placements in order to increase their employability.

However, the NEET problem has proved harder to crack than the Government might have hoped. Faced by rising numbers of NEETs and the failure of its policies to deal with the problem, the Government's attitude to NEETs has been curiously schizophrenic. Some ministers have claimed the problem does not even exist. For example, in February 2007 the Employment and Welfare Reform Minister announced, 'Youth unemployment has been virtually abolished'.[21] At the same time, other ministers have admitted there is a problem but insist that the number of NEETs has remained relatively stable since Labour took power: 'The proportion of 16- to 18-year-olds not in education, employment or training has remained broadly level for the last twelve years'.[22] The statement that youth unemployment has been virtually abolished is more than questionable, while the assertion that the number of NEETs has remained broadly level glosses over the fact that when this Government was elected, the number of NEETs was falling quite rapidly as overall levels of unemployment fell. It reached a low of 797,000 in 2001 and since then has

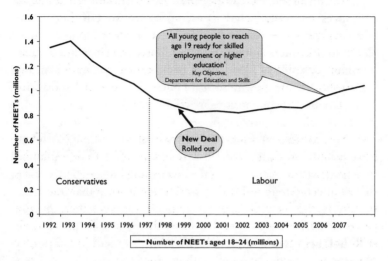

**Figure 8** The number of NEETs has been rising since 2001 (in spite of billions being spent on the New Deal)

risen by over 200,000 in spite of huge amounts of our money being liberally hosed on to the problem (see Figure 8).

Over a million young people have been on the New Deal programme. The Government claims huge success with 700,000 young people being helped into work.[23] Certainly, some participants have found jobs, but the rise in the number of NEETs since the New Deal was rolled out seems to tell a different story.

In the UK, about one in five 16- to 24-year-olds are spending their time doing approximately nothing at all. This is twice the level of France or Germany and is truly astonishing in view of the rapid and sustained economic growth that we have experienced over the 11 years or so of New Labour. In a period when over 2.5 million new jobs have been created, our education system has prepared over a million young people so badly in terms of their knowledge and skills that they are both unwilling and unable to be employed. We have huge skills shortages in some areas of the economy – the building sector for example estimates that it needs about 430,000 more workers without taking account of possibly 10,000 more required for the Olympics. However, these labour shortages have not acted as a barrier to the UK's economic growth, as between one million and two million foreigners have come to work here and have taken the jobs that our young people have not filled. There have been various estimates of how much the NEETs cost in terms of benefits, crime and social support. About £10 billion a year would probably be a reasonable guess. As the economy keeps growing, we can continue to bear the enormous social costs of over a million young people who are increasingly excluded from normal society. However, if and when growth begins to slow, this ever more entrenched army of the disaffected may well cause some quite nasty social problems.

## INITIATIVE, INITIATIVE, INITIATIVE

In education, we seem to see a similar situation to what has happened in organizations like the police and the NHS. Massive increases in the amounts of our money being spent appear to lead to astonishingly small increases in the number of people who actually work directly with the people those organizations are meant to serve. While almost doubling the amount spent per pupil, this Government has given us about 10 per cent more teachers. There are also a lot more classroom assistants who might be costing a couple of billion a year. However, even they do not explain the £35 billion more each year now being spent on education compared to when this Government was first elected. So, one might well wonder where most of our money has gone.

Looking at the number of initiatives launched by this Government, one can start to see where much of our money might have found its way. For children starting school there have been Early Learning Partnerships, Transition Information Sessions, Parent Support Advisers and Parenting Early

Intervention Pathfinders. At primary school level there were the Primary Leadership Programme and Primary Strategy Consultant Leaders. For secondary schools we were given Social and Emotional Aspects of Learning Resources (SEALS), School Improvement Partners, Reading Recovery Teachers, the Secondary National Strategy, Learning Agreements and Excellence Hubs. We have also been blessed with the September Guarantee, School Sport Partnerships, Pathfinder Partnerships, Education Improvement Partnerships, Extended Schools, the Every Child Matters (ECM) programme, the Cross-Government Safeguarding Programme Board, Local Safeguarding Children Boards, Activity Agreements, the Apprentice Ambassador Network, Care to Learn, Aimhigher (the national outreach programme), Safer School Partnerships, the London Challenge, Chartered London Teachers, the 6th Form Presumption, the Early Adopters Programme, Making Mathematics Count, the Train to Gain Service, Youth Matters, Sector Skills Councils, National Skills Academies, the Trust Schools Toolkit, the Specialist Schools and Academies Trust, the Numeracy Taskforce, Safer Sector Partnerships, the Framework for Personal Learning and Thinking Skills, Diploma Gateway, Every Child a Reader (ECAR) and the School Attendance Strategy, to name just a few. Moreover, there was Personalised Learning – but as the Department for Education and Skills explained, this is 'not a new initiative, it is a philosophy'.

As the Department for Education and Skills explained in its 2007 report, all of these initiatives are apparently part of 'the Government's commitment to removing unnecessary administrative burdens and giving schools greater freedom and autonomy'.[24] However, an ignorant outsider might get the impression that this Government has created a vast, Byzantine empire of specialists and advisers – many with good salaries, expense accounts and index-linked pensions – all there to wander round the country, attend thousands of meetings, produce hundreds of thousands of documents, all to tell our teachers how to teach

# CHAPTER 6

# THE HOME OFFICE – HOUSE OF HORROR

The purpose of the Home Office is 'to protect the public and secure our future'. On its website it explains how it does this:

> The Home Office leads a national effort to protect the public from terror, crime and anti-social behaviour. We secure our borders and welcome legal migrants and visitors. We safeguard identity and citizenship. We help build the security, justice and respect that enable people to prosper in a free and tolerant society.[1]

The Home Office receives a substantial proportion of our money. Spending went up from just under £7 billion a year in 1997–8 to over £14 billion by 2007–8 – a doubling in pure cash terms, equivalent to over a 70 per cent increase once inflation is taken into account. According to the Cabinet Office's 2006 'Capability Review' (a report on the management capabilities and organizational effectiveness of government departments), the Home Office has been remarkably successful in using our money to achieve its goals:

> The Department ... achieved noticeable successes in terms of its performance against those targets. In particular, the Home Office has reduced crime and the fear of crime, improved police performance, increased the number of

offences brought to justice, and 'tipped the balance' towards
greater clearance of cases than applications in relation to the
deportation of failed asylum-seekers.[2]

So, as far as the Government was concerned, everything seemed
pretty much tickety-boo at the Home Office and we were getting
reasonably good value for our money despite the large increase
which the Home Office had received from us. At least that is the
way things looked until spring 2006, when the scandal erupted
around foreign prisoners, including rapists, child sex offenders
and murderers, being released into the community without even
being considered for deportation. The Home Secretary Charles
Clarke apologized profusely and vowed to fix the problem.
However, his boss Mr Blair had other plans and Charles Clarke
was quickly and somewhat ignominiously replaced by John Reid.
The new Home Secretary rather surprised us all. Instead of trying to spin out of trouble, he bravely (so it seemed at the time)
accepted that something had gone horribly wrong and made
his memorable admission that the Home Office was not fit for
purpose:

> in the wake of the problems of mass migration that we have
> been facing our system is not fit for purpose. It is inadequate
> in terms of its scope; it is inadequate in terms of its infor-
> mation technology, leadership, management, systems and
> processes.[3]

The Home Secretary vowed to knock things back into shape.
The newspapers loved the image of the big tough political bruiser
coming in to bang together the heads of a few incompetent civil
servants, and generally accepted the Government's version of
events – that we had all been let down by a bunch of useless
bureaucrats who were about to get their come-uppance.
However, the truth behind the foreign prisoners' scandal was not
quite as straightforward as the Government would have us

believe. Given that this scandal was such a seminal moment in the history of the Home Office, it might be worth spending a little time looking behind the scenes to examine the details of who really was responsible for the foreign prisoners' fiasco, particularly as much of the blame lay rather closer to 10 Downing Street than the Government has wanted us to discover.

## HITTING TARGETS, MISSING GOALS

One of the key functions of the Home Office is the management of immigration, and within the Home Office is a department called the Immigration and Nationality Directorate (IND). Deep within the bowels of the IND was a small group called the Criminal Casework Team (CCT), where a mere 22 of the IND's total of 14,500 staff worked in 2002. The CCT was responsible for ensuring that foreign prisoners were considered for deportation and deported where appropriate. Between 2000 and 2007, the number of foreign prisoners in British prisons almost doubled from around 5,600 to 11,100, while the overall prison population only went up by about a third.

Up until 2002, it had been policy that convicted foreign prisoners should be considered for deportation. However, nobody had really bothered enforcing this policy and prisons only told the CCT when they received prisoners that judges had already recommended for deportation. This inaction allowed about three out of every four foreign criminals to remain in the UK on release from prison. Worried about the rising numbers of foreign prisoners, the CCT did a small survey of prisons to try to find out where all the foreign prisoners were. Once they realized that the numbers of foreign prisoners were increasing, the CCT made a request for extra staff in December 2002. This was rejected by IND bosses due to budget constraints as the IND had overspent on other parts of its budget. By April 2003 the CCT was handling 1,700 cases with 30 staff – about 57 cases per person.

In 2003 the Government started on a whole series of initiatives and changes in the law that would vastly increase the CCT's workload. In April the law was changed giving even deportees, who had been recommended for deportation, the right of appeal. Most, of course, made use of this opportunity to prevent themselves being thrown out of the country and this made each deportation much more difficult and work-intensive than before. Then in October the CCT was also made responsible for deporting European Union criminals. By April 2004 the CCT was handling 5,000 cases with 40 staff – 125 cases per person – more than doubling their previous workload at the same time as making each case harder to process. However, the Government's 2002 pledge to halve the number of asylum-seekers trying to stay in the UK put clear but unwritten pressure on CCT staff not to try to deport anyone who might be able to claim political asylum, as this would make the Government's asylum figures look bad. It is much easier to deport foreign criminals to countries that are deemed stable and safe than it is to send them to countries where there is some form of civil unrest. Therefore, the CCT tended to concentrate its efforts on the criminals that could be sent to safe countries rather than those who should be deported for our safety.

In June 2004, to counter public concern about prison overcrowding, the Government introduced an early removals scheme for foreign prisoners and in September 2004 a new Prison Service Order was issued requiring prison governors to inform the CCT of all foreign prisoners. So the priority for the CCT changed from removing prisoners who would not try to claim asylum to removing as many as possible to meet Government targets. Naturally, this intensified the pressure on the CCT to choose the 'easiest' cases rather than those who represented the greatest danger to us, the British public. The CCT did get some more staff and by April 2005 it had over 9,000 cases and 85 staff – 106 cases per person, still around twice what they had handled prior to 2002.

In 2005 the priorities for the CCT changed again. Following the Prime Minister's promise to increase the deportations of failed asylum-seekers, the CCT was given 25 extra staff and told to deport as many failed asylum-seekers as possible. Moreover, in order to meet the Government's targets, CCT personnel were instructed to deport even prisoners with short sentences for very minor crimes who would previously not have been considered for deportation. This further pressurized CCT staff towards achieving their numbers rather than protecting the public from the most dangerous individuals. Added to that, each CCT employee had a personal target of achieving 85 per cent of removals within 28 days of release from prison – yet another target which pushed staff towards focusing on cases that were easy rather than those concerning the criminals who were most dangerous. Given that most CCT staff managed to hit their 28-day targets about 90 per cent of the time, IND top managers could congratulate themselves that all was going swimmingly. Apparently, at no time during all these years did it ever occur to senior IND managers that the CCT should be prioritizing for deportation those individuals who were most likely to commit serious offences on release into the community, rather than just trying to hit ever-changing government targets.

In 2005, when the Public Accounts Committee (PAC) started to get a feeling that something was wrong, Home Office bosses repeatedly supplied the PAC with figures that some members of the PAC considered to be misleading. Home Office chiefs first under-reported the number of foreign prisoners released without being considered for deportation – initially they clamed 403, then 609, and then admitted it was 1,023. They then claimed that none of these prisoners were serious offenders – a significant number were later found to be violent criminals, murderers and rapists.[4]

Certainly, Home Office staff and top managers seem to be guilty of extraordinary incompetence and negligence in their avowed duty to protect the public, but the Government's obsession with appearing to meet its own overly-simplistic, ever-changing targets without assigning sufficient thought or resources was also partly to blame for the whole foreign prisoners and 'not fit-for-purpose' fiasco.

## A THREE-LEGGED MONSTER THAT CANNOT COUNT

There are three main parts to the Home Office – the IND, the justice system and the prisons. Following the ructions of 2006, the Home Office was split up and a new Ministry of Justice was created to run the courts and prisons in 2007. A key responsibility of each government department is to produce a reliable set of accounts so we all know how and where our money is being spent. The Home Office accounts for 2004–5 were such a mess that the Auditor General refused to approve them. One of the many mistakes uncovered concerned an employee putting a long code number where a financial amount should have been, so that when the various debits and credits were added up there was an error of £26,527,108,436,994 – equivalent to about 2,000 times the actual budget of the Home Office and about 20 times the GDP of the whole of the UK.[5] On the personal recommendation of the then Chancellor Gordon Brown, Sir John Gieve, the head of the Home Office, was promoted to Deputy Governor of the Bank of England in charge of financial stability in the banking system.[6] A member of the Public Accounts Committee remarked, 'You might reasonably expect to see this in a Gilbert and Sullivan opera, but not in real life'.[7]

Although it does not really seem to know where our money goes, the Home Office still manages to spend a fair amount of it on the three important areas of immigration, the justice system and prisons. So I propose to look at each area in turn to see whether we taxpayers are getting value for our money.

## IMMIGRATION

In this section I will not be dealing with the political and moral hot potato of whether immigration is good or harmful for the country. I will only look at how much of our money the IND has used, what it has said it will do with this money and how effectively it has done it.

The IND was reorganized in 2007 and rebranded the Border and Immigration Agency. Over the last five years, as immigration has soared, spending on immigration control seems to have been reduced by about 20 per cent from about £1.85 billion in 2003–4 to a planned £1.48 billion in 2007–8. The IND's and its successor's job was 'to regulate entry to and settlement in the United Kingdom effectively in the interests of sustainable growth and social inclusion'. It can be judged on how it has performed in three main areas – dealing with applications for asylum, preventing illegal immigration and controlling economic migrants for the benefit of the country.

### The Lunatic Asylum

When this Government came to power in 1997, applications for asylum were around 30,000 a year. By 1999 applications had more than doubled to over 70,000 a year. They stayed at between 70,000 and 80,000 a year for four years, giving the UK the highest level in Europe until public concern forced the Government to take action. In 2002 the Prime Minister made a pledge to halve the number and sure enough the Government soon took credit for the numbers falling rapidly to reach 23,610 by 2006 (see Figure 9).

The Prime Minster also set a target for the number of removals of failed asylum-seekers to rise from around 7,000 a year to 30,000. However, this target was quietly dropped a year later in 2003 when the Government realized it was unachievable. Moreover, the impressive fall in overall numbers of asylum-

**Figure 9** The number of asylum applications has fallen, but most rejected applicants just stay anyway

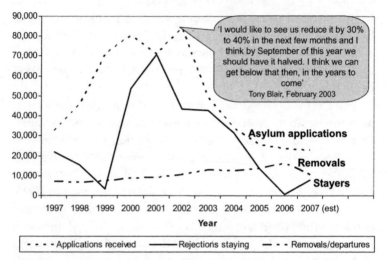

seekers masked a slightly embarrassing situation which the Government did not mention too often – although only around 20 per cent of asylum-seekers were granted the right to remain in the country, around 80 per cent stayed anyway. Of the 517,000 applications between 1997 and 2006, 107,000 (21 per cent) were granted leave to remain and 410,000 (79 per cent) were rejected. Yet most of those 410,000 (306,000) decided they quite liked living here and so did not return home (see Figure 9).

When the foreign prisoners scandal erupted in 2005–6, the Government once again quickly leapt into what it hoped looked like action and pledged to increase the number of deportations to what it called a 'tipping point', where the number of deportations exceeded the number of rejected applications. By doing this it could, it claimed, begin to cut into the backlog of failed asylum seekers who should have left the country. This 'tipping point' was theoretically achieved in 2006 when the IND claimed it had deported 18,235 rejected applicants against unfounded applications of 17,780 – thus cutting 455 cases from the backlog. Given that by 2007 the full backlog of rejected applicants staying in the country had reached around 450,000 people, at this rate of 455 cases a year it would have taken the IND almost 1,000 years to remove all the failed applicants. Anyway, the Government's calculation of the 'tipping point' was all but meaningless as it owed rather more to creative mathematics than to reality.[8] By 2006 the number of rejected applicants staying had plummeted to only about 700 people from a high in 2001 of over 70,000. However, once the Government and IND felt they had looked as if they had responded to the public's concern about rejected applicants staying here, the authorities relaxed and dropped the rate of deportations by over a third in 2007 compared to 2006. So once again many rejected applicants will just stay here and nobody will bother to do anything about it.

The Parliamentary Home Affairs Committee was clear in its view of the Home Office's handling of asylum applications:

> The United Kingdom's asylum policy has been undermined by the inability of the Home Office's Immigration and Nationality Directorate to deal promptly with asylum-seekers whose initial application to stay in the United Kingdom fails.[9]

The Home Office's reputation for dealing with asylum-seekers was not helped by unsubstantiated stories that some staff at its Croydon Lunar House building (affectionately known as 'Lunatic House') were offering to help asylum-seekers in return for sex, and by the story of two immigration judges who had sex with each other (which they filmed) before one of them went on to have sex with the other's Brazilian cleaner – whom he called his 'hot chili pepper' – whose immigration status was also dubious. Add to all this the group of illegal immigrants found working as cleaners in the Home Office's own buildings and the illegal immigrant working as a bodyguard for Gordon Brown, the

Prime Minister, and you have a government department whose incompetence almost defies belief.

Looking at Figure 9, it does seem as if the Government has been fantastically successful at meeting Blair's promise to more than halve the number of asylum-seekers. This may well be the case and perhaps the Government deserves our praise for its effective action. On the other hand, we may be witnessing yet another massive mathematical manipulation. There are two main reasons for claiming asylum – either a person is genuinely fleeing oppression or else a person already here has been threatened with deportation and they are using the asylum claim to delay, and hopefully avoid, being shown the door. So, as happened with releasing foreign criminals into the community, the fewer the authorities tried to deport, the fewer would need to consider claiming asylum. Thus, a possible explanation of the apparent dramatic fall in the number of asylum-seekers could be that the Home Office has once again instructed its staff to go easy on people who have stayed here illegally. By officials turning a blind eye and allowing illegals to stay, immigrants are less likely to try to claim asylum and so the Government can 'honestly' report that the numbers of asylum-seekers have fallen impressively. Some evidence that officials might be going easy on illegal immigrants could be found in the largesse the Home Office has displayed when handing out British citizenships. In 1996 and 1997 about 40,000 a year were being awarded. This soon shot up to 80,000 by 2000; 120,000 by 2002; 140,000 by 2004; and peaked at over 160,000 by 2005.[10] Why the number was allowed to increase so rapidly is not clear. However, the line of falling numbers of asylum-seekers from Figure 9 looks quite interesting when one superimposes the number of British citizenships granted (see Figure 10).

It could well be that these two sets of figures – numbers of asylum applications and citizenships granted – are not connected in any way, shape or form. On the other hand, Figure 10 may reveal that the Government has found a new trick for disguising

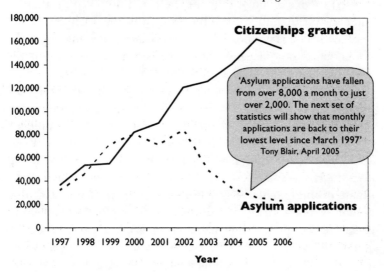

**Figure 10** While the number of asylum applications has fallen there has been a massive rise in citizenships granted

the true level of asylum-seekers in order to be seen as meeting its own targets: by freely distributing over a million British citizenships since 1997, the Home Office may be avoiding people claiming asylum and thus playing down the actual number of asylum-seekers. Moreover, one advantage for the Government of so many foreigners quickly and effortlessly becoming British citizens would be that official statistics would give the impression that there were far fewer foreigners in the country than was actually the case.

## Illegal Immigrants – Don't Know, Don't Care

If the Home Office's handling of asylum-seekers was almost laughable, its management of illegal immigration was pure comedy. When asked by the Home Affairs Committee how many people were illegally in the UK, the IND officer responsible replied, 'I haven't the faintest idea'. To the question, 'How many people are not complying with reporting requirements?', he said, 'I cannot give you those details, I do apologise'. When pressed to give a rough estimate, he could not even do that: 'I can't answer that question in the direct way you ask it'.[11]

Of course, it is not possible to know exactly how many people are in the country illegally. However, there are indications of the size of the problem. For a start, there are the 450,000 asylum-seekers whose applications were rejected but who decided to stay anyway as they seem to like it here. Moreover, in the four years up to April 2007, about one million National Insurance numbers were issued to non-Europeans. Given that the Government does know how many non-nationals have registered to work here, even the Home Office should have been capable of a rough guestimate of the number of illegal immigrants. Incidentally, of the million National Insurance numbers issued to foreign nationals, checks of the immigration status of the applicant were done in around 20,000 cases – just 2 per cent. A sizeable 98 per cent were given their NI numbers without anybody asking if they should be here or not. Perhaps this extremely low level of checking is further confirmation of the Government's unannounced policy of letting people stay to avoid them claiming asylum.

Yet another area of immigration where the Home Office seems to have just given up is in managing the numbers of overseas students allowed to study here. Around 300,000 people a year are granted visas to study in the UK. The Government has no idea how many stay, how many ever leave or how many even turn up for the courses they are meant to be studying. Once here, many foreign students apply for visa extensions, ostensibly to continue their studies. For most developed countries, just under 25 per cent of students coming here over a three-year period applied for extensions. However, for Jamaica, although only 1,690 students came to the UK during a three-year period, an astounding 27,525 student visa extensions were granted. Zimbabwe also did well with 4,270 students arriving in the three years and 25,420 of these being granted extensions, suggesting that coming to the UK as a 'student' is in many cases just a way of getting in through the back door.[12] Home Office personnel apparently noticed nothing odd that for some countries they were granting many times more student extension visas than there were students in the UK. Other countries that got more student visa extensions than there were students included Sri Lanka, Tanzania, South Africa, Mauritius, Ghana, Trinidad and the Ukraine. However, in early 2008 we learnt many of these supposed students hadn't actually needed to apply for extensions to their student visas at all. Although the Government acted tough by bringing in a new rule that students who overstayed their visas should be deported, the Border and Immigration Agency instructed its staff to ignore its own new rule as it didn't consider that deporting bogus students was a priority. This was a somewhat surprising decision given that the Home Secretary had just announced 'robust management' to ensure that all migrants 'played by the rules'.[13]

## Controlled Migration – Out of Control

The Government has repeatedly claimed that what it calls 'controlled migration' is good for the British economy. When the first batch of East European countries joined the EU in May 2004, only the UK, Sweden and Ireland of the existing 15 EU members allowed people from the new member states immediate access to their labour markets. The IND and the Government had apparently done their calculations and estimated that only somewhere between 5,000 and 15,000 economic migrants would come to the UK each year. Three years later, there were over 650,000. Then, in January 2007, Romania and Bulgaria joined. The Government and IND did their sums again and predicted another 10,000 or so migrants – within six months around 200,000 people from Bulgaria and Romania had visited the UK. Some may well have come to see the sights and enjoy the weather, but it is reasonably likely that most came here to work or check out the workings of the social security benefits system.

On 8 October 2007 the Government claimed that around 800,000 migrants had come to work in the UK since New Labour came to power. Then a few weeks later ministers admitted there had been a 'statistical error' and a more accurate number was 1,100,000 – apparently the Home Office had not noticed around 300,000 people (equal to three cities the size of Cambridge). However, one MP let slip that the true figure was nearer 1,600,000 – twice what the Government had claimed less than a month earlier.[14]

The Government was also very generous in giving our money to those who did come here to work. After 12 months in the UK, migrants were eligible for things like Tax Credits, Child Support and all the other payments that British workers could get. They could even get Child Support for children who were back at home and not in the UK at all. In 2006 only 42,620 Eastern Europeans had decided to claim benefits. By 2007 this had more than doubled to 112,000 claimants getting about £125 million in benefits.[15] By 2008 this will probably have doubled again.

By late 2007 the Government had realized that the public was becoming worried by hundreds of thousands of economic migrants taking British jobs and working for lower salaries than British workers would accept. With more than five million British citizens 'economically inactive', Prime Minister Gordon Brown promised the TUC conference an 'extra 500,000 British jobs for British workers', in spite of such a promise probably being illegal under EU freedom of movement and employment rules.[16] As the huge building programmes for 200,000 affordable homes and the 2012 Olympics suck in tens of thousands more workers from Eastern Europe, increasing housing shortages and forcing down wages, it will be interesting to see how the Prime Minister delivers on his (presumably illegal) promise.

## DOING JUSTICE AN INJUSTICE

Home Office spending on the justice system has gone up by almost 70 per cent from less than £6.8 billion in 1997 to over £11.5 billion in 2007–8. As usual with this Government's increasing spending of our money, within this wave of cash there were some worrying details. For example, although the amount spent on the probation service went up by 160 per cent, the number of probation service staff only increased by about 50 per cent from just under 14,000 in 1997 to around 21,000 by 2007. Moreover, there are indications that the number of managers and administration staff has increased much more than the number of fully trained probation officers, possibly echoing what happened with the police where a large rise in funding led to just a few more police, but many more administrative and support staff.[17] Another interesting set of numbers shows that over the last ten years or so the amount paid out for Criminal Injuries Compensation actually fell by 13 per cent in spite of a doubling in the number of violent crimes, apparently contradicting the Government's constant claims to be on the side of the victims of crime.

In its 1997 election manifesto, New Labour lambasted the Tories' allegedly incompetent handling of crime:

> The number of people convicted has fallen by a third, with only one crime in fifty leading to a conviction. This is the worst record of any government since the Second World War.[18]

New Labour called this gulf between the number of crimes and the number of convictions the 'justice gap' and promised to narrow the chasm by increasing the number of 'offences brought to justice' (OBTJ).

On gaining power, Blair, a former lawyer, leapt into action to prove his 'tough on crime' credentials. New Labour passed about

50 Acts of Parliament relating to crime and punishment, giving us thousands of new criminal offences ranging from impersonating a traffic warden to exploding a nuclear device. The age for criminal responsibility was dropped to ten and many new anti-crime initiatives were launched, several of which, such as marching yobs to cash machines, were quietly dropped within weeks of being announced. Many of the Government's criminal justice reforms were aimed at giving the police the power to issue fines and cautions in order to bypass the bothersome formality of taking people to court.

One key area where the Government had set out a target on which to be judged was its promise to increase the number of OBTJs. Sure enough, this leapt up from well under one million in 1997 to over 1.3 million by 2006. However, as with so many of this Government's figures, these statistics did not really stand up to any proper scrutiny. At the same time, the number of actual court convictions fell from 737,000 to 707,000.[19] So, the increase in OBTJs came from the relatively easy task of issuing penalty notices rather than from the more difficult task of ensuring court convictions. The fastest growing type of penalty notice was the Penalty Notice for Disorder (PND). In 2003–4, their first year of use, 49,000 PNDs were issued, comfortably making up for the fall in real convictions. One unfortunate side effect of issuing all these PNDs was that the level of violent crime would look as if it was soaring – something the Government clearly did not want. So the Government decided that while PNDs would count as OBTJs, they would not count against the performance assessment of police forces:

> as officers may be disincentivised to issue a PND in respect of a public order offence if in doing so it will lead to an apparent or misleading increase in violent crime.[20]

Thus, the Government could have the OBTJ without having the crime, meaning that the old adage of not being able to have one's cake and eat it had been disproven by New Labour's skilful manipulation of the figures. There is also strong evidence that the number of OBTJs had been boosted by focusing on children. It is much easier for the police to pick on children hanging around on streets or near shopping centres than it is to catch real criminals. As the number of adult convictions has fallen, the number of children drawn into the criminal justice system seems to have risen inexorably. In 1997 about 180,000 children were dealt with; by 2005 this had risen to 210,000.[21] At the same time, many more children were imprisoned rather than just being cautioned and so the number of 15- to 17-year-olds in prison increased by around 50 per cent under New Labour.[22] It would be a worrying development if thousands of children were being unnecessarily criminalized by police looking for a quick way to hit the Government's OBTJ targets.

The other target that the Government has claimed as key to its crime strategy is reducing re-offending. In 2004 New Labour set up the National Offender Management Service (NOMS). NOMS' goals were very clear:

> NOMS is the system through which we commission and provide the highest quality correctional services and interventions in order to protect the public and reduce re-offending. We have to make improvements to public protection and reduce re-offending. By 2010 NOMS aims to have made a significant reduction in re-offending rates. NOMS will protect the public, transform the way we punish and manage offenders, reduce re-offending and cut crime.[23]

There appear to be two sets of figures about re-offending rates. There are those published each year by the Home Office which indicate that re-offending rates have remained stable at around 59 per cent of criminals being reconvicted within two years of release from prison. Then there are special reports produced by

NOMS with the help of some clever number-crunchers at the Office for National Statistics. These special reports magically 'prove' that the Government is successfully reducing re-offending. Curiously, when the overall crime figures showed that violent crime had risen by 5 per cent in just one year, the Government claimed this was 'not statistically significant'. However, when the Government's carefully recalculated figures suggested re-offending might have fallen by 3.6 per cent over three years (just 1.2 per cent a year), this was hailed as a great achievement. Apparently, statistical significance is not some kind of mathematical absolute, but rather a flexible concept depending on whether or not the numbers have gone the way the Government wishes. Oddly, although NOMS' motto is 'Working together to reduce re-offending', nowhere in the 20 targets against which it continually reports its impressive progress is there any mention of rates of re-offending.

NOMS' brave but dubious efforts to look after criminals and decrease re-offending appear to have been somewhat undermined in 2007. After already spending £155 million of our money on a £244 million computer system to provide what ministers described as 'end-to-end offender management', NOMS found after endless problems and delays that it did not work properly. However, it would have to pay the supplier more than £50 million of our money if it was to cancel the project. NOMS is now reviewing the programme and it is currently expected that a much reduced version of the system may be working in 2009 or 2010, or never. In the meantime, those responsible for monitoring and rehabilitating offenders will just have to carry on working with the 200 or so disparate prison and probation service databases, thus hugely increasing the chances that dangerous criminals will slip through the NOMS net and commit new serious crimes against us.

## PRISONS – LOCK THEM UP

Under this Government, the number of people in prison has risen dramatically from around 65,000 in 1997 to 88,583 in 2007, giving a prison population well in excess of prison capacity. Under pressure to explain why our prisons are so overcrowded, the Government claimed it had provided 20,000 extra prison spaces since 1997 and would build another 8,000. However, it turned out that around half the 'extra' 20,000 prison spaces were merely achieved by jamming more prisoners into cells built for just one person. In 1997 there were 9,498 prisoners who were two to a one-person cell. By 2007 this had reached 17,974. There were a further 1,113 prisoners held three to a cell designed for two.[24] As the prison population rose 33 per cent over the last ten years, this seems to have created more problems than it has solved. Over the same period, the number of extra prison officers and prison spaces increased by only around 10 per cent, so that we have more prisoners crowded into a limited space and staff given less time to get to know and help rehabilitate prisoners. This pressure also meant that the average time prisoners spent out of their cells fell by over 10 per cent.

It costs just over £40,000 to keep a prisoner for a year, so the cost of these extra 20,000 prisoners is over £800 million a year and the overall cost of keeping 88,000 people locked away is in excess of £3.5 billion a year. With 150 people in prison per 100,000 of population, the UK now has more prisoners per head of population than any other main European country – in comparison France has 85 prisoners per 100,000 of population and Germany has 93. Yet, in spite of locking up so many people, the UK still has the highest crime rate in Europe.

In its 1997 manifesto, as part of its 'tough on the causes of crime' promise, New Labour said it would find 'better ways of tackling crime' through early intervention, push crime prevention down to a local level and give a new focus on drugs crime, guided by a 'drugs tsar' who would be a 'symbol of our commitment to tackle the modern menace of drugs in our communities'. However, it is far from clear that there has been any consistent policy for dealing with crime. On the one hand the Government has been keen to show that it is 'tough on crime' and has increased sentences for many offences and imposed mandatory minimum sentences for others. Yet at the same time, it has potentially reduced sentences by passing legislation, such as the 2003 Criminal Justice Act, which gives any prisoner with a sentence greater than four years the automatic right to be considered for parole after just half of their sentence. Moreover, the Government has launched early-release schemes for prisoners nearing the end of their time in prison in order to reduce overcrowding. So, on the one hand our judges were being pressured into imposing longer sentences, while on the other Government policies meant that many prisoners did not have to serve these longer sentences anyway.

There are serious questions about whether many of the prisoners should have been in prison in the first place. Given that re-offending rates for young prisoners are over 74 per cent, there are indications that the 10,000 or so younger offenders are more likely to become repeat criminals if imprisoned than they would if they are treated in the community. Of the 4,000 plus women in prison, more than half were there for non-violent offences (drugs and robbery) and two-thirds had children. It is estimated that each year over 17,000 children are separated from their mother by imprisonment.[25] Again, one could ask whether society has been best served by locking these people up. The social profile of prisoners suggests that education, and not imprisonment, is what they need to turn their lives around – more than half have no qualifications, half have poor reading skills and two-thirds have numeracy skills below those expected for an 11-year-old. Two-thirds of prisoners were unemployed before going to prison; similarly, around two-thirds regularly used drugs. While our short-term security may be helped by cramming all these people together in prison, with high re-offending rates it is far from clear that the Government's obsession with overfilling our prisons is doing anything to improve our long-term safety.

Another worrying set of numbers concerns prisoners on remand while awaiting trial and sentencing. There are about 13,000 remand prisoners, two-thirds of whom are non-violent and half of whom will not get prison sentences anyway. Yet through being held on remand many will lose jobs, marriages and homes – all this making them more, rather than less, prone to become criminals. However, the largest group of people who possibly should not be in prison are drug offenders. Under New Labour the number of those imprisoned for drug offences has risen more than for any other category and the average sentence length has increased the most (by 24 per cent). About 13,000 people are in prison for drug offences. Moreover, several studies, including one done by the Prime Minister's own Strategy Unit, have found that over 50 per cent of all criminal offences are connected to drug use – most thefts and robberies are believed to be carried out to get money to buy drugs.[26] Heroin is the drug behind most of these offences. If substantially more heroin addicts were to be treated in the community or if heroin was to be legalized and provided on NHS prescription, there could be a massive fall in the number of crimes committed and in the number of people in prison.

## IDISASTER

As we look forward, the next great project on which the Home Office will be spending eye-watering amounts of our money is to give us ID Cards. The Home Office currently forecasts this will cost us at least £5.4 billion. When reviewing the Home Office accounts chaos, one of the members of the Public Accounts Committee wondered how a department that could not even produce a set of accounts could successfully deliver such an ambitious project: 'How can we have any confidence that your department is now introducing identity cards without there being a monumental waste of public money?' The new head of the Home Office, who replaced the apparently accident-prone Sir John Gieve, replied, 'We have recruited a chief information officer, a very senior IT person to lead the identity card project'.[27] This answer was curiously similar to the one given in 2003 by the NHS when asked how they could ensure that the new NHS IT system would not be a complete disaster:

> What we have done is to secure for ourselves Richard Granger, who is Director-General of NHS IT. He comes from the private sector. He has experience of putting in large computer systems.[28]

At the time this was said, the NHS IT system was due to cost about £2.3 billion. Four years later, the NHS had admitted it would cost over £12 billion and would be up to ten years late. We should not be surprised when ID Cards go the same way.

# PART 2

## EMPTYING OUR POCKETS

# CHAPTER 7

# TAX BECOMES MORE TAXING

## RAKING IN BILLIONS

In its 1997 manifesto this Government made clear that it would use taxes as a means of redistributing wealth in the interests of fairness and that it would not impose excessive taxes on ordinary families: 'New Labour is not about high taxes on ordinary families. It is about social justice and a fair deal. This goal will benefit the many, not the few.' Moreover, the Government also insisted that we could trust them on taxes: 'New Labour will establish a new trust on tax with the British people. The promises we make we will keep.'

After having lambasted John Major's Government for its tax increases, 'Since 1992 the typical family has paid more than £2,000 in extra taxes – the biggest tax hike in peacetime history, breaking every promise made by John Major at the last election', New Labour set off on a series of tax rises that would make anything done by the much-criticized Major Government look like collecting small change. In the period 1997 to 2007, tax revenue went up by over 80 per cent from £293 billion to £529 billion (see Figure 11).[1] At the same time, average earnings only increased by just under 29 per cent for private-sector employees and by about 35 per cent for those in the public sector. So, over ten years our taxes will have gone up by around 2.5 times the rise in our earnings.

**Figure 11** In spite of criticizing Tory tax rises, New Labour has increased tax much more than the increase in average earnings

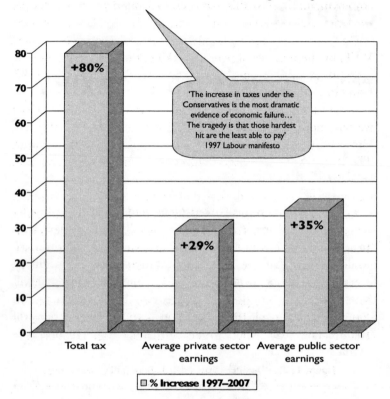

Clearly, different people will pay different levels of tax depending on their income, their consumption, the ingenuity of their tax advisers (if they can afford them) and whether (like private equity and non-domiciled multi-millionaires) they have managed to get this Government to give them special tax breaks that are not available to ordinary mortals. However, one simple way to get an idea of the average employee's growing contribution to the Government's spending addiction is to divide the total taxes directly paid by wage-earners (income tax, council tax, inheritance tax and stamp duty on homes) by the number of people working. In 1997 this came to about £3,400 tax per person in employment; by 2007 this had risen to around £6,200 in tax per working person. Were you to divide the total tax collected (including things like National Insurance, corporation tax and VAT) by the number of people working, the figures come out at a slightly more worrying £11,100 per working person in 1997, rising to £18,200 by 2007.

It has almost become conventional wisdom that under Labour we pay more in taxes and under the Conservatives we pay less. However, the figures suggest that this is not completely accurate. The Adam Smith Institute think tank calculates each year how long we have to work to pay taxes before we start earning money for ourselves. They call the day that we start working for ourselves, rather than for the Treasury, 'Tax Freedom Day'.[2] For the first five years of New Labour, Tax Freedom Day came later as taxes rose. Then it moved earlier for a couple of years as rapid economic growth outstripped tax increases. Since 2004, with rising taxes overtaking economic growth, the day has come later again. When New Labour came to power, Tax Freedom Day was 28 May. By 2007 it had moved to 1 June (see Figure 12). However, using the Tax Freedom Day analysis, it is clear that although taxes are now

**Figure 12** Tax Freedom Day under Labour and Conservative

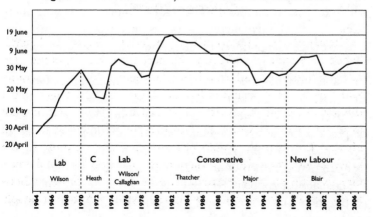

rising as a proportion of our national income, the highest our over-all taxes have ever been compared to our income came under the Conservatives during the recession of the early 1980s.

As the graph shows, the Labour Governments of Wilson (1964–70) and Wilson/Callaghan (1974–9) introduced major increases in taxation. Tax fell under Edward Heath's period in office (1970–4). However, it was actually during Margaret Thatcher's time in power (1979–90) that our taxes reached their highest level. Although Thatcher managed to bring down the share of our income paid in tax, by the time she was replaced by John Major tax was still around the highest point it had previously reached under Labour and near the highest level it has been under New Labour.

## NOT SO STEALTHY

In its 1997 manifesto, the Government promised not to increase the rate of income tax: 'To encourage work and reward effort, we are pledged not to raise the basic or top rates of income tax throughout the next Parliament'. Instead, it chose to increase the amount the Government received from income tax by using what is called 'fiscal drag' – not increasing the earnings levels at which taxes start, in line with increases in inflation. People often refer to this method of increasing tax as 'stealth taxes' because the Government takes in more of our money without actually having to provoke public hostility by being seen to openly raise tax rates. Probably no Chancellor has ever been as successful as Gordon Brown in claiming to be reducing tax rates while actually increasing overall tax revenues through fiscal drag. With income tax, despite the lowest tax rate being halved from 20 per cent to 10 per cent in the 1999 budget and the basic rate being reduced from 23 pence in the pound to 22 pence in the 2000 budget, the tax take almost doubled over ten years (see Figure 13). Similarly, corporation tax was cut by 2 per cent in 1997, yet over the following ten years the tax revenues went up by around 65 per cent. Those taxes that have increased most, for example inheritance tax and stamp duty on private homes, have done so from fiscal drag. (Stamp duty on private home sales is not included on the graph in Figure 13 as, in order to show its huge almost 600 per cent increase since 1997, the scale on the graph would have to be changed so much that the differences in the increases in the other taxes would be difficult to see.) One fact is clear from the chart – the largest tax increases have been those which affect individuals and families. Businesses have been less affected by the former Chancellor's tax hikes, in spite of many consistently making record profits during the last 11 years of economic growth.

The ex-Chancellor has also managed to largely avoid responsibility for the doubling of council tax because people tend to blame their inexorably rising council tax bills on their local councils. In this way, they overlook the fact that it is the decisions

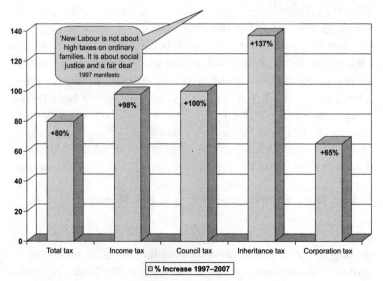

**Figure 13** Taxes on families have increased much more than taxes on business

taken by the Treasury in allocating funds to councils each year that largely determine how much council taxes have to rise.

## Income Tax – Ever Upwards

Income tax demonstrates quite neatly the difference between what the Government promised in its manifesto and what it actually did to take ever more of our money. In its 1997 election manifesto, the Government announced, 'Our long-term objective is a lower starting rate of income tax of ten pence in the pound'. Sure enough, to his credit Gordon Brown introduced this in his 1999 budget, but then he abolished it again in his 2007 budget. In the manifesto New Labour claimed, 'We will uphold family life as the most secure means of bringing up our children. Families are the core of our society.' Yet in its 1999 budget the Government scrapped married couples' allowances and mortgage interest tax relief, thus removing two forms of fiscal encouragement for stable family homes. The Government also committed to use tax policy to 'encourage employment opportunities and work incentives for all'. However, by failing to raise tax thresholds in line with inflation and wages growth, the Government increased the numbers paying the top rate of tax from around two million to approaching four million people. Moreover, National Insurance, a tax on employment, also went up above annual earnings growth when in 2002 the Government increased this by 1 per cent, netting around £8 billion a year extra as the tax take rose in just one year from £64.5 billion to £72.5 billion. In the year 2007–8, National Insurance is expected to bring the Treasury over £95 billion – almost 20 per cent of all our taxes.

## Stamp Duty on Private Homes – the Money Pours In

Labour's election manifesto demonstrated its commitment to supporting the principle of home ownership: 'Most families want to own their own homes ... Labour's housing strategy will address the needs of homeowners and tenants alike.' The Government also claimed it would 'reject the boom and bust policies' of the Tories. However, over the last ten years massive house price inflation has put owning a home beyond the reach of most people on average salaries. Moreover, the boom in property prices has led to a massive increase in the level of rents, much greater than the rise in salaries. Those fortunate enough to have jumped on the housing-boom bandwagon have made millions from increasing property prices and millions more from rising rents. These lucky few include many MPs who can have their mortgages paid for by taxpayers and yet the MPs (rather than taxpayers) take all the profits when the MPs' homes are sold. Meanwhile, for those left behind, the prospect of ever owning a property has receded. By not increasing the thresholds at which the different levels of stamp duty are paid, the Treasury has increased its tax take from around £675 million in 1996–7 to over £4.6 billion by 2005–6.[3] Unfortunately, as more and more properties become liable for stamp duty, this makes it ever harder for first-time buyers and those on average salaries to even contemplate home ownership.

## Inheritance Tax – Captured Dead or Alive

Inheritance tax (IHT) was once restricted to the reasonably wealthy. Mainly through rising house prices, many middle-income families are now being afforded the luxury of paying this wealth tax. Labour did not mention IHT in its manifesto and has enjoyed the benefits as tax revenues have increased from just under £1.7 billion to close to £4 billion a year. IHT gave us probably the most entertaining political spectacle of 2007. After ten years of half-hearted and ineffective opposition to New Labour, the Tories, possibly more through serendipity than design, came up with the idea of taxing some of the UK's growing army of non-domiciles in order to provide cash to increase the inheritance tax threshold to £1 million. To the Government's (and possibly also the Tories') surprise this idea seemed rather popular with the ordinary masses struggling under the ever-increasing burden of Brown's tax machine. There was immediate panic at Number 10 as the Prime Minister's plans for a snap election humiliatingly crumbled to dust, and the Government had to quickly botch something together that from a distance looked and smelt a bit like the Tory proposal without actually reducing the Government's tax revenues.

## Council Tax – Much More for Much Less

True to its proclaimed belief in devolution of power, New Labour proposed that good local government could be achieved by freeing councils from Westminster's control: 'Local decision-making should be less constrained by central government, and also more accountable to local people'. However, this Government vowed it would keep a watchful eye on how much local councils could choose to tax us: 'Although crude and universal council tax capping should go, we will retain reserve powers to contain excessive council tax rises'. The Government's approach seems to actually have been a mixture of hands-off and hands-on. Councils have been allowed to increase taxes by well above the rate of inflation for every one of the years New Labour has been in power, while at the same time cutting back services such as weekly rubbish collections, meals on wheels and care for the elderly. So while inflation has gone up by around 20 per cent, council tax bills have increased by a more respectable 100 per cent. However, by an odd and fortuitous coincidence, the 238 districts with the lowest council tax rises in 2006–7 just happened to be those where there were local elections in May 2007.[4]

For the Government, one of the less welcome results of the huge rise in council taxes has been the sight of pensioners who would rather go to jail than pay 100 per cent more council tax for ever-worsening services in the same period as their pensions went up by only around a quarter as much. In 2005, faced by a general election, the Government skilfully defused the growing grey revolt

by niftily slipping pensioners a £200 council-tax rebate to calm
them down, no doubt buying themselves a few votes in the process.

## Corporation Tax – Catching Minnows

Corporation tax has also provided some interesting sights for the
avid tax-twitchers amongst us. New Labour has always been
keen to demonstrate its business-friendly credentials. In its manifesto it declared, 'New Labour offers business a new deal for the
future … We see healthy profits as an essential motor of a
dynamic market economy.' Key to the Government's hug-a-cap-
italist approach was improving the UK's industrial competitiveness: 'We will build a new partnership with business to improve
the competitiveness of British industry for the 21st century leading to faster growth'. True to their word, in the Government's
first budget it cut corporation tax by 2 per cent. From then on
things seemed to go in pretty much exactly the opposite direction
to the one intended by the Government.

Firstly, crushed by increasing energy bills, new workers' rights,
a mountain of EU regulation and the Government's decision to
open our markets to global competition, our manufacturing
industries continued their sad decline. Other countries like France
and Germany vigorously protected their manufacturing by ignoring both the flood of regulation spewing out of Brussels and international pressure to expose their key industries to global
competition. So while the Government's overall corporation
tax take increased by about 37 per cent between 2000
and 2007 (the period for which comparable figures are available),
the amount extracted from manufacturing industry declined
from £5.5 billion in 2000 to £4.6 billion – a drop of almost
17 per cent.[5]

However, things were much more upbeat in the headquarters
of our major banks. As manufacturing withered away under New
Labour's botched attempts to help it grow, our banks and other
financial services providers were making more money than they

knew what to do with. Year after year, almost all of them declared record profits. In 2005 we had headlines such as 'Bank branches close as profits soar' and 'HSBC records latest record profits'. These continued into 2006 with 'Banking on record profits' and 'Barclays to unveil record profits'. And yet again, in 2007 we had 'Record profits at HSBC', 'British debt crisis rockets as Barclays make record profits', 'RBS-NatWest surges to record profits' and 'Banks' £40 billion profits record'. Given the almost unimaginable amounts of our money being hoovered up by the banks, one might have expected that a Government dedicated to strengthening our 'industrial competitiveness' and promoting social justice would have ensured that a reasonable proportion of the banks' booty found its way into Treasury coffers to be used to help manufacturing companies and poorer families. However, this was not quite what happened (see Figure 14).

Between 2000 and 2007, probably the most profitable years in the history of British banking, financial institutions' gross

**Figure 14** Small companies have been worst affected by New Labour's tax increases (large companies and banks have been allowed very effective 'tax planning')

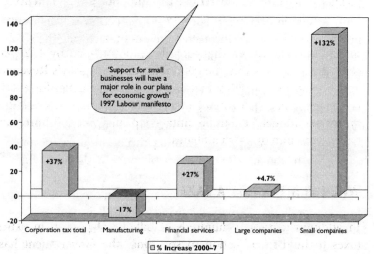

operating surpluses more than doubled, yet the corporation tax they paid went up by a modest 27 per cent from £8.4 billion to £10.7 billion. In the face of criticisms of 'excess profits', a leading Government Treasury Minister almost seemed to defend the banks' profits and devastatingly effective tax planning:

> My starting point as a Treasury minister is this: what more can I do – can we do together – to support and enhance the critical role that the banking industry plays in our economy?[6]

Moreover, as the banks appeared to be making more and more money and yet paying proportionately less and less tax, the same minister praised the banking industry for its corporate social responsibility: 'I understand that it is your success and the strength of our economy that enables you to fulfil your wider social responsibilities'.

Perhaps the most disturbing aspect of this Government's collection of corporation tax has been in how it appears to have ruthlessly squeezed smaller companies, which were meant to be the ones creating the most new jobs, while allowing our larger businesses to substantially reduce the amounts they paid in taxes. Between 2000 and 2007 the amount of tax paid by large companies inched up by a pathetic 4.7 per cent while taxes paid by small companies more than doubled, zooming up by 132 per cent. It would seem that the good folk at Her Majesty's Revenue and Customs doggedly pursue our smaller companies for every last penny in tax while smiling benignly or even helplessly as large businesses funnel billions in untaxed profits into offshore tax havens and into overseas affiliates.

## WHEN IS A TAX NOT A TAX?

In addition to raising hundreds of billions of pounds in extra taxes to fund its addiction to spending, the Government has raised billions more by getting us to pay for goods and services that were previously either supplied or subsidized by the state. In its manifesto New Labour did warn us that we would be paying a lot more for higher education: 'Higher education: the improvement and expansion needed cannot be funded out of general taxation'. True to its word, it introduced tuition fees at universities. There are over one million UK-domiciled students in full-time education and another 743,000 part-time students.[7] Of these, just under 200,000 get full grants and another 50,000 or so get partial grants.[8] If we do a conservative calculation and just take the full-time students – while assuming that the 800,000 who are not getting grants are paying an average of £2,500 a year in tuition fees – this gives around £2 billion a year. For most families these are new costs that were previously paid for by our taxes and so can be seen to represent a new form of taxation.

Under this Government we pay more for council services, private schooling, dental care, medical treatment and care for the elderly than ever before, either because services have been cut back in spite of our paying higher taxes or else because we do not have confidence in the quality of service provided by the Government. The self-evident failure of many of our schools, in spite of Government claims of improving standards, has driven more and more parents into coughing up to buy private education for their children in spite of an almost 40 per cent rise in private school fees over the past five years. The sight of ever more people being killed in filthy, hopelessly-managed hospitals, in spite of the Government claiming it has 'transformed' the NHS, has driven people to prefer private provision to that offered by the state. Moreover, this Government's future plans promise less state provision in many areas and more for us to pay directly. For example, the Government's intention to cut railway subsidies will force up fares by about 14 per cent in 2008, and each time the Government mentions the word 'environment' most people know that this means a new tax or that an increase of an existing tax is just around the corner.

## UNDER PRESSURE

The way households spend their money has changed quite
dramatically under this Government. The amount we use for
food and non-alcoholic drinks has gone up in line with inflation
and increases in average earnings (see Figure 15). Our expenditure for goods and clothes has increased by a bit more, probably
due to the spending spree it seems that many people have been
on for the last few years. Rising world energy prices and a lack of
effective competition in utilities like gas and electricity have
pushed our energy costs up by over twice the rate of inflation,
ensuring generous profits that are quickly pumped abroad by our
(mostly foreign-owned) power companies. Because of rising
house prices our mortgage loans have shot up by an impressive
125 per cent. However, perhaps the most significant statistics are
the amounts people have borrowed in unsecured loans (loans for
other purposes than buying property) and the change in the
household savings rate (the percentage of our income we save).
Our borrowing (not including mortgages) has increased by about
100 per cent from £92 billion in 1998 to over £184 billion in
2006 – equivalent to a rise for each person in employment from
around £3,200 in 1998 to about £6,400 in 2006 (see Figure 15).

Given that this massive rise in personal borrowing will actually
be confined to a small part of the working population – say 20 per
cent to 30 per cent – this large jump in debt suggests that rising
taxes and mortgage repayment costs are putting many people
under a great deal of financial pressure. This picture is reinforced
by the collapse in the rate of household savings from around 10
per cent before this Government came into power, to 7 per cent
in 1998, to just 5 per cent in 2006 and around 2.5 per cent in
2007. At a time when pension provision for private-sector workers is weakening, this flight from personal savings is a worrying
phenomenon, particularly under a Government that pledged 'to
promote long-term saving'.

**Figure 15** Our borrowing has increased and our savings have declined dramatically

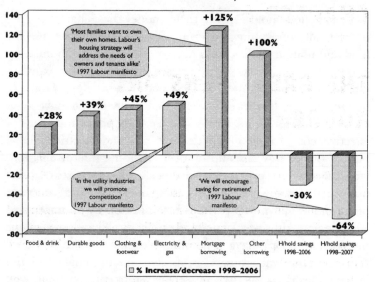

□ **% Increase/decrease 1998–2006**

## A NEW TRUST ON TAX WITH THE BRITISH PEOPLE?

So did we get a new trust on tax with the British people? And did the Government keep the promises it made? In its first years in power, New Labour did keep its promises to introduce the 10 per cent starting rate and not to raise the upper rate of income tax. Also, it lowered corporation tax. However, looking at how the Government has siphoned away ever-increasing quantities of our money, how its taxes have hit average families hardest and how many huge companies, banks and multi-millionaires hardly know what the word 'tax' actually means, it seems as if New Labour has consistently failed to deliver on almost any of the broader intentions laid out in its 1997 election manifesto.

# CHAPTER 8

# THE GREAT PENSIONS ROBBERY

The Government and the public sector have found many ingenious ways of taking, and mostly wasting, ever-increasing amounts of our money. However, perhaps nothing has been so brazen and so shameless as the politicians' and public sector's pillaging of our pensions while ensuring a comfortable and financially secure retirement for themselves.

If you work in the private sector and earn less than, say, £150,000 a year, you might want to look away now and perhaps move on to the next chapter as the description of what is happening to your prospects of a happy, healthy and prosperous retirement is not likely to leave you in an enormously good mood. However, if you work in the public sector, you should be cracking open the champagne at the thought of how generously private-sector workers will be pouring their hard-earned cash into funding your future retired bliss.

## BASIC FACTS AND FIGURES

There have been some fairly hair-raising newspaper articles about pensions in recent years such as 'Whose pension are you paying?', 'Civil service pensions cost up to £27 billion in year' and 'Private payments for public pensions',[1] so it might be worth laying out a few basic facts and figures before going on to look at how this Government's policies will force private-sector employees to hand over hundreds of billions of pounds of their money to look after the retirement of their public-sector colleagues.

There are currently just under six million people working in the public sector and another 23 million in the private sector. Under this Government, the number in the public sector has increased by over 600,000 and their salaries have gone up faster than those in the private sector.

About 90 per cent of those working for the public sector have 'defined benefit' pension schemes (also called 'final-salary' schemes). These guarantee them an inflation-linked pension for the rest of their and their partners' lives. The amount paid out is based on how long they have worked and the level of their final salary. Most of these pensions are what is called 'unfunded' – this means they are paid for out of future tax revenues and are not based on any financial assets such as savings and investments. Politicians, the judiciary, civil servants, the police, NHS workers, teachers, the fire service and the armed forces all have unfunded pensions that will be paid out of our taxes. The cost of these pensions will increase significantly each year, partly due to the population's rising longevity and partly because New Labour has both increased the number of public-sector employees and given them generous pay increases. Local government workers are part of a funded scheme whose cost shoots up every year also due to their rising salaries and generally increasing longevity. In 2001–2 the employers' contributions to the Local Government Pension Scheme in England were around £2.6 billion (about £125 per household); by 2005–6 these had increased by almost 60 per cent to £4.1 billion (almost £200 per household) and they have certainly gone up even more since then.[2] This is one reason why council taxes have doubled since 1997, yet we also see reductions in services. Much of the extra money is needed to pay for the growing cost of the pensions of more than 1.5 million local-government workers into whose pension funds we have to pay ever-increasing amounts.

Most private pension schemes are 'defined contribution' rather than 'defined benefit'. Defined benefit is clearly the best scheme as it gives you the complete security of a guaranteed pension based on your final salary and places all the financial risk with your employer who must find the money to pay for your pension for as long as you and your partner live. With defined contribution, you and your employer pay an agreed percentage of your salary each year and the level of your eventual pension is then dependent on the performance of your pension fund and the level of annuity rates when you retire. Once you retire, your employer has no obligations to look after you – so the person paying into the scheme bears all the risk. When this Government came to power, about 36 per cent of private pension schemes were 'defined benefit'. This has since halved to just 18 per cent as companies have rushed to avoid the financial risks of providing guaranteed pensions for all except their senior managers and directors.

Out of the 23 million private-sector workers, fewer than half pay into a pension scheme. The rest seem to be relying on the basic state pension (£87.30 a week in 2007) plus about another £25 a week in Pension Credits, which is not a smart thing to do if you want to have some fun in your old age – not too many world cruises for them. Moreover, the number of people saving in private pension schemes has fallen every year under this Government in spite of New Labour's 1997 manifesto pledge: 'We will encourage saving for retirement'. Those who have saved for their pensions have about £1.8 trillion invested in private pension schemes. This may sound a lot, but is actually pitifully small compared to the number of people who expect this sum to provide for them in retirement. If you divide the £1.8 trillion invested for future private-sector pensions by the 10 million or so people actually saving for a pension, this gives £180,000 per person to cover future pension liabilities. Current annuity rates are about 6.4 per cent, but for an index-linked joint pension the rate falls to around 3.8 per cent. So the average index-linked joint pension that the £180,000 would buy will be near £6,800 a year. By the time most pensioners have paid their taxes (including their ever-mounting council tax), they are going to be looking at a very modest lifestyle – not too many world cruises for them either.

## SPONSOR A RETIRED PUBLIC-SECTOR WORKER

We often receive junk mail asking us to sponsor a needy child, an impoverished family or a destitute village in a Third World country. However, a mixture of our Government's and the public sector's deceit and self-interest means that each person working in the private sector is now paying more into the pension of a retired public-sector worker than they are into their own funded pension savings each year. Unfortunately, private-sector employees' unwitting sponsoring of retired public-sector workers often leaves them little left over to give to possibly more deserving candidates for their money or even to put in their own pension savings.

There are two important numbers to consider when looking at how much public-sector pensions cost us. The 'big number' that anti-Government newspapers like to quote is the 'pensions liability' for public-sector pensions. This 'liability' is the amount of money that would have to be put aside now in order to provide a fund to pay for future public-sector pensions. According to the Government's own figures, this has shot up from around £360 billion in 1999 to an estimated £877 billion by 2007.[3] For example, the liabilities of just the civil servants' pension scheme, covering only one in ten public-sector workers, has gone from £54.4 billion to £128.7 billion in eight years, and in just two years the NHS scheme's liabilities jumped a staggering 58 per cent from £104.2 billion to £165.4 billion.[4]

Worryingly, some of the actuarial assumptions on investment rates and life-expectancy used by the Government may well understate these amounts and the real cost of future public-sector pension liabilities is probably comfortably north of £1 trillion. However, even at £877 billion, this equates to a shocking approximately £40,000 per private-sector worker, or more than £80,000 for every private-sector worker who actually pays into a private pension scheme. This 'pension liability' figure, though good for generating eye-catching newspaper headlines, is an artificial number as we will never actually have to put all this money into a fund to pay for public-sector pensions. They will be paid for by our future taxes. However, the dizzying speed with which public-sector pension liabilities have increased does give a useful indication of how much our taxes will have to rise in the future to pay for this Government's generosity to its politicians and its own employees over the last 11 years.

A much more relevant number is how much we taxpayers actually pay each year for the pensions of already retired public-sector workers. In 2005 the two million or so retired public-sector workers in unfunded schemes (directly paid out of taxes) cost around £18.6 billion. By 2007 this had risen to around £20 billion (1.5 per cent of GDP). In 2005 private-sector employees paid about £15.1 billion into their funded pension schemes and by 2007 this had probably risen to just over £17 billion.[5] This means that private-sector workers are now paying more into the pensions of currently retired public-sector workers than they are putting into their own funded pensions. These payments to existing pensioners do not yet take account of the Government's 600,000-person expansion of the public sector and the inflation-busting pay increases awarded to many public-sector workers, especially civil servants and senior public-sector managers, many of whom have had 50 per cent to 100 per cent salary increases under New Labour. When the Government's munificence with our money towards its own employees filters through to retirement payments over the next few decades, the Treasury expects public-sector pensions to rise about 40 per cent to around £28 billion a year (2.1 per cent of GDP): 'The annual cash payment from unfunded schemes will rise gradually from about 1.5 per cent of GDP now to 2.1 per cent by the middle of the century'.[6] Unless they dramatically increase their own pension savings, private-sector employees can expect to be paying about one-and-a-half times as much each year for public-sector pensions as they will for their own. If, as seems likely, the Government is using actuarial assumptions that understate public-sector pension liabilities, and their estimates prove to be as inaccurate as many other official predictions, then public-sector pension costs could go above £30 billion a year. If this happens, then within our lifetimes we may well be paying almost twice as much each year into the pension of already retired public-sector workers as we do for our own retirement. The Treasury, whose staff all get guaranteed index-linked pensions paid for out of our taxes, maintains that 'public sector pensions remain fully affordable'.[7] This view might not be shared by some of the people unable to save for their own retirement due to the amounts they are already paying to guarantee retirement security for their public-sector brethren.

## WELCOME TO PENSION PARADISE

The best pension scheme in the UK is the one enjoyed by our Members of Parliament. This is probably unsurprising given that we have granted them the power to decide the size of their own pensions. Naturally, they have shown admirable generosity to themselves and in 2002 voted themselves a large pension increase for which we will have to pay. Every year that an MP works, they accrue 1/40th of their final salary as an inflation-linked pension. This is equivalent to a payment into each MP's pension fund of around £50,000 each year. MPs tend not to mention this when they complain that they are not paid enough. In 20 years an MP will have a pension of half their final salary. One newspaper calculated that a private-sector worker would have to save around £2 million to retire with the same pension benefits as the average politician.[8] The judiciary have equally generous pension arrangements. In comparison a nurse, teacher or local-government worker would have to work 40 years to have a pension of half their (considerably lower) final salary. Theoretically, MPs' retirement age is 65, but if they have been in Parliament for 20 years or more by the time of their 60th birthday, they can retire early on a full pension. Most years, the MPs' pension scheme has a considerable deficit, so MPs just vote to increase the amount of our money paid into their scheme for their retirement. Usually this vote is unanimous.

There are several ways in which MPs can hugely increase their already satisfactory pensions. Many Labour MPs also serve as ministers or secretaries in some government department or other. For example, in the Treasury there are five MPs all getting tens of thousands of pounds in extra salary and in extra pensions from roles such as Chancellor, Chief Secretary, Paymaster General, Financial Secretary and Economic Secretary. In most other departments there are four or five MPs similarly on the salary and pensions payroll. A large number of MPs serve on the huge array of Parliamentary committees that do a lot of talking but are mostly powerless to take any action. Again, all this adds to salaries and pensions. Moreover, many MPs also have a string of well-rewarded private-sector directorships and consultancy jobs (the standard rate for a decent-sized company looking to get some juicy government contracts seems to be around £100,000 a year), while already being paid handsomely to represent the interests of their constituents.

Cabinet ministers also get extra pension add-ons. In the week that Dr David Kelly's death was announced, one piece of news seems to have slipped out almost unnoticed: Prime Minister Tony Blair had his 'Cabinet Office Allowance' increased from £47,000 to over £90,000 a year. In combination with his existing pension of around £100,000 per year, this now guaranteed him an inflation-linked pension of close to £200,000 a year for the rest of his life.[9] This can, of course, be boosted by earning millions from part-time consultancy work (at over £500,000 a year), speaking engagements and book deals. Even previously rabid left-wing cabinet ministers have been expeditious in taking up lucrative private-sector consultancy positions to supplement their political earnings.

Some other happy inhabitants of pension paradise are 603,000 working and 558,000 retired civil servants. With somewhere between 1/50th and 1/80th of a year's salary (depending on the scheme they choose) for each year worked, they accrue their pensions more slowly than MPs. However, if they spend their whole career in the civil service, they can retire at 60 with a full pension of at least half their final salary plus a lump sum payment equal to three years' pension. So a reasonably senior civil servant on £150,000 a year will get a one-off payment of £225,000 plus an inflation-linked pension of £75,000 a year. Some civil servants are even luckier. Sir Nigel Crisp, head of the NHS at the time when the spending of record amounts of our money led to record budget deficits, was reported to have been allowed to retire with full pension and a peerage at just 54 years old.[10] Several other senior civil servants have also been given gongs and magnanimous amounts of our money after similarly unconvincing managerial track records.

The employees of over 200 public-sector organizations are part of the civil service pension scheme. The pension liability of looking after these civil servants has increased at a staggering rate under this Government (see Figure 16).[11] At the same time, private-sector pension savings seem to be stagnating.

The Government claims it needs to look after its civil servants if it is to get high-quality staff. However, the extraordinary amounts of our money that have been wasted by civil servants, including over £20 billion being spent on management consultants to tell them how to do their jobs, may suggest that we are often paying for diamonds and getting dross.[12]

Another group of public-sector employees that lives its life sheltered from the harsh realities of greater longevity and falling returns on investment is the mass of about 2.8 million working

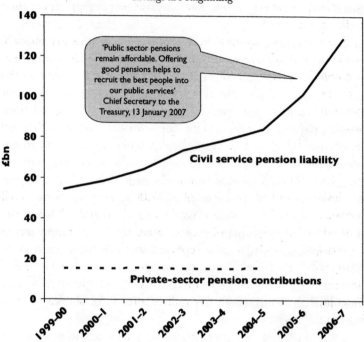

**Figure 16** While the amount they will have to pay for civil-service pensions has risen rapidly, private-sector pension savings are stagnating

and 2.1 million retired members of the big five unfunded pension schemes for teachers, the NHS, the armed forces, the police and the fire service. Ordinary teachers and NHS employees accrue benefits at 1/80th of a year's salary for each year worked and can retire at 60 with a tax-free lump sum equal to three years' pension plus a fully index-linked pension. The police and firefighters gain their benefits faster and so can retire earlier – staff with 30 years' service can retire at 50 with a pension of two-thirds of their final salary. Many then get jobs in the private sector to improve their standard of living. One fire chief reportedly even managed to retire at 55 with a £250,000 payout plus full pension and then get rehired to do his old job at a salary of £100,000 a year.[13]

Despite (or perhaps because of) their generous pension entitlements, many public-sector workers seem to be prevented by ill health from working all the way until their comparatively early retirement ages. In the private sector, less than 20 per cent of employees retire early due to ill health, in spite of the retirement age being 65. However, our hard-pressed public-sector staff must suffer from an awfully varied range of grievous medical conditions. About 68 per cent of firepersons, 49 per cent of police, 30 per cent of local-government employees, 23 per cent of NHS staff, 25 per cent of teachers and 22 per cent of civil servants seem to believe that they have valid health grounds for taking retirement even earlier than the already low official retirement ages permitted by their taxpayer-funded pension schemes.[14] On taking early retirement, many find that their health suddenly improves and that they are sufficiently well to take up jobs in the private sector to keep themselves occupied and to supplement their public-sector pensions.

## THE IMPOVERISHMENT OF THE PRIVATE SECTOR

The world of public-sector pensions resembles a land of milk and honey for those blessed to live there. In comparison, private-sector pensions increasingly look like a barren wilderness populated with starving outcasts. Since this Government came to power, there has been a rapid collapse in private-pension provision. In 1997 there were 97,900 private-sector occupational pension schemes; by 2005 this had dropped by a third to 65,500 and it has kept on falling since. In 2000 there were 34,700 defined benefit schemes (the best kind to have); by 2005 this had collapsed by about two-thirds to just 12,000 schemes and has kept on going down. In 1997 about 34 per cent of the active workforce was covered by a defined benefit scheme; by 2005 this was just 19 per cent and is still dropping further (see Figure 17).

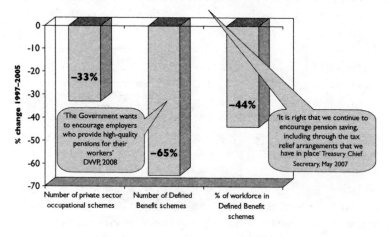

**Figure 17** There has been a worrying decline in private pension schemes, particularly final salary schemes

We have seen that, with Government pension schemes, changed actuarial assumptions (around longevity and investment returns) have led to the liabilities increasing by about 140 per cent since 1997. This indicates that funds in private schemes would have needed a similar increase to keep pace with their rising liabilities. However, unable to keep pace with their ever-growing pension burden, most companies have closed their defined benefits schemes and reduced, or even eliminated, their pension liabilities by having their employees pay into defined-contribution schemes whose assets are invested in stocks and bonds. This has meant that total private-pension savings have only gone up by about 29 per cent from around £1.4 trillion in 1997–8 to about £1.8 trillion in 2007–8, hardly more than the rate of inflation (see Figure 18). This enormous gap between the Government's hugely increased provisions for public-sector pensions and the minimal rise in private-sector pension savings does not bode well for the retirement prospects of private-sector employees. New Labour promised to create greater fairness with pensions. Instead, it has created a large and ever-widening chasm

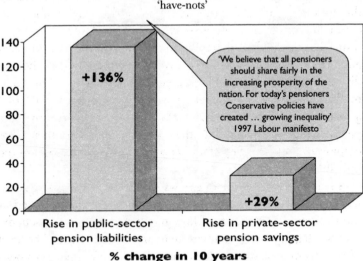

**Figure 18** New Labour has created greater pension inequality between the public-sector 'haves' and the private-sector 'have-nots'

between the fortunate few in the public sector and the great majority excluded from the public-sector pension paradise.

Despite pressure from the Government Regulator to cover their pension deficits, many companies are failing to put in the necessary money. Reviewing the recovery plans submitted by 1,292 private-pension schemes in late 2007, the Pensions Regulator felt that many had not taken sufficient account of increasing life expectancy and therefore had larger deficits than they were admitting.[15] However, companies seem to be losing the appetite for pouring ever more money into the pension-deficit black hole and such household names as Marks & Spencer, United Biscuits, Rolls-Royce, Unilever and Friends Provident are reported to have all reduced the generosity of their pension schemes.[16]

Industry leaders have often criticized the Government for its failure to deal with the rising cost of public-sector pensions. The president of the Confederation of British Industry (CBI) is quoted as saying, 'There has been a tightening down of the way companies fund their pension schemes, meanwhile the Government blithely goes on offering all the benefits to their staff. They are mortgaging the future.'[17] However, the moral authority of the bosses to comment on generous public-sector pensions could seem to be somewhat dented by the revelation of how well they have looked after their own pensions. The average pension pot of the top directors of the UK's 100 largest companies is now about £5.3 million, giving an annual pension in the region of £320,000 a year. So private-sector bosses do not seem to be sharing the pension belt-tightening that they are imposing on their own employees and that they would apparently like to impose on the public sector.

A study carried out by one newspaper makes disturbing reading for people with private pensions. The newspaper looked at the two key determinants of how much pension private-scheme savers will get: returns on investment and annuity rates. The level of returns on investment determines how much a person's pension fund can grow while they are working and saving. The annuity rate decides the amount of pension income the saver's funds can buy when they retire. Since 1997 the returns on investment have halved. At the same time, annuity rates have fallen from well over 7 per cent to under 6 per cent as a result of declining interest rates and the fact that people are living longer. Taken together these two changes mean that if a person had paid £200 a month into their pension fund for 20 years, they would have got a pension of around £20,000 a year if they started saving in 1977 and retired in 1997, but only just over £4,500 a year if they started saving in 1987 and retired in 2007.[18] Many annuity experts are concerned that annuity rates are now so low that about 75 per cent of people are buying pensions with little to no linkage to inflation. On retirement this gives them a noticeably higher income (just over 6 per cent of their fund value compared to about 3.8 per cent for an inflation-linked pension), but they will spend the rest of their lives living with the worry that any large rise in inflation will severely impact their standard of living.

Another factor that should concern private-sector employees is the increasing sophistication used by annuity companies in deciding how long someone might live and therefore what pension to pay them. By using such indicators as postcodes, annuity providers can make more accurate estimates of longevity. Life expectancy rates vary significantly in different parts of the country. A man living in the London Borough of Kensington and Chelsea can expect to live to 80.8 years and a woman 85.8 years, compared to Manchester's 72.3 years for a man and 77.4 years for a woman, or Glasgow's 69.9 for a man and 76.7 for a woman. The annuities chief from one company explained: 'Postcodes will mean we are able to more accurately assess and so price the longevity risk for each customer'.[19] The result will be that those living in more prosperous areas, where people tend to live longer, will get comparatively smaller pensions than those from more deprived districts.

## Profiting from Plundering our Pensions

However, it is not just the Government and its civil servants who appear to have set their hearts on feeding off our pension savings. Perhaps the biggest risks to private-pension provision come from the instability of financial markets and the large number of hungry and resourceful predators who hunt in them. Public-sector pensions' defined benefits are guaranteed by the Government, but with almost all private-sector companies having closed their defined benefits schemes, most savers' money is invested in stock markets and bonds. This leaves them vulnerable to fluctuating investment returns, poor investment decisions, greed and dishonesty. Around 230,000 people have lost their pensions due to their pension schemes collapsing following insolvency or being pillaged by financial manipulators in search of easy pickings. The more than £1.8 trillion in UK pension savings makes a very tempting target for city traders and speculators, all eager to increase their often multi-million-pound bonuses.

One common trick pension managers use is 'churning'. Each time pension savings move from one investment to another, fund managers, brokers and advisers all take a pay-off. So while it might be in savers' interests to keep the money in a few stable high-performing investments, it often benefits city insiders to keep on moving (churning) our pension savings from one investment to another in order to boost their own profits and bonuses.

Another danger to our savings is the growth in questionable investment vehicles. This Government likes to attribute the City of London's extraordinary international success over the last decade to its 'light-touch' regulatory approach. However, it tends not to mention that much of this so-called 'success' has been built on allowing City institutions to push our pension savings into ever more complex, poorly regulated and dubious financial instruments. As the collapse of hedge funds and the US sub-prime mortgage débâcle showed, many pension managers are throwing our savings into products they do not really understand and sometimes they are not even aware of how much of our pension savings have ended up in such high-risk investments. One pension management conference in mid-2007 was more like a sharks' feeding frenzy than a gathering of sober-suited financial experts – ever more intricate financial constructions were being snapped up by fund managers with little real comprehension of what they were buying with our money. One of the world's best-known investors famously said, 'Only when the tide goes out do you discover who has been swimming naked'.[20] A shock to the global financial system could expose many of the investments containing our pension money as being considerably less well-appointed than we would have hoped. The collapse of a few of the more imaginative and therefore risky financial constructions could wipe out billions of pounds of our pension savings.

A third danger to our pension savings comes from a few specialist financial services firms (in 2007 there were about 20) who specialize in buying private-sector pension schemes so they can make money from fund management fees and clever financial engineering techniques. Some of them even buy whole companies just so they can get their hands on the pension funds which can be worth more than the companies they buy. They then keep the pension funds and sell off the companies. Normally, these financial services firms make massive profits if their financial engineering is successful, while it's the pensioners who lose out if the financial engineering implodes.

A fourth and very real threat to private-sector pension savings is from private-equity firms. They take on high levels of borrowing to buy target companies and then have to squeeze profits out to pay back the loans. The Government's favourable tax treatment of private-equity profits and their often non-domiciled bosses has led to an 'unprecedented private equity buyout binge' accounting for about a fifth of private-sector business activity.[21] The billions of pounds lying in firms' pension funds have in many cases proved irresistible to this new breed of tax-avoiding financial buccaneers. By moving money around their many companies, they can effortlessly siphon off workers' pensions, leaving the pension regulator helplessly looking for excuses for failing to protect our retirement funds. A Labour MP, many of whose constituents were left destitute as a result of pension fund collapses after a private-equity takeover, expressed his views of the behaviour of one private-equity company with close links to the Government:

> I think these people need flogging. I feel so angry on behalf of decent upright citizens robbed of their basic human rights … These are greedy, selfish capitalists who live on the backs of others … We are a party of social rights and justice. It's why I joined the Labour party. We can't pretend it's nothing to do with us.[22]

A leading pensions expert who examined the case said, 'The company took advantage of all the loopholes in pensions law and ensured that there was as little money as possible in the pension scheme'. However, the Department of Work and Pensions commented:

> Opra (the pensions regulator) and the Pensions Ombudsman were satisfied that the activities surrounding the ... pension scheme did not break pensions legislation. There are no plans to hold further investigations.

## IT'S NOTHING TO DO WITH US

There has been much heat and noise but little clarity from politicians and the business community about who is responsible for the virtual meltdown in private-pension provision. The Tories and business people have tended to blame Gordon Brown for his pension fund tax grab, when in 1997 as Chancellor he abolished the Dividend Tax Relief for pension funds, giving him about £5.4 billion a year extra in tax revenue to lavish on supposedly improving public services. However, the Chancellor was only following the example of a Tory predecessor, Norman Lamont, who reduced the level of this tax relief from 25 per cent to 20 per cent in 1993, handing the Conservatives £500 million in additional tax.

Brown's 1997 move has proved to be controversial. When reducing the amount that pension funds had to invest by appropriating this £5.4 billion a year, the Chancellor curiously claimed he had 'removed a bias against investment which has been built into the tax system'.[23] For years the Treasury tried to prevent the documents relating to the decision from being made public on the basis that their release would undermine the decision-making process taken by ministers. However, the Information Commissioner ruled that it was in the public interest to release the papers. The Treasury first tried to claim that they abolished the tax relief on the advice of business leaders. This was vigorously denied by those business leaders. Then the Treasury claimed they had only followed civil servants' advice:

We decided on the basis of civil service advice to go ahead because this was the best thing for the long-term investment of the UK economy. The suggestion that the decisions were made not on the basis of the best civil service advice … is not true.[24]

However, the internal Treasury documents seemed to tell a quite different story. One warned:

The general message is that the big employer pension schemes will be able to cope at some cost to employers. But members of money purchase schemes would all be potential losers … We agree that abolishing tax credits would make a big hole in pension scheme finances.[25]

Internal Treasury forecasts predicted 'a shortfall in existing assets of up to £75 billion' and that 'employers would have to contribute an extra £10 billion a year for the next 10 to 15 years to get pension scheme funding back on track'.[26]

Finally, the Treasury just denied that the decision could have had an effect on the financial health of pension funds:

Anyone who pretends these decisions have led to the funding problems of pension schemes in recent years, while ignoring the impact of the dotcom crash, the pension holidays in the 1980s and 1990s and the rise in life expectancy, is simply distorting the facts.[27]

It is true that in comparison to the £1.8 trillion in pension savings, Brown's £5.4 billion a year tax grab is quite insignificant. However, it looks much more disturbing compared to the £17 billion or so that private-sector employees pay into their pensions each year. The real significance has probably been that it moved the pensions industry to what has now become fashionably known as a 'tipping point'. On its own, the extra tax could probably have been easily absorbed by the pensions industry. However, added to falling investment returns, greater longevity and new financial reporting regulations introduced by the Government, it significantly increased the amount companies would have had to pay into their pensions funds to cover final-salary pensions (defined benefit) liabilities and so led to a mass closure of defined benefit schemes, significantly disadvantaging people unfortunate enough to work in the private sector.

As if to add insult to injury, the Government pulled off yet another coup in its embezzlement of our pension savings with an announcement made in March 2004: from April 2006 the Government would impose a Lifetime Pension Fund Cap of £1.5 million for the year 2006–7, rising each year to £1.8 million by 2010–11. This meant that anyone able to accumulate pension savings above this amount would be subject to a new tax of 55 per cent. Naturally the pensions of politicians, judges and senior civil servants were exempt from this officially sanctioned plundering of our pensions.

## THE RICH GET RICHER

With pensions, there is just one thing on which almost everyone seems to agree – somebody else's pension should be reduced in order to avoid a financial crisis in the future. However, pensions reform is something that most governments shy away from. After all, reducing some people's pension entitlements is just going to make you a lot of enemies and the economic benefits for the over-all economy will not be seen for 30 to 40 years. So why bother? In 2005 the Government did make a half-hearted attempt to control the cost of public-sector pensions by suggesting an increase in the retirement age for many public-sector workers from 60 to 65. However, faced with union opposition, the Government backed down and only made the higher retirement age applicable for new recruits, so there will not be any economic benefits for taxpayers for about another 40 years. Conversely, while all current public-sector employees keep their early retirement, the Government is vigorously changing pension rules so that private-sector staff will have to work well beyond 65 before they can receive their pensions.

In spite of all its claims to be working towards a fairer society, this Government has actually created a clearly delineated four-tier society. At the top are the super-rich – tax-avoiding city financiers, senior politicians, judges and top civil servants all with six-figure pensions and complete financial security for themselves and their partners. Next are the mass of public-sector employees who will also enjoy a financial security and early retirement that is beyond the wildest dreams of 99 per cent of private-sector employees. Third are private-sector workers who are saving for a pension but who will have to work longer and save more to pay for public-sector pensions that will be significantly greater than their own. At the bottom will be 10 to 15 million pensioners living in virtual poverty on just the basic state pension and a few means-tested additional benefits handed out by civil servants who are all happily immune, thanks to the taxes paid by working people, from pensioner poverty themselves.

# CHAPTER 9

# GIVING IT ALL AWAY

In 2007–8 the Government plans to distribute about £156 billion of our money to 30 million of us through around 40 different types of social security benefits and Tax Credits.[1] This amount has risen from around £90 billion when the Government was first elected, an increase of over 70 per cent in cash terms and just over 48 per cent once inflation is taken into account. Since it was elected, the Government has handed out around £343 billion more in benefits than it would have done had benefits stayed at their 1997–8 level. This vast extra benefits expenditure has happened in spite of record economic growth and rising numbers of jobs in almost every year this Government has been in power (see Figure 19). If benefits were well-targeted, one might have expected that they would actually reduce as more people were working and people got wealthier.

Around £141 billion of the £156 billion will be handled by the Department for Work and Pensions (DWP), with another £15 billion given out by HM Revenue and Customs (HMRC) as Tax Credits. The purpose of this money is 'to build a fair and inclusive society which promotes opportunity and independence for all'.[2] Giving away so much of our money also costs money. The DWP has about 130,000 staff to process all these various benefits. They cost us £7.73 billion – around £59,000 per person including all their salaries, offices costs, pencils, paper and computer systems. At the HMRC there are close to another 8,000 staff

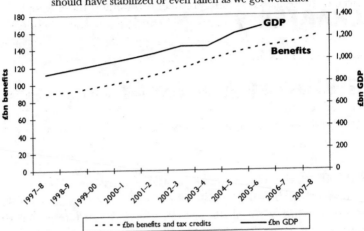

**Figure 19** Benefits have risen in line with GDP, whereas they should have stabilized or even fallen as we got wealthier

working with Tax Credits, costing perhaps another £400 million. So in all about £164 billion – around 30 per cent of the money spent by the Government – gets gobbled up by the benefits system.

This is a lot of money. However, most taxpayers probably would not object to our Government's largesse with our cash as long as the money really was well-targeted to achieve its aim of 'promoting fairness and opportunity for all'. There are three main groups at whom the Government directs the benefits money:

> Helping households into work 'to promote work as the best form of welfare for people of working age, while protecting the position of those in greatest need'.

> Relieving child poverty 'to ensure the best start for all children and relieve child poverty in 20 years'.

> Providing financial security for pensioners 'to combat poverty and promote security and independence in retirement for today's and future pensioners'.[3]

The Government claims to have achieved stunning success in all three of these areas: 'There are over 2.5 million more people in work today than there were in 1997, and the number of children in absolute poverty has halved'.[4] In addition, the Government says that its Pension Credit, launched in 2003,

> has helped to lift over one million pensioner households out of relative poverty and over two million pensioner households out of absolute poverty, a reduction of over 75 per cent between 1996–97 and 2005–06.[5]

It should be a relatively simple task for a government to better people's lives by just giving them a pile of our money – handing out mountains of cash ought to be much easier than trying to improve health, education or policing. However, a closer look at how well the Government has managed this money, and whether the Government really has achieved what it claims, might lead those of a nervous disposition to begin to worry about whether our £164 billion is being well spent. I will review two areas: the Government's administrative efficiency in distributing our money; and whether the money has actually achieved the goals of helping the unemployed, children in poverty and poorer pensioners.

## ADMINISTRATION AND ANARCHY

Unfortunately for us, our thrice-elected Government seems to have been a bit accident-prone when it comes to administering this £164 billion. The DWP, which handles most of the cash, has had its financial accounts rejected for the last 18 years. The high level of fraud and errors meant that the Auditor General did not have sufficient confidence in the DWP's figures to sign off the department's accounts. In one year the DWP claimed to have halved the amount of fraud, but the auditor rejected this as just a 'reclassification' of figures that did not 'represent a real improvement in tackling fraud or conversely a diminution in the level of error'.[6] The level of fraud estimated by the DWP varies by type of benefit from between 5.8 per cent (Income Support) and 9.0 per cent (Jobseeker's Allowance), though seasoned department-watchers might suspect it is really significantly higher.[7] Each year the DWP claims to have reduced the rates of error and fraud, but not all observers seem convinced by the department's version of events. The chairman of the Public Accounts Committee (PAC) explained:

> For the last eighteen years, the story has been the same: the Department for Work and Pensions loses enormous amounts of money to fraud and error and as a result has its accounts qualified.[8]

However, the DWP's problems with the numbers seem like small beer compared to the chaos over at HMRC when it introduced Gordon Brown's pet project – Tax Credits. Tax Credits are paid to around six million families. In each of the first two years more than £2 billion a year was overpaid. When the mistakes were discovered, HMRC tried to reclaim this money, causing some of the most financially vulnerable people to lose homes and jobs and driving many families into financial misery.[9] One hundred million calls were made to the Tax Credit helpline, most of which went unanswered. However, there were some very satisfied customers who did manage to navigate their way around this complex new system. These were fraudsters. They managed to steal the identities of 13,000 DWP staff and another 30,000 Network Rail staff, and using the Tax Credits website they siphoned off possibly hundreds of millions of pounds of our money. Unfortunately, HMRC did not shut down the website until almost three months after it was warned about this type of fraud. One of the members of the PAC appeared more than displeased with HMRC's dismal performance: 'Tax Credits are one of the most popular initiatives that this Government have introduced, but your incompetence and mismanagement have brought it into disrepute'.[10]

In 2007, HMRC once again provided world-class entertainment for the nation when it mislaid a couple of computer disks containing the names, addresses, National Insurance numbers and bank details of the 25 million people who received Child Benefit. At first, the Government claimed it was all due to a mistake made by a junior official, but later revelations showed a culture of slovenly incompetence reaching all the way up to senior management as this fiasco was just the latest of more than 2,100 security breaches at HMRC over the previous year. HMRC then sent apology letters to all the families involved – unfortunately, many thousands, containing confidential information, went to the wrong people. The merging of the Inland Revenue and Customs and Excise was meant to be one of Gordon Brown's major achievements, but it just seems to have created an expensive shambles. Even staff at HMRC do not seem too impressed by the quality of their own colleagues. One said, 'The new kids who apply to work here don't have to have any GCSEs. It used to be that you had to have five but lots don't have one.' Another complained, 'The training is a joke and new recruits cannot do fractions or percentages so they cannot do what is required to help people properly'.[11] The HMRC even seemed to confirm the poor educational level of its staff when its website informed potential new recruits, 'If you have no formal educational qualifications, you can still apply'.

However, perhaps the star performer in terms of administrative incompetence is the Child Support Agency (CSA). This was originally set up by Thatcher's Tories in 1990, but it seemed to reach Brobdingnagian levels of uselessness when New Labour paid close to £1 billion of our money to its favourite management and IT systems consultants to modernize, automate and improve the CSA's operations.[12] The results were depressingly predictable – 330,000 cases stuck in the backlog for months, 19,000 cases having to be processed by hand due to computer problems, 25 per cent of applications taking more than two years, £3.5 billion uncollected and only 297,000 out of 1,449,000 absent parents making any payments at all.[13] When he was Work and Pensions Secretary, David Blunkett described the CSA as a 'shambles' and in 2007 the chairman of the PAC called the Government's reform of the CSA 'one of the greatest public administration disasters of recent times'.[14] Following this massive squandering of our money, it looks as if the CSA will be wound down and replaced in 2008 by a new organization, the Child Maintenance and Enforcement Commission (CMEC). One could imagine that the CMEC will inherit both the CSA's problems and its apparently incompetent but spendaholic management.

Behind these entertaining but expensive examples of Government and civil service bungling lies a less obvious haemorrhaging of our money – the benefits system for helping the less fortunate has become so complicated that it is almost unmanageable. Each government seems to add to the complexity by dreaming up new variations without simplifying what is already there. With six new Acts and 364 new statutory instruments affecting the law on social security between 2000 and 2004, this Government has taken complexity to an entirely new level of unmanageability. Many of the 40 available benefits overlap so that the more you get of one, the less you get of another. Increasing complexity means increasing administrative costs and increasing errors. There are now, for example, 24 files of guidance just on Jobseeker's Allowance and another 14 volumes on Income Support. Studies have shown that very few DWP staff can master the encyclopaedic array of rules and regulations. The administrators of one project to get benefits for 87 users of community mental health services found that they had to complete 169 forms, write 788 letters, attend 436 interviews and make about 900 telephone calls.[15] This benefits maze is so impenetrable that many staff do not know which benefits to propose and so the most vulnerable claimants often give up and do not get their full entitlement. On the other hand, some groups have become so sophisticated at navigating their way round the labyrinth that they can extract huge sums without anyone noticing that we are being defrauded. A former Labour mayor and his wife, for example, were reported to have fraudulently claimed almost £37,000 in Disability Living Allowance and Income Support which they used to pay for their daughter's private school fees.[16] The DWP states that one of its key objectives is 'to modernise welfare delivery so as to improve the accessibility, accuracy and value for money of services to customers'.[17] It does seem as if there is still much more to do.

## EMPLOYING THE EMPLOYABLE

This Government's claim that more than 2.5 million more people have found work during its time in power does represent an achievement that probably no other government has ever managed. However, one unfortunate fact that casts doubt on how much credit we should give this Government for this success is that most of the fall in unemployment occurred in the three years before, and during the first three years of, its time in office, before it really began spending our money on job creation. The level of unemployment actually began rising after 2004 when the Government's spending to decrease unemployment should have been having an effect (see Figure 20).[18]

Most statistics can be interpreted in many ways to suit whatever story one wishes to present. One possible explanation of Figure 20 is as follows. There were huge increases in unemployment under the Conservatives in the early 1980s and again in the early 1990s, partly due to two recessions and partly due to the Tories' almost wilful dismantling of our manufacturing industries – in particular steel, car manufacture and mining. It is clear that unemployment was already falling rapidly under the last years of the Tories and that New Labour merely inherited this trend. This

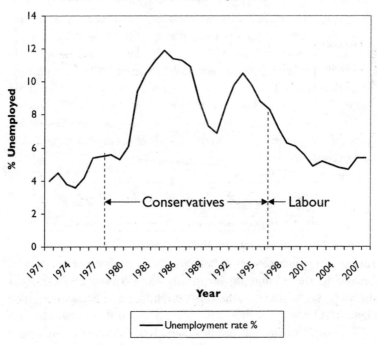

**Figure 20** Unemployment was already falling rapidly when New Labour came to power

fall in unemployment continued under New Labour until around 2002 and then resumed again from 2003 until 2005, due to both economic growth and the 600,000 extra jobs that the Government created in the public sector. With the budget deficit spiralling out of control in the NHS and other public-sector administrative costs also shooting up, recruitment in the public sector stalled around 2005 and unemployment started to rise as the private sector did not manage to grow as fast as the workforce.

But there is another, more probable explanation for the fall in people claiming unemployment benefit – namely that successive governments (particularly this Government) have been hiding the real level of unemployment by allowing many people to move

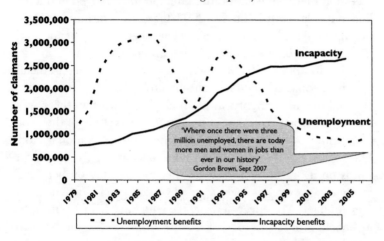

**Figure 21** As the numbers claiming unemployment benefit have decreased, the numbers claiming incapacity have increased

from getting unemployment benefits to receiving other benefits – the rise in those claiming incapacity since 1994, for example, almost perfectly matches the supposed fall in unemployment (see Figure 21).[19]

The number of people on incapacity benefits keeps on increasing. By 2007 around 2.7 million people of working age were being paid almost £8 billion in disability benefits in addition to billions more in other support. About 4,000 claim they cannot work because of gout, another 2,000 believe they are too fat to work and tens of thousands more are prevented from working because of dizziness, depression, phobias and headaches. The UK now has the highest proportion of people of working age with a disability in the developed world. Given improvements in the general population's health around the world thanks to better nutrition, advances in medical science and increased spending on healthcare, either the British population is bucking the international trend of improving health or else incapacity benefit has become a convenient place for governments to park and hide employable but unemployed people in order to make the unemployment figures look low. At the height of the 1985/6 recession there were about three million unemployed and a million on sickness benefit. By 2007 there were around 900,000 unemployed and 2.8 million on sickness benefit. If you add in an increase in people claiming single-parent benefits from around 500,000 to about 850,000, then there were more economically inactive people living off benefits in 2007, when the Government claimed unemployment was at an all-time low, than there were during the worst recession of the last 70 years. One of the problems with incapacity benefit, identified by the National Audit Office (NAO), is that up till now it has increased each year a person is on it, 'creating a perverse incentive to stay on benefit'.[20] Strangely, the average age of people on incapacity benefit is getting younger. Moreover, few people who have been on incapacity benefit ever return to work. As the former Work and Pensions Secretary said, 'If you have been on incapacity benefit for more than two years, you are more likely to retire or die than ever get another job'.[21]

Thus by 2007, in spite of a decade of economic expansion, around 13 per cent of the British population still lived in households where nobody worked, compared to 11 per cent in France, 10 per cent in Italy, 5 per cent in the US and 3 per cent in Japan. In the UK, there seems to be a hard-core of around 2.5 million households that have nobody in work and nobody looking for work. The NAO has estimated that these households cost us just under £40 billion a year. They receive about £12.7 billion every year in direct benefits and another £25.4 billion each year in other forms of support.[22] This is a problem that this Government has inherited from the previous Conservative administration which was responsible for the number of workless households more than doubling to their current level.[23]

As Chancellor, Gordon Brown said that Labour was determined that every household would have at least one member who was acquainted with the 'world of work'.[24] This Government has showered this group with new schemes and initiatives to get them into some kind of employment. There have been the New Deal for Lone Parents, New Deal for Partners, New Deal for Young People, Pathways to Work, Workstep, Local Employment Partnerships, Employment Zones and, from April 2007, the City Strategy. All these efforts have cost us close to £6 billion. It is unclear how many people have been helped into work, as many participants in these schemes find temporary work for a few months and then end up back on the scheme. The Government claims that over three million people have been on these schemes and that almost two million participants have found work.[25] However, a study done by the NAO suggests that the real figure for people who have found work as a result of a government programme is nearer to 400,000. This means that each person who has moved from a scheme to a job has cost us around £15,000, with some schemes costing over £20,000 per person employed.[26]

Administration costs on some of these employment programmes seem high and can be as much as 60 to 80 per cent on a couple of the less well-attended initiatives. Some people unfortunately do not seem to benefit from these schemes – over half a million people have been on the New Deal programme twice and of these around 172,000 have taken part three times or more.[27] In addition, the Government's claims of high participation rates do not completely match up with a study done by the NAO, suggesting that at any time less than 5 per cent of working-age recipients of benefits were on any Government scheme to get back into work. For one of the Government's initiatives, only 0.003 per cent of benefit recipients took part.[28] So, while the Government has certainly made some progress in dealing with a massive social problem largely created by the Conservatives, its real achievements have probably been much more modest than those it claims. However, in attacking the Government's supposed failure to tackle the problem of the hard-core unemployed, our friends in the Conservative Party seem to have conveniently forgotten that it was during their time in power that the whole situation reached its current, almost epic proportions.

In the US, the Clinton administration, supported by a Republican Congress, signed the Personal Responsibility and Work Opportunity Reconciliation Act in 1996. The Act is generally seen as one of the greatest changes in US welfare. This abandoned the previous 'something for nothing' welfare payments where people who were fit for work could receive support indefinitely even though they were not looking for work. Instead, welfare payments were substantially cut after people had claimed for two years and nobody was allowed more than five years welfare dependency in a lifetime. In the ten years since the Act, the number on welfare in the US has dropped by around 60 per cent. Despite much higher immigration per 100,000 of population than the UK, the US has managed to maintain the proportion of workless households at less than 40 per cent of the UK level. The US has sought to reduce poverty by getting people into work. In the UK, both political parties have tended to avoid tackling some of the underlying causes of workless households and so around 80 per cent of benefits are paid without placing any obligation on the recipients to try to improve their situation. Reducing the 'something for nothing' principle of benefits payment may not be the solution for the UK's problem, but so far neither of the main parties seems to know how to tackle this £40 billion a year drain on our country's resources.

Numerous studies have shown the importance of work in terms of giving people a purpose and a social network, and also the negative effects of being out of work and marginalized. The question arises as to whether we are getting value for the money this Government spends on the economically inactive. If we are genuinely helping the disadvantaged back into the productive mainstream of society, most people would probably feel the £40 billion is being well spent, but if the Government is merely throwing our money away by putting off the day of reckoning and, even worse, encouraging and entrenching rather than solving the problem, then we could be forgiven for wishing that this money was put to better use. It was the Labour Government, not the Tories, who produced a report called *Welfare isn't Working*,[29] and yet the Government has not had the courage to act on the conclusions of its own report. The Government states that it is spending all this money to create fairness, but in too many cases it appears only to be contributing to unproductive dependency.

## LOOKING AFTER OUR CHILDREN

Childhood poverty more than doubled in the 1980s and 1990s, matching the rise in unemployment under the Tories (see Figure 22). There seems to be a few years' delay between unemployment rising and the measurement of childhood poverty reflecting that rise, but the link between the two is clear. By the time this Government was elected, there were an estimated 3.4 million (26 per cent of 13.1 million children) living in poverty, giving the UK the shameful distinction of having one of the highest levels of child poverty in the developed world.

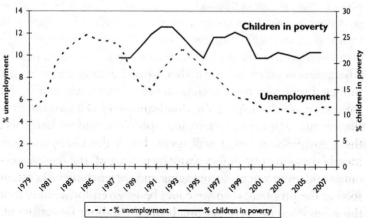

**Figure 22**  The level of children in poverty closely reflects the level of unemployment

One of this Government's key social pledges was to get to grips with the problem of child poverty and it committed to: 'halve the number of children in relative low income households between 1998–99 and 2010–11, on the way to eradicating child poverty by 2020'.[30]

At first sight, the Government has had quite a bit of success as by 2004–5 it had moved around 700,000 children out of poverty, reducing the level to 2.7 million and leading the Work and Pensions Minister to state, 'We have made considerable progress against our historic goal to end child poverty in the UK'.[31] However, an obsessive graph-watcher could claim that the number of children in poverty would have fallen anyway, even if the Government had done nothing at all, as the trend line of children in poverty would simply have followed (with only a few years' delay) the downward trend in unemployment of the Tories' last years in government. It's even worrying that, in spite of all the money the Government is spending, child poverty has not continued to decrease in line with falling unemployment. But this is because unemployment has not really fallen under this Government. The unemployed have just been moved onto other forms of benefit and so child poverty has stabilised at a high level.

The social consequences of poverty on children's lives have been frequently documented – low educational achievement, poor health, failure to establish themselves in the job market and higher than average levels of crime and addiction. One study found that even by the age of three, children from disadvantaged households were already one year behind children from more prosperous backgrounds.[32]

By 2005–6, the number of children in poverty had started to rise again to 2.8 million. The Tories' quickly berated the Government for this rise: 'Today's depressing figures show that poverty is increasing, inequality is rising, and the incomes of the poorest fifth are in decline', once again seemingly oblivious of the fact that it was their shaky economic management that pushed so many children into poverty in the first place.[33] To reverse this unwanted development, in his 2007 budget the then Chancellor Gordon Brown announced:

> The Budget 2007 decision to uprate the child element of the Child Tax Credit by £150 over the average earnings index- ing from April 2008 will set child poverty on a renewed downward trajectory by lifting roughly a further 200,000 children out of relative poverty.[34]

There seems to be a tendency for those in the child poverty busi- ness to suggest that the solution is always to throw more of our money at the problem. Some felt that the Government was not supplying enough cash. A spokesperson from Save the Children commented, 'It is only too clear that Gordon Brown's budget announcements last week will not be enough to get the govern- ment back on track'.[35] This view was echoed by Barnardo's, who suggested that the Government's priorities might be wrong and that it would be better to push more cash at child poverty than at other projects:

> If we can afford the Olympics – and I am delighted we can – if we can afford Trident, if we can afford to build 8,000 new jail spaces, we can most certainly afford to halve child poverty.[36]

This 'we need to give more money' approach is always laudable and morally pleasing, but it may unfortunately oversimplify more complex problems and ultimately do disservice to, rather than help, those who clearly need support.

There appear to be both deep-rooted social and administrative issues contributing to child poverty that a pile of gold, however big, might not actually solve. Although unemployment has sup- posedly plummeted since the inglorious peaks of Tory rule, the number of workless households has decreased by less than 20 per cent. Today, about 1.74 million children live in households where nobody works. Many of these are also included in the 1.7 million children who live in the care of alcoholics and drug addicts.[37] The incomes of the most disadvantaged households are being reduced by such social changes as rising economic inactivity in spite of rising employment, increases in the number of children born to single parents, and the UK having one of the highest divorce rates in Europe. There are also administrative barriers to reducing the number of children in poverty. One report suggested that child poverty could be halved by handing out another £4 billion to poorer households.[38] However, in 2007 about £9.4 billion in means-tested benefits was not being claimed by those who were entitled to it and an additional £4.5 billion of Working Tax Credits and Child Tax Credits also went unclaimed – this combined £13.9 billion far exceeded what the experts claimed was necessary to make a major reduction in child poverty.[39] This problem of child poverty has not been helped either by the utter incompetence and administrative chaos which have accompanied this Government's attempts to introduce Tax Credits, or by the Government wasting almost £1 billion on consultants to 'modernize' the Child Support Agency which now has over £3.5 billion in outstanding payments, most of which will never be made.

All this has meant that in spite of having one of the strongest economies and highest employment rates of the G8 countries, by 2007 the UK had more children in poverty than 21 out of 25 European Union countries, with over one in five children living in poverty. So, it is not immediately obvious that all the money the Government has already spent on reducing child poverty has been particularly effective. In 2007 Prime Minister Gordon Brown, when Chancellor, stated that:

> As a result of these reforms to the tax and benefit system, by April 2009, households with children will be on average £200 per year better off … and households with children in the poorest fifth of the population will be, on average, £350 per year better off.[40]

This equates to about 55p per day per household for households with children and 96p per day per household in the poorest households. It could appear rather over optimistic to believe that these seemingly modest sums will really make much of an impact on the high levels, underlying causes and baleful results of child poverty.

## PROTECTING OUR PENSIONERS

In 1997 over 30 per cent of the UK's 11 million pensioners were living in either what economists call 'relative poverty' or 'absolute poverty'. To pay pensions and to focus on the problem of pensioner poverty, in 2002 the Government set up the Pension Service as part of the DWP. Each year the Pension Service costs us around £830 million to run and pays out about £60 billion. The Pension Service's aims are 'to combat poverty among today's pensioners, provide security for those likely to rely on state provision and further improve and modernize services for today's and future pensioners'.[41]

The Government has stated that it has lifted around one million pensioners out of relative poverty and another two million out of absolute poverty. The main means used to improve the lot of pensioners has been the Pension Credit, introduced in October 2003 to replace the previous benefit called the Minimum Income Guarantee. About 2.7 million pensioners receive Pension Credits, hence the Government's claim to have lifted about three million out of poverty. However, in making this claim, the Government seems to be forgetting that 1.7 million pensioners were already getting the Minimum Income Guarantee, so although more pensioners are getting more money than ten years ago, the difference is not quite as large as the Government would like us to think.

The problem with the British state pension is that it is really just a form of minimum subsistence payment, not a reward for a lifetime of working and paying taxes. The average European state pension is around 57 per cent of average earnings – in the UK it is just about 17 per cent of average earnings. The UK pension is now so low that, if you have no pension savings, it is not worth paying National Insurance to qualify for a state pension. Many people retiring today are finding that although they have paid tax and National Insurance all their lives, they get pretty much the same amount of money as someone who has never paid a penny in either tax or National Insurance.

The state pension, which was introduced in 1948, has almost a 100 per cent take-up rate, but despite spending about £25 million on advertising, the Pension Service seems to be struggling slightly to get pensioners to take all the money that we want to give them. For example, while the overall take-up rate for Pension Credits is somewhere between 60 per cent and 70 per cent, only about 27 per cent of pensioners living in relative poverty claim it.[42] With the other two main benefits for pensioners, the take-up rate is similarly dismal. Around 29 per cent of pensioners living in relative poverty claim Housing Benefit and about 30 per cent claim Council Tax Benefit. Because of this failure of benefits to reach those who most need them, it is estimated that there are still over 2.2 million pensioners living in poverty in the UK.

Various studies have found that poor coordination between the Pension Service and local authorities, over-complex claimant procedures and excessive form-filling cause many poorer pensioners to give up trying to get the benefits to which they are entitled. The NAO singled out the eligibility assessment for disability benefits as being particularly impenetrable. What is more worrying is that take-up rates of Housing Benefit and Council Tax Benefit have been falling over the last three years in spite of the Pension Service being allocated an extra £85.5 million to ensure that pensioner benefits reached those who most need them. One study estimated that an additional 500,000 pensioners would be lifted out of poverty if they simply received the full

Council Tax Benefit, Housing Benefit and Pension Credit to which they were entitled.[43] Another study estimated that many pensioners are losing about £50,000 in unclaimed benefits over their lifetime.[44] The Government set a target for three million pensioners to be receiving Pension Credits by February 2006; the Pension Service achieved 2.7 million. The target for 2008 is 3.2 million but, despite all the money it has received, the Pension Service does not expect to meet this target either.[45] The reason the Pension Service gives for not reaching its targets is that they were 'unrealistic'. It has apparently not occurred to the Pension Service that its own impenetrable bureaucratic procedures and administrative incompetence might be partly to blame for depriving our pensioners of what is rightly theirs.

Perhaps the most significant cause of pensioner poverty is that pensions are increasing at only a fraction of the rates of increase of many of the items for which pensioners have to pay. Each year the basic state pension and other benefits are increased in line with the Consumer Price Index. However, due to the Government's failure to regulate utility companies, services on which pensioners rely, like gas, electricity and water, have all increased in price by many times the rise in pensions. The Government estimated that in the winter of 2006–7 about 25,000 pensioners died because they could not afford to heat their homes properly. Although there are winter fuel payments of £200 for each household with a resident over 60, and £300 where there is a resident over 80, the average pensioner winter fuel bill is estimated to have increased from £572 in 2003 to £924 by 2007.[46] Moreover, council tax in most areas has risen by about four times the increase in pensions. In one year pensions were famously increased by only 75 pence per week, ludicrously less than the increase in most pensioners' weekly bills. One study showed that in 2006–7 the inflation rate for pensioners was around 9 per cent, while pensions increased by less than a third of that.[47]

This leaves many older people in severe financial difficulties and prey to unscrupulous businesses seeking to profit from pensioner poverty. Some pensioners are falling victim to companies offering dubious equity release schemes and are surrendering the value in their homes for extremely poor returns because the Financial Services Authority seems to prefer a 'light touch' regulation of financial services providers. Or else pensioners are being conned into selling their homes on the understanding they can rent them back for the rest of their lives and then find that they get thrown out on to the street a year or two after the deal is done. There are many indications that hundreds of thousands of pensioners are finding their financial situation unsatisfactory. Over one million are still paying off mortgages, with an average remaining debt of £38,000. About two million more pensioners are working now compared to 1997. Perhaps many of these pensioners are able to do so because people are healthier and want to work past retirement age to maintain their social networks and avoid boredom. However, surveys suggest that the majority of them are working out of necessity, rather than voluntarily.[48]

The problem of pensioner poverty would be significantly reduced if the Pension Service got its act together and actually modernized the provision of benefits by such steps as simplifying applications procedures; linking benefits together instead of making people fill in forms in duplicate, triplicate or quadruplicate; communicating effectively with local authorities; and making more payments automatic (like the state pension) instead of putting pensioners through the indignity of having to jump through a long series of often unnecessary bureaucratic hoops in order to get the money to which they are entitled. Judging by the Pension Service's current progress, we may be waiting some time before our pensioners receive the financial security the Government has so often promised and for which most pensioners have paid all their working lives.

# PART 3

# POWER TO THE PROFLIGATE

# CHAPTER 10

# A PROFUSION OF PLUNDERING POLITICIANS

## KEEPING ITS PROMISES

In its 1997 manifesto this Government promised to funda-
mentally change the way this country was governed: 'Our aim is
no less than to set British political life on a new course for the
future'. The most radical proposals concerned the distribution of
power away from Westminster: 'Over-centralisation of government and lack of accountability was a problem in governments of
both left and right. Labour is committed to the democratic
renewal of our country through decentralisation.' The new
Government planned to address this over-centralization in
two main ways. One was by devolving powers to Scotland and
Wales:

> We will meet the demand for decentralisation of power to
> Scotland and Wales, once established in referendums ... As
> soon as possible after the election we will enact legislation to
> allow the people of Scotland and Wales to vote in separate
> referendums on our proposals.

The other was by giving London an assembly and a mayor:

> London is the only Western capital without an elected city
> government. Following a referendum to confirm popular

demand, there will be a new deal for London. With a strategic authority and a mayor, each directly elected.

These were two of New Labour's promises that it did actually deliver and the result has been quite expensive for us British tax-payers.

## AN ODD WAY TO SAVE MONEY

The first to start spending our money were the Scots. In May 1999 the 129 Members of the first Scottish Parliament (MSPs) were elected and by July they had full legislative powers. As one of the first acts of preparation for the new Parliament, the Scots decided to start building a fine new home in which the future MSPs could conduct their important business. In the Government's original White Paper, 'Scotland's Parliament', published in July 1997, New Labour had envisaged us spending somewhere between £10 million and £40 million to provide a building for the new Scottish Parliament – possibly from adapting and refurbishing an existing building. However, the MSPs had much more ambitious plans for accommodating themselves. They did not want a tarting up of an existing building; they wanted a bright shiny new symbol of their power, in the most expensive part of Edinburgh, designed by a top international architect – after all, it was mostly the remainder of the UK that would be paying for the thing.

In January 1998 a great competition was launched to find a designer capable of delivering Scotland's great ambitions. On 17 June 1999 the MSPs held their first Parliamentary debate on the project, approved the designer's proposal and voted themselves a budget of £109 million of taxpayers' money – considerably more than the Government had originally intended. As costs began to soar effortlessly past £109 million, the MSPs held a second debate on 5 April 2000. During this, they upped the budget and set a maximum cap on the project of a mere £195 million. A year of chaos and mismanagement followed and several key people on the project were gently replaced. In a third debate on 21 June 2001, the MSPs generously decided to lift the maximum cap on how much of our money they would be using so that by November 2001 the cost had gone up to £241 million – stratospherically higher than New Labour's first estimate.

However, the MSPs were not finished yet – not by a long way. Another year of incompetence, infighting and possibly dubious contracting practices went by, during which several construction companies filled their bank accounts and the cost jumped, first to £266.4 million by March 2002 and then to £294.6 million by October. After what was certainly a very jolly Hogmanay for those who were snaffling immense quantities of our money, the new year just brought more of the same. In January 2003 the cost reached £323.9 million, by June it was £375.8 million and by September the MSPs managed to push the cost up to £401 million. By February 2004 the price had increased yet again to £430.5 million. The Holyrood building was finally occupied in August 2004 and on 7 September 2004 the Scottish Parliament met there for the first time. In a final gesture of brazenness so shameless that it defies description in polite English, the MSPs claimed that they had actually managed to reduce the cost of the building when they triumphantly announced, 'The final cost of the Scottish Parliament Building has been reduced by £16.1 million. The cost to the taxpayer will therefore fall from an estimated £430.5 million to £414.4 million.'[1]

Throughout the farrago, the MSPs did commission various supposedly independent and always expensive reports, studies and reviews in the interest of public accountability. With each one, those involved claimed 'important lessons had been learnt', yet the mismanagement continued unabated.

## WE ONLY COST £600,000 EACH

Another 'difficult' decision the MSPs had to make was how much to pay themselves. After consulting various remuneration experts, they chose to link their pay and allowances to those paid to MPs at Westminster and set their salaries at 87.5 per cent of the MP level. This was quite modest given that the average salary in Scotland was about 92 per cent of the UK average. It was on their expenses though that the MSPs decided to show more unrestrained generosity towards themselves, as these seemed to keep on increasing well above the level of inflation. For example, on average MSPs claimed expenses of around £69,000 each in 2004–5, rising to over £74,000 by 2005–6 as MSPs apparently got better at manipulating their various allowances – a comfortable increase of around 8 per cent: over three times the rise in the cost of living.

Eventually, a series of scandals in 2006 rudely interrupted some MSPs' milking of the system. One Labour MSP was reported to be claiming £7,000 a year for housing costs while living at his son's flat. A Lib Dem MSP allegedly broke the rules by pocketing £9,000 a year on a house he jointly owned with his wife. Another Lib Dem MSP allegedly managed to buy two Edinburgh flats using his Parliamentary allowances. One MSP got caught claiming mileage allowances for driving around his constituency when he was actually abroad. There were also questions about MSPs' taxi fares, with some Parliamentarians claiming up to £8,500 a year, and the Scottish Parliament refusing to release details of some members' expenses. Following the public outcry about the waste and dishonesty, the Scottish Parliament decided to publish all MSPs' expenses in a bid to restore public trust in an institution that had become too used to treating taxpayers' money as its own. The Parliament claimed this new openness proved that Scotland had 'one of the most open and accountable systems of any parliament in the world'.[2] However, it took almost eight years of massive waste and dubious expense claims to achieve this transparency.

Overall, the whole paraphernalia of the Scottish Parliament costs around £79 million a year to run – equivalent to over £600,000 per MSP.[3] MSPs get paid about £53,000 a year. However, there are many ways by which they can boost this sum other than through the more obviously outrageous ones already mentioned. If they use their annual accommodation allowance of up to £10,900 to buy a property for use when in Edinburgh, instead of staying in a hotel or renting, this adds the equivalent of over £18,000 before tax (at 40 per cent) to their income. Then there is up to £58,000 which can be used to employ staff, who can be members of the MSP's own family. There is also free travel, 12 free trips a year for each member of the MSP's family, meals, trips to Europe, freebies from lobbyists and a one-off payment of thousands more should an MSP be careless enough to lose their seat. In addition, MSPs have one of the best pension schemes in Scotland, with early retirement on full pension and accumulating almost twice as much for each year of service as most other public-sector workers (see Chapter 8: The Great Pensions Robbery). Nevertheless, the Scottish Parliament has recently launched a review of MSPs' pensions (presumably with the aim of finding some excuse to increase them) and we should not be surprised if they soon discover excellent reasons to re-examine their salaries and expenses arrangements as well.

## ANOTHER GREAT BUILDING 'SUCCESS'

The Welsh Assembly members also seemed to like building things for themselves with the UK's cash. Fortunately for us taxpayers, they are nowhere near as ambitious as their Scottish partners in crime. The project to build the seat for the National Assembly for Wales' 60 members was kicked off in 1998. It was due to be completed and fully operational by 2002 and should have cost £12 million. Richard Rogers, one of the UK's most famous architects, was given the commission and work started.

By July 2001 the project was not progressing quite as planned. The project was stopped[4] and his partnership made a claim against the Welsh Assembly for nearly £400,000 in unpaid fees, which was upheld. The Assembly made a counter-claim for over £7 million, but this was thrown out. The project was halted for two years. The President of the Royal Institute of British Architects, who tried to intervene as an honest-broker, said that the 'incompetence on the client's side frankly beggars belief'.[5] By January 2003 the project was relaunched as a Private Finance Initiative (PFI). However, the building costs had now risen to £55 million and it would not be completed until August 2005. In spite of the cost increasing by more than a factor of four and the time needed going from four years to seven years, the Welsh First Minister called the new fixed-price contract 'a major achievement' and claimed:

> We can now go forward secure in the knowledge that the cost of the project has been fixed at a level which will deliver value for money and a flagship building for Wales.[6]

The building finally opened in 2006 and ended up costing £67 million – over five times the original budget. The usual bunch of local politicians all gave speeches proclaiming what a wonderful building it was and clapped themselves on the back for their great success. Little mention was made of the cost, chaos and incompetence that had wasted so many tens of millions of our money over the previous eight years. Critics characterized the whole sorry episode as an exercise in self-aggrandizement at the taxpayers' expense. One of the first debates held in the new building was to decide whether the Welsh NHS could afford to provide new life-saving drugs including Herceptin.

The Welsh Assembly costs the taxpayer around £37 million a year to run – just over £600,000 per Assembly member and very close to the annual cost per MSP. Salaries of Assembly members are slightly lower than for MSPs, but some of the expenses limits are more generous, allowing Assembly members many creative and tax-free ways of supplementing their official 2007–8 salaries of £46,496.

## WONDERFUL WESTMINSTER – LESS WORK, MORE MONEY

By handing over most of their powers to either the devolved Parliaments in Scotland and Wales or else to the ever-expanding Euro-Superstate, Westminster MPs have less and less to do. Yet curiously their salaries, expenses and other costs keep going up. One study concluded that in May 1997 about 40 per cent of legislation affecting the UK was initiated and authored in the EU. By 2001 this had reached 55 per cent and, according to an answer given in 2007 in the German parliament (the UK Government has refused to provide the same information), 84 per cent of their legislation now comes straight from the EU.[7] There are whole areas of our government where Westminster has become almost irrelevant – agriculture, customs, fisheries, free movement of goods and competition policy are just some of these. For example, when the Inland Revenue wanted to alter some regulations to let it crack down on a multi-billion-pound VAT fraud, it had to ask permission from the EU and had no need to consult our own Parliament at all. Incidentally, the EU rejected all but a small part of the Revenue's request, thus protecting the multinational fraudsters against our tax authorities. Similarly, when a 2007 television documentary exposed the massive scandal of thousands of tons of edible fish being thrown back into the sea because of EU quotas, our Government was powerless to act and instead had to ask the EU bureaucrats if they could look at the problem.

A hint that our parliamentarians are actually at a bit of a loose end as to what to do with their time came in late 2007 when the Government announced that it was considering giving MPs an extra 12 days holiday over the next year, starting with an extra week off at the end of October 2007 when MPs had only just returned from their 12-week summer break. The reason for this additional time off was that the Government had run out of legislation to put before Parliament. One leading member of the shadow cabinet admitted that MPs did not have enough work to fill their time: 'We are just not doing anything at the moment'.[8] In 2002, as part of its attempt to improve the government of our country, New Labour announced that it would be shortening the summer holiday and that each year MPs would return to work in September rather than October. However, that plan was quietly dropped. Instead, under this Government, MPs' hours have been significantly shortened, with late-night sittings scrapped to make the House of Commons more family-friendly. Moreover, MPs already have 91 days holiday a year, over three times the 28 days a year granted to almost all other British workers.

If you owned a corner shop and you lost most of your customers, you might consider reducing your staff and even paying yourself slightly less. That is fairly classic economics. However, Westminster seems to work according to different economic principles. In spite of losing a large proportion of their work to the EU and the devolved assemblies, our leaders have never considered cutting their numbers to match their greatly reduced workload. In fact, they keep awarding themselves larger salaries, increased pensions and ever more allowances to do around half the amount of work that they were doing just over a decade ago when New Labour first came to power.

In the last five years alone, the amount of money our MPs have taken in salaries and expenses has gone up by a satisfying (for them) 64 per cent, from less than £100 million in 2001–2 to over £155 million in 2006–7. This took the direct cost of an MP from about £146,000 in 2001–2 to over £240,000 in 2006–7.[9] Part of this large rise comes from MPs awarding themselves inflation-busting salary increases. Part also comes from them claiming ever more expenses – the number of expense claims submitted by

MPs has almost doubled in five years from just over 30,000 a year to close to 60,000. A third reason is that MPs have employed more staff. As the House of Commons Annual Report explains, 'The number of Members' staff on the payroll has increased significantly since 2001 as a result of the introduction of the Staffing Allowance'.[10] In the last five years the number of staff employed to help MPs do less and less work has gone up by over a third from around 1,800 to over 2,500. Now that MPs have decided to grant themselves another £10,000 each as a Communication Allowance, the cost of our Westminster MPs will go even higher and each year we will be bombarded with another £6.4 million of junk mail that almost all of us will bin immediately. We can probably assume that the Scottish and Welsh representatives will look at the Communication Allowance, consider it a terrifically good idea and will also vote to award it to themselves at our expense, unnecessarily destroying several large forests as a result.

A Westminster MP's salary is only £60,675 and over the last three years MPs have had below-inflation pay rises.[11] However, their generous pension scheme adds the equivalent of another £50,000 per MP per year to their modest salaries. Also, the 646 Westminster MPs' ever-increasing expenses allowances further generously compensate them for low increases in salaries and make the expenses paid to the 189 MSPs and Welsh Assembly members look decidedly diminutive. Over £22,000 a year is offered to cover the costs of staying away from their main residence to MPs from constituencies outside the capital. If this is genuinely used for hotels or renting, then it can not be seen as additional salary. However, if this is used to purchase property, then at a tax rate of 40 per cent this is equivalent to an extra salary of over £36,000 a year, taking MPs' salaries comfortably close to £100,000 a year. The rules generously allow MPs to decide which of their homes is their 'main residence'. This has apparently allowed some senior government figures with free accommodation in London to use this money to pay off the mortgages on their homes in their constituencies. Gordon Brown, for example, was reported to have claimed £17,017 in the most recent year in spite of having lived rent-free in Downing Street for as long as some of us can remember. Others living extremely close to Westminster nevertheless feel that they are so far from the seat of government that they too deserve the extra allowance, intended solely for MPs who have to stay away from their main home.

There is a staffing allowance of over £87,000 a year which, of course, can go partly or wholly to members of an MP's kith and kin, making a useful addition to the household's weekly shopping budget. At least 70 MPs are known to employ partners, children or other relatives; the real figure is probably much higher. On top of that there is over £20,000 Incidental Expenses Provision to cover office and such-like costs (see Figure 23).

In addition, MPs have unlimited free travel in the UK on Parliamentary business, 15 free trips to London for the MP's family, three visits to Europe a year and mileage for MPs' cars, motorbikes and even bicycles. MPs are allowed to claim for 350 miles a month at 40p a mile without providing any proof of their travel. So even though they also get free train travel and can claim for taxis, some MPs maintain they are driving over an improbable 40,000 miles a year and are thus managing to claim over £10,000 a year for mileage, almost enough to buy a new car every year. Whatever they choose to buy themselves, MPs do not have to provide receipts for any expense below £250. In fact, while working as an MP, it is quite difficult to find anything on which to spend one's own money. MPs fought bitterly for years to prevent the details of their expenses being revealed, in the process using many tens of thousands of pounds of taxpayers' money.

Few MPs, however, have to live on these generous piles of our cash. Cabinet ministers all get a salary of about £138,000 a year. Most whips, deputy whips, speakers and deputy speakers pick up over £100,000 a year each. Many government MPs hold obscure roles in civil service departments like health, education, defence, justice and so on, adding many tens of thousands of pounds to their takings. Other MPs of all parties sit on a plethora of

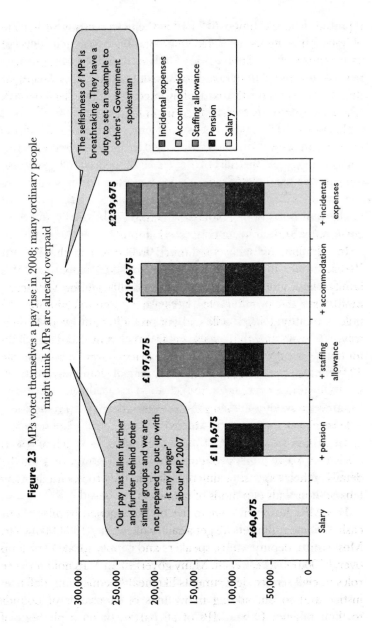

**Figure 23** MPs voted themselves a pay rise in 2008; many ordinary people might think MPs are already overpaid

committees, most of which are completely powerless talking-shops, but which nevertheless considerably boost their members' meagre earnings. Yet our MPs often seem to forget how much of our money they are all really pocketing and try to make out that they are poorly rewarded compared to other 'professionals'. Some of them are peering greedily at the £100,000 plus being earned by GPs, school heads and senior civil servants, and are wondering aloud and often why they should not be receiving similar amounts. At the start of 2008, MPs appeared to be setting an admirable example of self-sacrifice for other public-sector workers by only voting themselves a modest 1.9 per cent pay rise when they had been hoping for 2.6 per cent. This meant foregoing about £440 each in increased pay. However, at the same time, they granted themselves up to £10,000 each in extra staffing allowances – money that they could pay directly to members of their own families – so their supposed altruism was far from as painful as they would have us believe.

In addition to the money paid directly to MPs for salaries and expenses, we also pay another £210 million a year for administration, support services and subsidized food and drink at Westminster. Although most commercial companies are constantly able to reduce administration costs through improved computer systems and communications, the Westminster administration has increased by around a third, from £159 million, in only five years, again at a time when our MPs have had less and less to do. The total cost to us of our MPs is now over £366 million a year. If we reduced the number of MPs to match the recent halving of their workload, we could save around £180 million a year. We could also shove all the remaining MPs back into Westminster, flog off the rather luxurious Portcullis House and use the money raised by the sale to build a few schools and hospitals, or else distribute it to the country's 500,000 poorest pensioners. Moreover, now that our Prime Minister has rushed into signing the EU Constitution-by-another-name without asking our permission, more powers will soon move to Brussels, leaving even less work for our MPs. Yet, rather than prudently pruning the number of MPs and their costs to match their ever-decreasing workload, we can expect that sooner or later the Government will give in to MPs' pressure for further increases in salary, pensions and allowances.

## Meanwhile, Over at the EU Millionaires' Club

Being an MSP or member of the Welsh Assembly is extremely lucrative. Being a Westminster MP is even more rewarding. However, nothing quite compares with being elected to the European Parliament. This can truly be called a millionaires' club as you can easily pocket over £1 million from serving just one five-year term there.

Up until after the 2009 European elections, MEPs' salaries are fixed at the same level as MPs in their country of origin. This allows Italian MEPs to take home over £90,000 a year while some MEPs from the Eastern European countries get little more than a tenth of that. However, it is on their expense allowances that MEPs really cash in. In most businesses and even in the various British parliaments and assemblies, there is normally some kind of relationship, however vague, between what a politician spends in expenses related to their work and the amounts they can claim in reimbursement. For example, Westminster MPs are required to provide proof that they are using their £22,000 accommodation allowance and that they actually are employing the staff they claim to be employing. In the European Union no such link exists as expenses are paid on a so-called 'flat rate' basis regardless of whether the person claiming them has ever used the money in the first place. As all expense reimbursements are tax-free, MEPs can pocket more than considerable sums from the control-free and audit-free expenses procedures that they have granted themselves.

The biggest pot of money MEPs can dip into is for employing staff. Currently this stands at about £120,000 per MEP per year. Many MEPs use this to pay members of their own family – one estimate suggested that around 70 per cent of MEPs employed one or more family members.[12] Yet the amount is so generous that an MEP can easily afford to slip their partner or offspring £40,000 to £50,000 a year and still have enough loose change to employ a full-time secretary and a couple of researchers. Some MEPs disburse with the formality of handing the cash to a family member and just pay most of it to themselves. In early 2008, an internal EU report found evidence of widespread fraud in how Euro-MPs used their staff allowances. However, only MEPs on the Parliament's budget control committee were allowed to see the report and to do so, they had to apply to enter a special room protected by biometric locks and security guards – they were not allowed to take notes and they had to sign a confidentiality agreement. When asked whether this was part of a cover-up, an official explained, 'The document is not secret. It is confidential. It can be read by Euro-MPs on the budget control committee, in the secret room but not generally. That is not the same as a secret document nobody can read'.[13]

Being an MEP also gives immunity from prosecution unless your colleagues vote to suspend your immunity. In several EU countries, rich fraudsters, feeling the hot breath of the forces of law and order on the backs of their necks, have quickly 'bought' themselves seats as MEPs by making large contributions to local political parties and thus, as long as they maintained their lucrative but legal Brussels 'jobs', could stick two fingers up at the police and at those they have defrauded. In many cases, by the time they eventually left the EU Parliament, local statutes of limitations meant they could no longer be prosecuted for the crimes they perpetrated before hurriedly decamping to the safety of Brussels.

The next big money-spinner for MEPs is their office allowance of about £30,000 a year. Here, too, no receipts are required to get this money – as one MEP said, 'there is no need to present receipts for office expenses and there's no audit. You could use the allowance for any purpose you like.'[14] One trick many MEPs use is to pay an extra £660 a month into their pension plans from their office expenses money. In theory, they are then supposed to reimburse this money from their salaries. But everything relies on the MEPs' honesty: there are no checks that any of them actually do repay this money.

MEPs get an accommodation allowance of around £20,000 a year, which most use to buy a flat or house in Brussels. After five or ten years of this, they have probably paid off much of the property which can then be sold, usually for a huge profit when the MEP either retires or loses their seat. MEPs can benefit in other ways from this allowance – there have been numerous stories of MEPs buying properties that are much larger than they need and then making it a term of employment for their staff that they rent a room in the MEP's Brussels home, often for a healthy sum.

In spite of this accommodation allowance for MEPs to have a home in Brussels, they can also claim an attendance allowance of almost £200 a day tax-free for every one of the 155 days of the European Parliament sessions. The British MEPs call this the 'sign on and sod off' allowance, as all you have to do to get it is to sign in before 10.00 a.m. Some MEPs even get their researchers to sign in for them. There is no requirement to attend a single debate or committee session. What you do for the rest of the day is up to you. In theory, this money is for meals, but as there are over 15,000 lobbyists in Brussels (3,000 more than there are in Washington – the Sodom and Gomorrah of political lobbying) this means there are around 20 lobbyists for each MEP. Consequently, MEPs seldom have to pay for their own food – there are always plenty of lobbyists with bulging expense accounts eager to take MEPs to the restaurant of their choice in return for the opportunity to influence the thousands of rules and regulations that pour out of Brussels in favour of the lobbyists' paymasters.

MEPs also get very generous travel expenses. They can claim weekly flights from their constituencies. Here, they do need to provide proof of travel. However, they just have to submit the stub from their boarding pass – they are not asked for any information as to how much they have paid for their ticket. They are then reimbursed at a set rate per kilometre which often comfortably exceeds the business class fare. By buying cheap weekend return tickets or by travelling on budget airlines, many MEPs can rake off more than £500 a week. For the 30 plus weeks that the European Parliament works each year, an MEP can thus skim off around £15,000 tax-free, equivalent to £25,000 before tax at 40 per cent. MEPs also get over £2,000 a year for travel around the EU and around £1,000 a year taxi allowance should they happen to be out carousing after 10.00 p.m., when the EU limousine service stops.

Adding all this up, a typical British MEP will be getting around £330,000 a year in salary, pension and expenses – over £1.5 million for each five-year period in Brussels. With a bit of judicial financial management (for example, by buying a property in Brussels, paying 40 per cent of their staff allowance to a family member, by booking cheaper airline fares and cadging a few meals from lobbyists), British MEPs can ensure that at least £180,000 a year ends up in their own pockets. Add to this their fantastically favourable pension arrangements and most MEPs easily take home over £1 million for just five years of supposedly representing our interests. If you are the EU candidate for one of the main British political parties, you have about a one in three chance of scoring your EU million – all in all, much better odds than trying to win the Lottery or Premium Bonds or else correctly answering all the questions on 'Who Wants to be a Millionaire?'.

There have been repeated attempts by renegade MEPs to have the expenses system changed to a more honest one where MEPs would be reimbursed only for legitimate expenses. Time and again these get voted down and their supporters are shunned by their Brussels colleagues and in some cases expelled from their parties. In 2004 one such effort – to grant MEPs large salary increases in return for their agreeing to be paid only for expenses actually incurred – was blocked by the German and French MEPs on the basis that the timing was wrong. They did not want voters in the 2004 EU elections to see their MEPs being effectively 'bribed', with large amounts of taxpayers' money, to give up one of the world's most fraudulent expenses reimbursement schemes. In 2005, under pressure to clean up their act, MEPs did finally agree to move to an 'actual-cost' expenses scheme after the 2009 EU elections. One MEP claimed, 'MEPs have made real progress by putting the reputation of the European Parliament before their personal financial interests'.[15] However, the changes are complex and may not be quite as 'open' and 'transparent' as the EU might like us to believe. There appear to be a number of important opt-outs. For example, one reliable report stated that the new scheme would only be compulsory for new MEPs – all those who had become MEPs before the 2009 elections and were re-elected would apparently be allowed, if they wished, to continue with the existing system of almost printing their own money.[16]

## LONDON – PAYING A LOT, GETTING A LITTLE

Since their election in 2000, the Mayor of London and the 25 members of the Greater London Authority (GLA) have also become quite prolific spenders of our taxes. The GLA's main areas of responsibility are transport, the metropolitan police and its own administration. Spending on all three seems to have increased considerably more than the results each have delivered.

For the London Underground, operating costs have gone up by 17 per cent from £1.8 billion to £2.1 billion in the four years since 2002–3, yet the number of passenger journeys has gone up by only 7 per cent.[17] On the buses the difference is somewhat more dramatic, with costs shooting up by 64 per cent from £1 billion to £1.64 billion compared to a rise in passenger journeys of just 22 per cent. One of the reasons for this explosion in costs seems to be the generous amounts paid in wages to ever-increasing numbers of staff at Transport for London (TfL). Average TfL wages have gone up from just over £26,000 in 2003 to around £33,000 in 2007 – a rise of 24 per cent compared to the average London wage rise of 14 per cent. One study found that train drivers on London Underground were paid around 20 per cent more than drivers on mainline train services and had 43 days of paid holiday a year compared to just 30 days for overland train drivers. In 2006–7 the Commissioner of Transport for London received a salary of £320,000 plus a bonus – considerably more than the Prime Minister's salary of £188,848. In fact, there were 16 people at TfL who earned more than the Prime Minister. In the same year, over 112 TfL staff had salaries in excess of £100,000, several times more than at the Ministry of Defence.

Over at the Metropolitan Police (MPA) there has been a similar picture. A 65 per cent increase in budget from around £2 billion in 2001–2 to nearer £3.3 billion in 2006–7 has resulted in only 25 per cent more police officers, but a much more impressive rise of 61 per cent in the number of other staff.

At the Mayor's office there seemed to be few limits on how much money the politicians felt they could take from taxpayers to spend on their own schemes. The London Band D council tax has gone up from £150.88 in 2000–1 to £288.61 in 2006–7 – a 91 per cent increase, over double the 41 per cent increase for the whole of England for the same period and more than six times the rate of inflation.[18] However, the £832 million paid each year by London's council tax payers only represents a tiny 9 per cent or so of the £9.644 billion spent by the GLA each year – up 28 per cent from £7.517 billion in only three years. Just over half the money (about £5 billion) comes from central government grants, meaning that each taxpayer in the UK is selflessly handing over about £180 a year to pay for the running of London.

Over the next few years, the GLA's spending will rise even further as it is given more power over areas like planning and housing. And, of course, the GLA will be one of the major players in spending our billions to bring us the triumph of the 2012 Olympics – but that's another story (see Chapter 14: Olympic Gold-dust).

depends on the definition of a quango that one uses. Some studies suggest there has been an increase while others point to a slight decline. Finding the truth was made slightly more difficult when the Government decided to rename many quangos as NDPBs (non-departmental public bodies) because the name quango had become discredited, and then it stopped publishing all details of the ones that existed on the basis that it would cost too much to collect the information. One Parliamentary study suggested that in the UK in 1998 there were about 867 national executive and advisory quangos with 9,522 appointed members, in addition to their full-time employees.[4] It also found 4,534 local public-spending bodies with over 50,000 appointed members (approximately three times the number of elected local councillors). Another set of government figures identified 1,128 quangos in the UK – about 880 quangos in England and the other 248 in Scotland, Wales and Northern Ireland.[5] Between 1997 and the end of 2004, New Labour added around another 113 quangos (more than one a month).[6] These included such vital contributors to our well-being as the Better Regulation Taskforce (18 unpaid volunteer members) at a time when the Government was powerless to influence the tidal wave of regulation sweeping in from the EU; the British Educational Communications and Technology Agency (BECTA) (2006–7 budget £33.6 million and chief executive's salary £107,810) to do a job that should have been done by some of the over 4,600 bureaucrats at the Department for Education and Skills; and the Commission for Patient and Public Involvement in Health (2006 budget £26.9 million and acting chief executive's salary over £115,000) when the Government was centralizing control of the NHS and introducing widespread privatization and hospital closures against the will of most local communities.

One study found that between 2005 and 2007 another 200 or so quangos were born and immediately started hungrily feeding off our taxes.[7] Then, in his first seven weeks as Prime Minister, Gordon Brown – he of the 'bonfire of the quangos' quote – introduced no less than seven new quangos (one a week), including a Business

Council for Britain (when we already had thousands of civil servants at the Department of Trade and Industry, rebranded the Department for Business and Enterprise), a Council on Social Action (to add to the several other social work quangos created by this Government) and the Independent Statistics Board (in spite of Blair having created the Statistics Commission in 2000). When asked why the Government had created so many new quangos, a cabinet office spokesman said, 'Public bodies are only established where this is the most effective and efficient method of conducting government business'.[8]

Not only did someone apparently forget to light the much-heralded bonfire, but most quangos that existed before this Government's election and most that have been created since have also hugely increased their budgets, numbers of employees and pay to their chief executives since New Labour came to power. According to the Government's own figures (before they stopped publishing them), spending on quangos shot up from £79.6 billion in 2003 to £123.8 billion in 2006 – a rise of over 55 per cent in just three years.[9]

To be fair to the Government, it did make a half-hearted attempt to give the impression that it was about to do something to regulate quangos. In 1997 the Government published a Consultation Paper, 'Opening Up Quangos'. However, this 'consultation' only resulted in a non-statutory guidance framework, 'Quangos: Opening the Doors', which quangos could choose to follow if they felt it was 'practicable and appropriate'. All in all, this amounts to a little less than the great 'sweeping away' (Blair) and 'burning' (Brown) that had once been promised.

## QUANGOPHILIA IN SCOTLAND AND WALES

Like the British Government, the Scottish and the Welsh governing bodies also claim to be quangophobics and yet show clear signs of really being closet quangophiles.

A greater percentage of the Scottish workforce holds public-sector jobs than in the UK as a whole, and this seems to be reflected in the popularity of local quangos. Echoing Gordon Brown's 1995 pledge for a 'bonfire of the quangos', in 2001 the Scottish First Minister promised a similar culling north of the border. Yet by 2006 there were 11,400 Scottish people working for quangos, around 3,000 more than when the 'cull' was first announced. A spokeswoman for the Scottish Executive said, 'NDPBs do have a valuable function which is crucial to the Executive's priorities'.[10] However, this did not really explain why a supposed cull had turned into an almost uncontrolled population explosion.

A report written in 2007 found that Scotland had around 43 quangos just involved in inspecting, auditing and regulating other public services and other quangos. The direct costs of these inspectorates had increased by over 50 per cent in three years from £60 million in 2002–3 to £92 million in 2005–6.[11] There were also massive extra costs imposed on those being inspected – officials in Glasgow estimated that one social work inspection alone cost them around £155,000, mostly in staff time. Many departments found they were being inspected by several different quangos each year. The Leader of Glasgow Council explained, 'Many of the inspections ask for the same information. There is a huge amount of wasteful duplication.'[12] One of the proposals of the report was to merge these 43 quangos into one organization, but that would mean 42 fewer chairpeople and 42 fewer chief executives. Given that many of the people appointed to run quangos appear to be best mates with Scotland's makers and shakers, it will be interesting to see what really happens, or more likely does not happen, with this latest attempt at quango-control.

The Scots had another shot at quango-bashing at the SNP's annual conference in late 2007 when Alex Salmond pledged to abolish a quarter of the country's 200 quangos: 'We don't need 200 and we don't need overlap, duplication and people falling over each other'.[13] This commitment was commended by business leaders:

I would welcome anything that reduces government over-heads, especially this huge number of non-elected decision-makers which is a big burden on the taxpayer and just adds an additional layer of bureaucracy.[14]

However, political opponents accused Salmond of 'shifty accounting' and claimed that many of the cuts had already been agreed by the previous Labour–Lib Dem Executive.

In Wales, there were an estimated 1,800 people working for quangos in 1997, administering £825 million of our money. About 715 quango positions were political appointments and of these 405 were paid. As plans were made to set up the new Welsh Assembly, the Welsh Secretary said that the Assembly would be funded by a 'bonfire of the quangos' – a phrase that was becom-ing somewhat familiar to quango-watchers and quangocrats. One of the most reviled quangos was the Welsh Development Agency. It had a budget of £150 million and was involved in a string of scandals in which large quantities of taxpayers' money had found their way into the wrong pockets. The Welsh Secretary promised to abolish more than half of the Welsh quan-gos within the first three years of the Assembly: 'We can put behind us the days of "jobs for the boys" and people appointed on the basis of who they knew or where they had lunch'.[15] Then not much happened except that the existing quangos got bigger and spent ever more of our money. About seven years later, in July 2004, the Welsh First Minister announced that the country's three largest quangos, with 1,600 staff and an annual budget that had grown to £920 million (70 per cent of Welsh quango fund-ing), would be axed. It seems though that no staff or spending reductions were planned. Instead, the employees would simply be transferred to the Assembly in order to strengthen its powers:

The shape of the assembly government will become more governmental, because by merging the staff currently employed by the quangos with our existing departments it will give us more firepower, more critical mass, more ability to generate Wales-oriented policies.[16]

Three years after this announcement and 18 months after the actual merger, about 70 staff costing around £2 million a year were still waiting to be found jobs. It seems that it never occurred to the politicians that if after 18 months they could not find jobs for these people, then they might not be that essential to the running of Wales and therefore could be fired to save taxpayers a bit of money. All this showed that the quango cull was only about consolidating political power and nobody showed any interest in reducing bureaucracy or costs.

## MONEY, MONEY, MONEY

Quangos seem to use up an awful lot of our money by being extremely generous to their own bosses – the quangocrats. The heads of the largest 100 quangos all get paid well over £100,000 a year each, in addition to long holidays, early retirement and generous inflation-linked pensions. Some may be doing difficult and challenging jobs – but most are definitely not. One might wonder whether their remuneration is really warranted by the tasks they are fortunate enough to be employed to perform. For example, Kew Gardens is very pleasant and interesting, but does its boss deserve over £155,000 a year plus many thousands more paid into his pension? The Construction Industry Training Board may feel it does a terrifically important job, but does its chief executive merit over £240,200 a year – almost £50,000 a year more than the Prime Minister? Similarly, does the head of the Tote, an organization most of us will never come into contact with, absolutely need to be paid a salary of £330,000 a year with benefits and a bonus of £351,000, giving a total of £681,000 for 2006–7 – more than three times that of the Prime Minister?

Those involved in protecting our national cultural heritage also seem to do very nicely, thanks to our generosity – according to one review of quangos, the boss of the Tate reportedly got paid £191,000, the British Library over £175,000, the Natural History Museum £175,400, across the road at the Victoria and Albert Museum more than £168,000 and the National Gallery more than £176,000, to list just a few.[17] We taxpayers apparently even pay the head of the Design Council over £138,000 a year for managing a modest 69 staff. Being a culture vulture has clearly become an extremely lucrative occupation. Moreover, one must assume that all of us taxpayers have become much more cultured over the last decade as we appear to have decided to massively increase the pay of the bosses at our art galleries and museums – the Museum of London went up 103 per cent, the Natural History Museum up 90 per cent, the National Portrait Gallery up 82 per cent, the British Library up 78 per cent in just six years, the National Gallery up 58 per cent and the National Maritime Museum up 57 per cent.[18]

The total salaries paid just to the quango bosses probably cost us more than £100 million a year out of our taxes. Moreover, under New Labour, however wonderful or appalling their performance, leading quangocrats have enjoyed the kind of pay rises of which most of us could hardly even dream. At the same time as the Government has urged pay restraint on nurses, firefighters and other public-sector workers who actually deliver something useful to us, the quangocrats have been almost drowning in a sea of our cash. The head of the Qualifications and Curriculum Authority (QCA) was reportedly paid just over £43,000 in 1998. Following the A-Levels marking chaos of 2002, the Government beefed up the QCA by adding staff and pouring in cash. By 2006, with our exam system almost totally discredited and many schools and universities casting around for a more reliable way of assessing pupils' abilities, the boss was getting £273,000 in pay and benefits. In 2007, after the QCA demonstrably and abjectly failed to do what it was meant to do – provide a curriculum and exam system in which the public had confidence – the decision was taken to split the QCA into two organizations. However, it is unlikely that any of those involved will see a reduction in their take-home pay in spite of a halving of their workload. In fact, by splitting the QCA, the Government has created two quangos where previously there was only one – that probably means two chairpeople, two chief executives, two management boards and ever more of our money.

Over at the Construction Industry Training Board (CITB) there was similar largesse with our money as the chief executive's salary leapt nimbly up from a mere £123,741 in 2000 to £240,200 in 2006 – a rise of 94 per cent in six years. At the same time it would appear that most of the jobs in the UK's construction boom were actually taken, not by British people schooled thanks to the selfless efforts of the CITB, but by some of the more than 1.5 million migrant workers who flooded unhindered into the country. At the British Waterways Board, the lack of any new rivers or canals to manage did not prevent the bosses finding good reason to whack up the chief executive's package from under £180,000 in 2001–2 to almost £280,000 in 2006–7 – an increase of over 55 per cent in five years. Any frontline public-sector worker being told that the Government cannot afford above-inflation pay rises just needs to look at how New Labour has hurled our money at its favourite quangocrats. We would all be affected if nurses or the police went on strike even for a day or two – it is unlikely any of us would notice if some of the quangocrats downed tools for a few weeks, months, years or even the rest of their lives.

## BIGGER BUT NOT BETTER

In addition to almost smothering their bosses in our money, quangos also seem to absorb large amounts of our taxes to fuel their own usually impressive growth without always displaying correspondingly impressive results. At the same time as it demonstrably failed to provide sufficient skilled staff for the UK's building boom, Construction Skills, an organization dedicated to 'life-long learning' and 'skills for sustainability' for plasterers, plumbers and bricklayers, managed to expand from around 978 employees in 2000 to 1,423 in 2006 (a 45 per cent increase) while more than doubling its spending from £121 million to £246 million. The Prescription Pricing Authority seemed eager to consume a sizeable chunk of our money as it pumped up its workforce from 1,981 in 1997–8 to 2,849 eight years later. This 44 per cent increase in the number of staff, however, led to a 74 per cent rise in salary costs from £29.8 million to £51.7 million. Some people might think that this £21.9 million a year increase in salaries could have bought an awful lot of life-saving medicine rather than being spent on ever more bureaucrats. The Sea Fish Industry Authority is one of the few quangos that has not become ever more bloated. As the EU has decimated our fishing industry and handed over fishing rights in our waters to a Spanish armada which we have to subsidize, the Sea Fish Industry Authority admirably reduced its staff from 117 people in 2005 to 104 in 2007 and only increased its overall budget by around 4 per cent. However, fewer staff did not mean less money for the bosses. In 2005 the board and main directors pocketed around £431,000 between them for managing this tiny body; by 2007 this had risen 26 per cent to about £545,000.

Those of us desperate for our children to learn something in school will hopefully be reassured by the fact that the Training and Development Agency for Schools went from 112 staff in 2001 to 308 by 2007. However, while staff numbers increased by 2.75 times, the salary bill leapt up by over 4.1 times from a modest £3.63 million to £15 million in 2007. Perhaps one day we will see a flood of better-trained teachers as a result. Just in case reading about this gargantuan waste drives some readers really mad, staff at the Mental Health Act Commission have doubled under this Government.

Occasionally, a quango is phased out. Usually its death throes are long-drawn-out and horrifically expensive for the taxpayer. The Millennium Commission, for example, was set up in 1993 by the National Lottery Act and was one of the 15 bodies that distributed money from the National Lottery. As it explains on its website, 'the Commission was created as a short-life organization with a specific aim: to fund projects to celebrate the end of the second millennium and the start of the third'. This 'short life' ended up as 12 years. The Commission began spending our money in earnest in 1994, a comfortable six years before the end of the Millennium. It survived until November 2006, a similarly comfortable six years after the Millennium. During its life, it distributed around £2 billion (which could no doubt have been handled by any of the other 14 organizations giving out Lottery funds) and spent over £100 million on its own administration and management. It is quite difficult to know how much of our money actually went into the pockets of the Millennium Commission's directors as some years one of the four directors 'declined to disclose' how much they were getting paid – never a good sign. They were probably all getting between £100,000 and over £130,000 a year in salary and benefits. In its penultimate year, the Commission had 36 staff. In its last year it had only 24 staff but apparently still needed the four directors. In addition to their salaries, these directors were given payoffs of close to £300,000 in total (again, we do not know the actual figure as one director 'declined to disclose') because 'The Commission operates a terminal payment scheme on behalf of its own employees to retain staff over its short life'.[19] It was this Commission that brought us the Millennium Dome disaster. We could all have saved a lot of money had the Commission's life been shorter or, better still, if it had never existed at all.

## JOBS FOR THE BOYS (AND GIRLS)

Perhaps one of the reasons why governments have been slow to kill off quangos is that they provide a very useful way of rewarding friends and helpers at the taxpayers' expense. The chairperson of a decent-sized quango can comfortably pocket £30,000 a year plus expenses and pension benefits from just attending a few meetings. A chief executive would be most careless if they were earning less than £150,000 a year plus many benefits.

Parachuting the party faithful into comfortable quango sinecures has become a ritual for the political classes. In the final years of the last Tory government, there were six times as many chairs of quangos appointed from Tory supporters as from Labour supporters. By 1999 this situation was almost completely reversed, with five times as many Labour supporters being chosen. Five of the 12 appointees of the Big Lottery Board, which distributes £2.3 billion of Lottery money both to good causes and to themselves, were Labour Party members. Over at the Department for Communities, four of the ten members of an equal opportunity board were Labour supporters. The serving government always takes the lion's share of appointments for its own faithful followers, but, to keep everyone happy, the other parties are also allowed to get their snouts gratifyingly deep into the trough of our quango cash. In just one year, 394 Labour activists were appointed to public bodies, as were 96 Conservatives and 78 Liberal Democrats. Some political insiders seem to pick up quangos like the rest of us pick up parking tickets. One good lady, unofficially known as the 'queen of the quangos', was a member of 16 public bodies. Theoretically, people are appointed to quangos on the basis of ability and experience. In practice, quango appointments usually avoid the scrutiny of the Public Appointments Commission, and so time served brown-nosing one's political masters is often much more helpful for securing one or more lucrative quango sinecures than a weighty curriculum vitae.

There is another advantage from stuffing quangos with one's own supporters. Should anything unpleasant ever leak out into the press, the Government can immediately get an appropriate, supposedly 'independent' quango (ideally a 'watchdog') to conduct a 'thorough investigation', 'leaving no stone unturned' and to appear on breakfast television confirming that the Government is not responsible for anything, has never been responsible for anything, is taking 'robust measures' and doing 'everything humanly possible' to protect the public, when usually the exact opposite is the case. And if things should ever go really badly wrong, the Government can give the impression that it is doing something by sticking some minister or other on television to solemnly announce that 'important lessons have been learned' and 'to ensure this can never happen again, we are setting up a new regulator with tough new powers'. In this way yet another cash-hungry quango, stuffed with pro-government self-serving apparatchiks, is born.

## MOST USELESS OF THEM ALL

It is difficult to choose which is the most utterly pointless and wasteful quango. Different people seem to have their own favourites. Some observers have chosen the British Potato Council (BPC), whose website is imaginatively and appropriately www.potato.org.uk.[20] Our long-suffering potato farmers have to fork up over £4 million a year for the BPC's many useful services, such as its regular updates on the Euro-Potato. About £170,000 of this levy goes straight into the pockets of the chairman and chief executive. Taxpayers may also wonder why the BPC exists when the impending obesity crisis means we have to try to wean our citizens off crisps and chips, though, when answering her critics, the head of the BPC (salary about £80,000 a year) appeared in no doubt about her contribution to our well-being:

How can they say we are the most useless? You would have to know what every quango does to appreciate their value. I think our work is quite important. It is about learning the difference between a healthy chip and an unhealthy chip.[21]

The Coal Authority has always been consistent in mining our taxes. Its mission is 'to facilitate the proper exploitation of the nation's coal reserves whilst providing information and addressing the liabilities for which the authority is responsible in a professional, efficient and open manner'.[22] Since 1998 the amount of coal produced in the UK has decreased by almost 60 per cent and subsidence claims have gone down by over 70 per cent, but this huge decrease in the two main areas for which it is responsible has not in any way decreased the Coal Authority's appetite for our money. Over the last ten or so years, it has used around £40 million of our taxes in 'administrative expenses' each year. At the same time it has increased its employee numbers by 65 per cent and the salaries paid to its directors by almost 73 per cent from £268,285 to £463,468.[23]

In 2007, amongst all the other useful things it does, the Local Authorities Co-ordinators of Regulatory Services (LACORS) produced a key report on levels of salt in foods like chicken nuggets and pot noodles which 'found a high level of accuracy between salt contents shown on labels and the salt content of products tested'.[24] In addition to this less than earth-shattering conclusion, it did also identify that fewer than half the products met the salt reduction targets set by the Food Standards Agency. However, as these targets were planned for 2010, one might well ask why LACORS was wasting our money on a study of whether salt levels met targets three years before those targets were due to be met. Moreover, the whole matter of salt levels and food-labelling was a job for the Food Standards Agency whose 2,373 staff spend around £144 million of our money each year: 'The Food Standards Agency is concerned not only with the food we eat but with what it is sold in and how that is labelled'.[25] So why on earth was LACORS duplicating work that was being done in at least one other government department?

Some very tempting targets for the bonfire that will certainly never be lit are the regional development agencies. In England alone there are eight regional development agencies, all set up by New Labour, employing about 300 staff each (2,500 in all) and dispensing around £2 billion of our money (probably about £200 million of this for their own administration) each year. Some still call themselves by their old-fashioned titles such as the 'South East England Development Agency' and the 'East Midlands Development Agency'. Others have apparently brought in expensive image consultants and come up with much sexier names like 'Yorkshire Forward' and 'Advantage West Midlands'. Most of their chief executives pick up over £175,000 each a year, plus lots of benefits and very generous inflation-proof pensions. Then we pay tens of millions more for their other executives, board members, chairmen, auditors, lawyers, management consultants and so on. We do need some kind of development agency to provide financial assistance to encourage companies to invest in the UK. However, for the British taxpayer it is a complete and utter waste of money for different regions to compete with each other for business investment, especially if many of the jobs created are actually taken by foreigners.

In late 2007 we were given a brief look into the financial incontinence of some of the development agencies. The part-time chairman of one agency spent £51,489 on taxis and chauffeur-driven cars in just one year: £343 for each day of his contract. The agencies spend millions on overseas offices, all duplicating each other's work. In March 2007, eight of the agencies felt it necessary to send delegations to a property trade fair (famous for its champagne and lobster parties) on the French Riviera. Just one agency took 13 staff to the event and spent £24,000 on dinner and brunch amongst other things; another one spent £61,000 at the event; and the agency promoting the West

Midlands held an £8,000 cocktail reception. Yorkshire Forward also reportedly spent £61,600 for a staff event in Center Parcs in Wiltshire and another £28,000 on a meeting at the Riviera Centre in Torquay to discuss efficiency savings.[26] If we scrapped all eight development agencies, got rid of all their managers and at least half their staff and handed their work back to the thousands of bureaucrats at the Department of Business and Enterprise, we could probably save over £100 million a year in unnecessary bureaucracy and hundreds of millions more in reduced local corruption and fewer wasted grants.

Then there is the Economic and Social Research Council (ESRC). Its mission in life is 'addressing economic and social concerns. We aim to provide high quality research on issues of importance to government.' As family breakdown has accelerated, as the prison population has soared, as social alienation has increased and as our streets have become palpably more dangerous, the ESRC has been busy producing mountains of 'high quality' but apparently ineffective research. Since 1998–9 we have allowed our Government to more than double the amount of our money that the ESRC spends from £69 million to £160 million. Much of the money that passes through the hands of the ESRC is given out in grants to fund research in various academic institutions. However, the ESRC staff have not been slow to divert increasing amounts of our money into their own presumably needy pockets. In 1998–9 the ESRC's 97 employees were paid £2,086,000 – a very modest £21,505 a head. By 2007 staff numbers had only gone up by 26 per cent to 122, but the cost of these people's salaries had exploded to £4,514,000, equivalent to £37,000 a head – a pay rise of 72 per cent in eight years. Of course, the ESRC is not responsible for rising social problems, but while spending ever more of our money, it does not seem to have done much to help solve them either. If the ESRC, all its grants and all its staff disappeared tomorrow, probably none of us would notice any difference in our lives and we would have £160 million more a year to spend on something more useful.

# CHAPTER 12

# REGULATORS WITHOUT REGULATION

The area of the UK's quangocracy that has seen the greatest growth under this Government is the number of organizations set up to regulate our lives. In almost any area of activity there is at least one, and more often several, of these so-called 'watch-dogs', all spending many billions of pounds of our money. In health, for example, we pay over £500 million a year for the services of such organizations as the Health Protection Agency, the Healthcare Commission, the National Patient Safety Agency and Monitor, the supposedly 'independent' regulator of NHS Foundation Trusts. Hundreds of millions more are spent on reg-ulating, auditing and inspecting things such as education, the police, social services and so on. Yet when things do go pear-shaped, as with the horrific cases of social workers failing to pre-vent at-risk young children being tortured, burnt and beaten to death (such as Victoria Climbié in February 2000, Leticia Wright in November 2006 and Peter Connolly and Trycia Balhous, both in August 2007), those responsible usually circle the wagons and deny responsibility for anything. A 'watchdog' (or two) is then sent in to conduct a 'thorough' investigation where 'no stone is left unturned', a report is written and everybody involved is absolved and often promoted out of trouble. For example, the report into the death of Jessica Randall published in early 2008 concluded that none of the 30 health workers who had seen her during her brief 54-day life bore any responsibility for failing to spot that she was being repeatedly beaten and sexually assaulted by her father. The hospital's medical director explained, 'The report was not a whitewash. We considered that it was the processes that were remiss. The individuals now know from training what they need to do in the future'.

Moreover, to dampen down public outrage and to show how determined it is to take action, the Government usually trots out the standard 'important lessons have been learned', followed by the announcement that it is setting up yet another regulator 'with tough new powers' so that what has happened 'can never happen again'. When social workers failed to do their jobs, we were given Area Child Protection Committees. When these proved inadequate the Government dreamed up Safeguarding Children Boards. All these were usually staffed by the same social-worker managers and local politicians that had been on the previous failed regulators.

We now have so many regulators and supposed watchdogs, it is almost impossible to find out how much they all cost or what they all actually do. So in this chapter, I propose to look at just one small group of regulators who influence a significant part of our household income – the regulators that deal with utilities: water, gas and electricity. We spend around £45 billion a year on these services – over £2,000 per household – including about £55 million a year on the main regulators. By looking at whether we get value for money from these utilities, we can assess the effectiveness of those paid to regulate them.

After this review, I propose to look at the mother of all regulators, the disgraced and politically subservient National Audit Office (NAO), as it should have been responsible for ensuring that the £540 billion or so of our money that the Government uses each year is well spent and achieves what the NAO likes to call 'value for money'.

## MONEY FOR NOTHING

When they privatized our utilities in the 1980s, the Conservatives set up regulatory agencies ostensibly to ensure that these new monopolies and quasi-monopolies did not exploit us, their captive customers. However, probably to make these privatizations attractive to investors, the powers given to these regulators were fairly minimal. So although we have spent close to £1 billion on the regulation of our water, gas and electricity companies since privatization, our utility companies have been so mouthwateringly profitable that many have been snapped up by foreign companies (often French, German and Spanish). They have then extracted billions in profit from us while most countries, especially France and Germany, prevented their utility companies from being owned by foreigners on the basis that they were 'strategic assets'. The case of Thames Water gives some idea of the billions that could be made in a short time by grabbing a UK utility company. In 2000, Thames Water was bought by the German company RWE for £6.8 billion (£4.3 billion cash plus taking on debts of £2.5 billion). In 2006, after having siphoned off over £1 billion in dividends, RWE sold Thames Water to a consortium led by an Australian bank for £8 billion (£4.8 billion cash plus £3.2 billion debt). Thus, RWE made more than £2.2 billion from its relatively brief six-year ownership of the water company. Similarly, the US company Entergy bought London Electricity for £1.3 billion in 1996 and then in 1998 sold it to the French EDF for £1.9 billion – an easy 46 per cent profit in just two years. This foreign takeover seemed to be encouraged by Blair who declared, 'liberalised energy markets and more open markets are good for business and for consumers right across Europe'.[1] However, it has left more than half of our utilities in foreign hands and resulted in us having to pay some of the highest water, gas and electricity prices in Europe.

In New Labour's 1997 election manifesto, it promised tough new regulation for the utilities:

> In the utility industries we will promote competition wherever possible. Where competition is not an effective discipline, for example in the water industry which has a poor environmental record and has in most cases been a tax-free zone, we will pursue tough regulation in the interests of customers.

So let us see how well New Labour has delivered on this unambiguous commitment to effective regulation of our utilities.

## WATER RIP-OFF

The regulator for water, Ofwat, was set up in 1989 at the time of the privatization of the UK's ten water companies. Ofwat's purpose is to protect customers: 'Our vision is for a water industry that delivers a world-class service, representing best value to customers now and in the future'.[2] In order to deliver this vision, Ofwat spends over £10 million a year, which is about £120 million since New Labour came to power. During this time, the salary for Ofwat's boss has increased from £107,974 to £158,831, so that he has earned well over £1 million since 1997. From 1991 till 2005, the most serious power that Ofwat had was to issue an 'enforcement order'. This would require a water company to comply with an Ofwat directive. Throughout the whole of these 14 years, Ofwat did not see fit to issue a single enforcement order. In 2005, Ofwat was given an additional power to fine water companies up to 10 per cent of their water business turnover. One company was actually fined – United Utilities were ordered to pay £8.5 million because for years the firm ignored Ofwat's request to stop overcharging its customers. However, as the fine was equal to just 0.7 per cent of the company's £1.2 billion turnover and just 1.76 per cent of its £481 million profits, many observers felt that the company was not overly concerned by Ofwat's action.

Ofwat is responsible for setting the prices that water companies can charge us and claims, 'The price limits we set companies are based on demanding efficiency assumptions'. However, this seems to be contradicted by the staggering level of profits made by the water companies. In 2004–5 the industry made profits of 29 per cent (£2.195 billion on a turnover of £7.520 billion). In 2005–6 this rose to 31 per cent (£2.577 billion on a turnover of £8.228 billion). Some of the foreign water companies regularly make profits of 30–40 per cent on their UK operations, while exactly the same companies only make profits of 5–10 per cent on their operations in other countries, especially in their home territories.[3] This would seem to suggest that despite its claims, Ofwat's price controls are not quite as rigorous as those in other European countries.

Ofwat also claims that it actively controls how much water companies lose through leakage: 'We monitor the level of water that leaks from each company's network and take action where the leakage is unsatisfactory'.[4] About a quarter of the water that is purified for our use is lost due to leakage – 894 million litres a day – equivalent to each household having another three full baths a day or flushing the toilet unnecessarily 30 times every day. Thames Water loses a third of its supplies through leakage. For six years Thames Water failed to meet Ofwat's extremely modest targets for reducing its levels of leakage and Ofwat did nothing – no enforcement orders and no fines. Finally, embarrassed by the 2006 drought, subsequent hosepipe bans and public outrage at the level of leakage, Ofwat started to talk tough: 'We view as very serious Thames Water's significant failure to achieve its leakage target'.[5] At first, Ofwat threatened Thames with a fine that could go as high as £66 million. However, Thames managed to avoid any fine by promising to increase its spending on repairing leaks by an extra £150 million over five years. At the new rate of pipe replacement agreed between Thames and Ofwat, it would now take about 128 years to fix London's leaking pipes. Ofwat's boss seemed pleased with his firm action: 'This will directly address the issue of London leak-age and achieve more secure supplies'.[6] This £30 million a year extra investment represented just 2 per cent of Thames' turnover. At the same time, Thames Water was allowed to raise its prices by 21 per cent and a month later it announced it was going to improve profits even more by sacking a quarter of its 6,000 employees, which would give annual savings of about £45 million.[7] One could have suspected that giving the boot to one in four of its staff might actually slow down the rate at which Thames Water could repair its leaking pipes. However, Ofwat does not seem to have noticed this possibility. Anyway, Thames Water's owners, RWE, hardly seemed to care – in that year the chairman earned £6.3 million in salary and bonuses and he could wash his hands of Thames and its leaky pipes as he was selling off the company for over £1 billion more than he paid for it. When asked about why RWE had been allowed to extract so much money from Thames while doing so little to run the com-pany properly, the Ofwat spokesman seemed to feel that Ofwat was not responsible, perhaps forgetting Ofwat's duty to pressure water companies to invest some of their massive profits to reduce leakage: 'We don't have any control over their dividends because we don't manage the companies. The companies' profits are a matter for them.'[8]

In spite of there being so many regulators, they seldom seem to be hauled in front of Parliamentary committees to explain what they have been doing with our money. Unfortunately for Ofwat, their performance was so utterly dismal that even the normally supine NAO could not help wondering what on earth, if any-thing, the water regulator had been up to for the previous 18 or so years. Following an unusually critical NAO report, Ofwat bosses had to appear before the Public Accounts Committee (PAC) in mid-2007 to justify their existence. They did not seem to impress the PAC. When asked why they had not acted against Thames Water earlier, Ofwat's chairman replied, 'We have contemplated an enforcement order in every year since Thames first started failing'. This prompted the response from the PAC, 'We are not interested in contemplation; we are interested in action'.[9]

Ofwat had previously been questioned by the PAC in 2002 and at the time the PAC had recommended that Ofwat work with the water companies to draw up proposals on how best to save water. When asked why little progress had been made by 2007, Ofwat explained, 'Following our previous appearance at the PAC in 2002, we have been working very hard with the companies to achieve that'. Again, the PAC was far from convinced about Ofwat's effectiveness: '*Working very hard*, but it is five years since the previous PAC report on this'.[10]

Overall, the PAC was damning of Ofwat's regulation of the water industry: 'you have been lacklustre in your performance and particularly passive in your dealings with Thames Water'.[11] The PAC chairman said, 'Ofwat has been passive in its regulation of the water industry. At the same time it has paid little heed to the interests of water users.' Ofwat brushed off this criticism by claiming that it 'protects consumers by keeping prices down, driving improved service and where companies fail to deliver, taking effective action'.[12]

In 2007, Ofwat finally seemed to find some backbone. It threatened to fine Southern Water £20.3 million because the water company had 'deliberately misreported its customer service performance to Ofwat and systematically manipulated information to conceal the company's true performance over an extended period of time'. Ofwat's chief executive explained why the company had been deceiving the regulator: 'The company benefited from this misreporting at the last two price reviews meaning Southern was able to increase its prices by more than it should have done'.[13] Given that Southern Water has a turnover of more than £570 million, the company probably earned many times the £20.3 million fine from overcharging its customers over at least five years between 1999 and 2004. Consequently, the company did not seem particularly concerned with the fine, even though it 'fully acknowledged'

Ofwat's action and the chief executive said he was 'really sorry' that the company had been cheating its customers for so long.[14]

## NO GEM

The gas and electricity industries also have a regulator – Ofgem, the Office of Gas and Electricity Markets. Ofgem apparently also exists to look after our interests: 'Protecting consumers is Ofgem's first priority. We do this by promoting effective competition wherever appropriate and regulating effectively the monopoly companies which run the gas pipes and electricity wires.'[15]

Ofgem costs us around £39.5 million a year and its boss gets paid about £200,000. The reason for requiring about four times what Ofwat costs probably has to do with the fact that it regulates a market worth around £37 billion a year compared to Ofwat's market of just over £8 billion. Ofgem seems to be vaguely aware that it costs us a lot of money as it writes in one annual report: 'The costs of Ofgem need to be seen in the context of what it achieves'.[16] Ofgem's annual reports include many pages detailing its long list of supposed successes, for example, 'In the markets area Ofgem will be leading with the Department of Business, Enterprise and Regulatory Reform on a project to enhance significantly the analysis and scope of a forward-looking report', whatever that means. However, it is only deep down in the Appendices that one discovers any concrete actions taken by Ofgem on our behalf. In 2006–7, Ofgem published 13 Impact Assessments (big, thick reports) and conducted just four investigations of energy suppliers. Although in three of these cases the companies involved had been found to have breached their operating licences, no penalties were imposed as Ofgem was content to accept the companies' undertakings that they would behave better in the future. In 2005–6, Ofgem published 12 Impact Assessments and conducted eight investigations. One company was found not to have breached its obligations. Of the seven that were found guilty of breaches, in four cases Ofgem accepted the companies' commitments that they would change their wicked ways and there was no action taken in the other three as the companies were in administration. In 2004–5, Ofgem seems to have been a little more forceful, conducting three investigations and issuing three penalties of £250,000, £450,000 and £1,000,000. The year before that, there were ten investigations and seven penalties, mostly fairly small – between £50,000 and £100,000.

Although Ofgem claims that its primary purpose is to protect customers, it seems to have been doing this so poorly that in 2000 the Government passed the Utilities Act which, amongst other things, led to the creation of Energywatch, yet another watchdog. Energywatch costs us about £13 million a year and its 'duties are to protect and promote the interests of energy consumers'.[17] To someone who is not an aficionado of the fine differences between our many regulators, Energywatch's goals could sound awfully similar to those of Ofgem. One of Energywatch's claims of success is how it has managed to get compensation and reduced bills for consumers: 'In 2006–07 Energywatch secured £7.4 million for consumers in compensation and reduced bills – our tally to date is £25.3 million.'[18] Unfortunately, in the six years Energywatch took to achieve that £25.3 million, the organization cost us well over £70 million.

As electricity and gas companies actually have to compete for our custom, the market should be a little bit more effective in preventing companies overcharging us than the water industry where there is no competition (and evidently little regulation). Profits for energy companies are usually around the 10–20 per cent level compared to the 30–40 per cent usually achieved by the water companies.

A big test of how effectively Ofgem and Energywatch protect consumers' interests came in spring 2007. From 2004 to mid-2006, wholesale gas prices doubled. A later investigation by EU authorities found that some of the largest energy companies had deliberately withheld gas supplies in order to force the price up.

Given this increase in wholesale gas prices (which several of the French and German companies had been complicit in causing), most energy companies quickly increased their prices to consumers (i.e. retail prices) three or four times in order to maintain (and usually increase) their profit margins. Scottish and Southern Energy (SSE), for example, had a 13 per cent increase in profits to £873.9 million and its top director saw his remuneration increase by 30 per cent from £803,000 in 2005 to £1,040,000 in 2006.

Between June 2006 and April 2007, wholesale gas prices fell by about 50 per cent. However, most energy suppliers maintained their high retail prices, claiming that they had gas contracts lasting three, six and even nine months and therefore could not pass any lower prices on to us. Finally, in April 2007, two of the 'big six' energy companies, British Gas and SSE, started to lower their retail prices, having both made record profits up until March 2007 – SSE's profits, having already gone up in 2005–6, jumped a further 23.5 per cent in the year ending 31 March 2007. Accused of profiteering, SSE's chairman said, 'SSE's first responsibility to shareholders is to deliver sustained real growth in the dividend'.[19] The reductions in retail prices to us were significantly less than the fall in the wholesale gas price. By mid-April 2007 two more companies, both German-owned – NPower (owned by RWE, the previous owner of the infamous Thames Water) and Powergen (owned by E.On) – also announced limited price cuts, but these would not come into effect until after 30 April, by which time winter would be over and most families would be using much less energy, having lowered or switched off their central heating. Pressure started to mount on the remaining two of the big six companies, French EDF and Spanish-owned Scottish Power, to follow suit. Both companies were even 'named and shamed' by Ofgem, though the regulator held back from any tougher action than this. Finally, both announced price cuts. Having previously been charging about 20 per cent more than most companies, EDF's price cuts merely brought it more in line with the rest of the industry.[20] Scottish Power's cuts looked impressive on paper – gas prices would fall by 16.5 per cent and electricity by 5.5 per cent. However, half of the company's 5.2 million customers, those who paid by cash or cheque (rather than by direct debit), would only get a 5 per cent cut in gas prices and no cut in electricity prices. Moreover, both companies' price 'cuts' would not start until 15 June.[21] Industry specialists estimated that before the price cuts, the big six were making profit margins of 30–40 per cent and, after the cuts, profits would still be close to 20 per cent.[22]

For many people, the 'price cuts' failed to put any cash back into their pockets. While reducing their prices, most energy suppliers maintained their direct debit customers' payments at the level they were before the price cuts, thus building up a cash mountain of hundreds of millions of pounds on which they could earn interest. While some journalists noticed and reported this apparent scam, Ofgem seems to have remained silent and done nothing. Perhaps more worrying was the way the energy companies treated their poorest customers. About 750,000 of the most deprived households in the UK have pre-payment meters. When prices went up, the energy suppliers demanded extra payments from these customers to cover the cost of the price increases between the date of the increase and the date when someone could visit the household to recalibrate the meter up to the higher price. However, when the price went down, most companies did not offer any refunds to these customers even though these customers might have paid too much for several months until their meters could be recalibrated down again to the new, lower price.

Compared to Ofgem's somnolent performance, Energywatch seemed to be slightly more awake to what was happening and probably gave an appropriate summing-up of how Ofgem had allowed us to be fleeced by the big six energy suppliers:

> I am concerned that the regulator has been asleep at the wheel. The recent price cuts have only been a fraction of the

rises over the past three years when gas has gone up 95 per cent and electricity by 65 per cent. Some have not even taken effect yet a year after wholesale prices fell by 50 per cent.[23]

By August 2007, Energywatch protested that the companies' prices were still too high:

UK consumers continue to pay among the highest prices despite us having what is supposed to be the most competitive market. Price cuts so far have not reflected the savings that suppliers have enjoyed over the last year and I call on suppliers to cut their bills.[24]

Fortunately for the power companies, Energywatch could only talk about the problem of predatory prices: it had no power to take any action. Ofgem, who had the power to act, seems to have done little to nothing. By 2008, Energywatch calculated that while wholesale gas prices had gone down by 50 per cent in 18 months, customer bills had only been reduced by around 15 per cent. The companies' obvious disregard for the regulators was made abundantly clear at the beginning of 2008, when NPower felt free to announce further massive rises in both gas and electricity prices, of 17.2 per cent and 12.7 per cent respectively. An Energywatch spokesman commented, 'companies are all too quick to pass on wholesale price rises, but far too slow to pass on price falls'.[25] Again, Ofgem did nothing. In early 2008, it was also revealed that the six largest energy companies had been meeting regularly and engaging in a large range of apparently anti-competitive practices aimed at fleecing consumers.[26] Energywatch again protested about the lack of competition:

The problem with the energy market is that it's lazy, complacent and uncompetitive. It has been able to drive out the possibility of any vigorous challenge to the prominence of the big six energy suppliers.[27]

It will be interesting to see if Ofgem reacts to these new disclosures.

Meanwhile, by becoming increasingly international, the energy companies have found that they can further boost profits by better 'tax planning'. In a presentation given in 2006 by the chief financial officer of one of the largest companies, he explained that while his company's profits were expected to grow significantly each year, the tax paid by the company would more than halve by 2008.[28]

In January 2008, Ofgem claimed that there was no evidence of collusion or anti-competitive activity in the energy markets. In February the main suppliers announced price increases well into double figures even though one of the largest companies had just announced a fivefold increase in profits from £95 million to £571 million and the companies had received a £9 billion wind-fall from the free allocation of EU tradeable emission permits. Following public outrage, Ofgem announced that it would launch an investigation into the electricity and gas markets and invited anyone with any evidence of collusion on pricing to make contact. However, given that the problem in the markets is exploitative, predatory pricing, which is easy to show, rather than collusion, which is much more difficult to prove, it is likely that when Ofgem's report does eventually emerge towards the end of 2008, the energy firms will once again be cleared of any wrongdoing.

## BOURN TO SPEND

The UK's most important regulator is the NAO. With about 845 staff and a budget of over £80 million a year, its 'aim is to help the nation spend wisely'.[29] The NAO has two main areas of work. It is the nation's chief bean-counter and signs off the financial accounts of government departments and many quangos. It also has an investigative responsibility whereby it can launch 'value-for-money studies' into any area of public-sector spending it chooses. These NAO reports are then presented to the Public Accounts Committee (PAC) to be used as a basis for interrogating officials about how efficiently they are running their departments. This strange dual role for the NAO poses the question as to whether the kind of people who get their daily kicks from adding up lots of numbers are really the sort of people who can ruthlessly investigate and best uncover all the devious tricks used by the heads of government departments to cover up their own profligacy and waste of our money.[30]

In 2007 the NAO had a bit of a well-deserved *annus horribilis*. An investigation by *Private Eye* claimed that the NAO's boss, Sir John Bourn, allegedly went on up to 15 foreign trips a year, taking his wife on about half of them, and usually staying at top-of-the-range hotels (often between £300 and £500 a night) and dining at the finest restaurants. Even when in this country Sir John was apparently living well, entertaining senior figures from government and business – again, courtesy of our tax bills – over 50 times a year at an average of £154 a throw. It was estimated that Sir John spent £365,000 of our money in travel expenses and another £27,000 in restaurant bills in just three years. Bourn had also apparently accepted hospitality such as expensive meals and attendances at a polo match, the opera and the British Grand Prix from companies whose multi-million- (and sometimes multi-billion-) pound public-sector contracts his organization should have been relentlessly investigating on our behalf.[31]

Sir John Bourn was at the helm of the NAO for 20 years until he retired at 73, 13 years beyond the normal civil service retirement age. There have been several indications that the NAO now fails in its principal business of holding government departments to account. (This may be why most of the world's other national audit institutions limit the tenure of their head.) Controversial criticisms seem to be side-stepped, hard-hitting reports are few and far between and apparently wasteful projects endorsed rather than condemned – regularly enabling ministers to quote helpful NAO findings in defence of lost billions. In recent years the NAO seems to have gone easy on scandals including the 2012 Olympic Games budgeting process, where a tripled budget represented a 'significant step forward', and the NHS IT programme, which one seasoned MP on the PAC described as 'easily the most gushing' of the 62 NAO reports he had looked at. Observers with any understanding of the programme could only see taxpayers' cash flooding out of health services and into the pockets of computer systems suppliers for IT systems that were years late and did not work. In the summer of 2007, the NAO said that the Financial Services Authority (FSA) was 'a well-established regulator with an impressive set of processes and structures to help tackle high-risk organizations and markets'.[32] A few weeks later the FSA's failure to spot the looming crisis at the 'high-risk' Northern Rock saw the first run on a British bank for 140 years.

Worse still, on perhaps the most wasteful policy in ten years of New Labour – the Private Finance Initiative (PFI) – the NAO has gone further than simply failing to act. It has actively encouraged it. In 2003 it produced a report claiming that PFI saved on building costs compared with traditional procurement. The report, which ignored the exorbitant financing costs of PFI, was repeatedly and comprehensively demolished by experts. However, for the past four years this same report has been repeatedly invoked by ministers and officials in Parliament in defence of PFIs. The deception suits the NAO, too. Under a bizarre agreement with the Treasury, every new PFI is deemed to save the taxpayer money, for which the NAO can claim credit as it is assumed to have made each deal cheaper through its work on the subject. The reality, of course, is that under PFI the UK will overpay for its infrastructure by many billions over at least the next 30 years. However, without these illusory 'savings', the NAO would miss its performance targets every year. Thus the country's public-spending 'watchdog' has a strong vested interest in pushing possibly the most misjudged public-spending scheme in memory

– which it does relentlessly through a stream of seminars, conferences and other love-ins with the PFI industry.

Criticism of the NAO and its junketing boss invariably receives the stock response that the auditor saves the taxpayer several times what it costs. Closer inspection, however, reveals that the figures behind this assertion do not add up. The NAO is judged on how much it saves the taxpayer through its audits and investigations. Its 2006 report boasts of '£582 million of savings identified this year as a result of our work ... exceeding our 8:1 target by some £22 million'. Not only is this figure largely made up of the fictitious savings on PFI schemes, the claim is also rendered meaningless by the fact that by the time the NAO investigates anything, our money has usually been spent and there is no way of getting it back – identifying wasted money is not quite the same as being able to put it in the bank.

The cosy consensus between this extraordinarily obedient and comatose watchdog and the Government has lasted so long because it keeps everybody happy. When criticized for policy failures, the Government can use NAO studies to claim the backing of an 'independent' auditor. The NAO does dish up the odd critical report – but never on anything too threatening or politically sensitive – enabling MPs on the PAC to fume very publicly and to be seen to be vigorously controlling public-sector waste. However, government departments are under no obligation at all to act on any of the NAO's or the PAC's recommendations – usually they just ignore them.

# CHAPTER 13

# NOT A NATIONAL TREASURE

Although quite a small government department with just around 1,000 employees and costing about £170 million a year to run, the Treasury is an important indicator of how well our money is being spent for two reasons. Firstly, it is the Treasury that has the crucial task of managing our overall economic policy. As the Treasury explains:

> The Treasury is the United Kingdom's economics and finance ministry. It is responsible for formulating and implementing the UK Government's financial and economic policy. Its aim is to raise the rate of sustainable growth, and achieve rising prosperity and a better quality of life, with economic and employment opportunities for all.[1]

Secondly, the Treasury is interesting because for ten years it was run by Prime Minister Gordon Brown when he was Chancellor, so it is here that we can get an idea of how effective he actually is as a manager.

One striking feature of the Treasury is that it costs an awful lot more to run now than it did when this Government was first elected. In 1998–9, Brown's first full year in charge, the Treasury's net administration costs were around the £100 million mark, yet by 2007 they had shot up to about £170 million (see Figure 24). As part of Gordon Brown's efficiency programme, he planned to reduce Treasury administration costs a couple of per cent a year to reach £158 million by 2010–11. However, even if this target is achieved, Brown would have still succeeded in increasing administration costs in his own department by about 60 per cent – hardly a sign of the Presbyterian prudence and tough economic management with which he usually likes to be associated.

Treasury apologists will no doubt claim that these constantly increasing costs are due to the Treasury doing more than it did before. For example, in one year it had some extra work linked to the UK's joint presidencies of G7 and G8. In another year it did some work for the Government's Spending Review and in another it took over some policy work from another department.[2] However, all this only added about £2 million a year for three

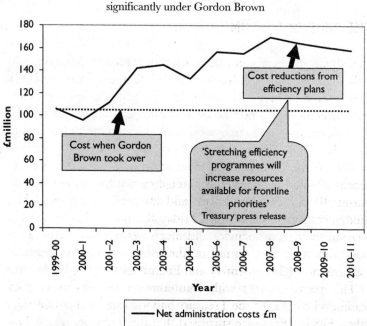

**Figure 24** Treasury net administration costs have risen significantly under Gordon Brown

years and hardly explains the £60 million to £70 million rise in administration costs since Gordon Brown took over the department. Moreover, there is a most curious phenomenon in the public sector – almost every time one government department says it is taking over some activities from another government department, the administration costs of both departments seem to rise.

During the last 11 years, the Treasury has made some interesting policy decisions. Two of the most significant in terms of the amounts of our money involved are the sale of over half the UK's gold reserves and the massive £180 billion PFI/PPP (Public Finance Initiative/Public Private Partnership) programme. I propose to look briefly at these before moving on to reviewing the Treasury's success in managing the economy to meet its aims of achieving growth, rising prosperity and employment opportunities for all.

## THE 'BROWN BOTTOM'

In 1999, Patricia Hewitt, then a Junior Treasury Minister, signalled the Treasury's intention to sell just over half of the UK's gold reserves as part of 'a restructuring of the UK's reserve holdings to achieve a better balance in the portfolio by increasing the proportion held in currency'.[3] The idea was that 415 tons of the UK's total of 715 tons of gold would be sold over a period of two to three years in a series of auctions and the money received would be invested in foreign currency – 40 per cent in euros, 40 per cent in dollars and 20 per cent in yen. The announcement was made on a Friday afternoon when most MPs were in their constituencies and much of the news media were busy reporting the results of the elections for the Scottish Parliament, Welsh Assembly and English local councils.

This plan was met with consternation by experts in gold trading who believed the Treasury had made several crucial mistakes. Firstly, they were surprised that the Treasury was selling gold when the price was at an all-time low, having fallen from around $835 an ounce in 1980 to around $290 an ounce by 1999. Secondly, by announcing that so much gold was going to be sold in a relatively short period, this was bound to drag the price down even further. One trader said:

> The timing of the decision was ludicrous. We told them you are going to push the gold price down before you sell. We thought it was a disastrous decision. We couldn't understand it.[4]

Not only did the Treasury ignore the advice of gold experts, it also appears not to have even asked the Bank of England for its views. Bank of England officials were quoted as saying they had 'little say' in the matter and that they were 'doing what they were told'.[5] Sure enough, just after the Treasury revealed its brilliant plans, the price of gold dropped by over 10 per cent to $256.45 an ounce, effectively knocking over £450 million off the value of the UK's gold reserves before any had actually been sold. This drop in the price of gold to the lowest it has been for the last 25 years is known in the trade as the 'Brown Bottom', in honour of the Chancellor who sold our gold at rock-bottom prices and made many gold traders rich at our expense.[6] The number of traders 'shorting' gold (betting the price would fall) went up eightfold in the run-up to the first auction as traders made millions from the Treasury's stupidity. One trader explained, 'The joke in the market was that Gordon had guaranteed he would get the worst price. The world and his grandmother shorted the market.'[7] Previously, when the banks of other countries such as Switzerland and Australia wanted to sell gold, rather than letting the market know their intentions in advance, they trickled the gold into the market in order to maintain the price and only announced the sales after they were completed.

The Treasury's strategy to sell gold not only surprised traders, it also seems to have been at odds with the plans of the other main central banks. The governor of the Bank of France explained the policy of the other banks:

> I will simply say that as far as I am aware – and this is not just the position of the Bank of France and our country but also the Bundesbank, the Bank of Italy and of the United States, and these are the four main gold stocks in the world – the position is not to sell gold.[8]

A day later, Alan Greenspan, chairman of the US Federal Reserve, confirmed the importance it put on holding gold and by September 1999, 15 European central banks published a signed agreement limiting the amount of gold that would be sold in order to prevent any other country 'destabilizing' the gold market as Brown's incompetent Treasury had done.

It was not just the timing of the sale that worried experts: they were also less than impressed by the way the Treasury was going to sell the gold in what were called 'uniform price auctions'. One explained, 'I was surprised they had chosen the auction method. It indicated they did not have a real understanding of the gold market.'[9] The folly of choosing this method has lost us taxpayers so much money that it is probably worth explaining how it worked to our disadvantage while earning billions for those who bought our gold. Potential buyers were invited to submit bids for the gold. The Treasury would then choose 'the lowest acceptable price' and everybody who had bid at this price or above would get their gold at this price, even if they had been willing to pay more.[10] This is a bit like announcing to a few neighbours in January that in July you are going to sell 100 kilos of strawberries from your garden. You then invite the neighbours to each put in bids for some of the strawberries and inform them that however much they choose to bid per kilo, they will all get the strawberries at the price of the lowest bid you accept. Of course, the first thing that happens is that they all discuss with each other how much each will bid, which pushes the price down, and then you lose even more money by allowing those putting in higher bids to get their strawberries at the price of the lowest bid you accept.

By 2004 the price of gold had shot up from the Brown Bottom and was over $450 an ounce. By 2007 it had reached about $670 an ounce, meaning that we taxpayers had lost over £2 billion compared with the price paid when our gold was sold. By 2008 the price had leapt to $914 an ounce, adding billions more to the value of the gold that we no longer had. The Bank of China alone was estimated to have made well over £1 billion by buying our gold at the Brown Bottom. As for the other central banks, they chose to keep rather than sell their gold so that by 2007 the US held 8,133 tons, Germany 2,422 tons and France 2,710 tons, compared to the UK's remaining paltry 300 tons. We will probably never find out why the politicians made the decision to sell our gold. There have always been suspicions that it was done in preparation for the UK abandoning the pound and replacing it by the Euro. The Brown Bottom is often compared to the Tories' Black Wednesday when the Conservative Government lost over £3 billion of our money trying unsuccessfully to prop up sterling and made many currency traders enormously wealthy in the process. However, Black Wednesday was a result of a bungling government being caught out by events beyond its understanding and largely beyond its control. The more than £2 billion lost from the Brown Bottom was an entirely self-inflicted, politically motivated own-goal scored by an inept Treasury that was not interested in asking advice from those with experience in the gold market.

## THE £180 BILLION PFI MONSTER

In its 1997 manifesto, New Labour promised to 'Reinvigorate the Private Finance Initiative' to improve national infrastructure like hospitals, schools, roads and so on:

> A Labour government will overcome the problems that have plagued the PFI ... We will set priorities between projects, saving time and expense; we will seek a realistic allocation of risk between the partners to a project; and we will ensure that best practice is spread throughout government.

Under PFI, private companies fund and build new hospitals, schools, prisons, roads, all manner of defence kit and much else besides. They then rent the facilities back to the taxpayer, typically for around 30 years, throwing in some additional services to boost their bottom lines. The presumed advantage is that the superior management skills of private companies will ensure that projects do not go over budget and that we get value for money. The disadvantages are that setting up every PFI contract costs millions in fees to lawyers, consultants and accountants, that private companies will be looking to make substantial profits and that it costs private companies far more to borrow the money to pay for PFI schemes than it would cost the Government. The taxpayer ends up paying for all these extra expenses, profits and the increased borrowing costs.

One political advantage of PFI projects is that the Government does not have to borrow any money to pay for them – PFI schemes will be paid for with future tax revenues. So the huge commitments do not add to national debt levels that, had they been included, would by now have breached the limits imposed by Gordon Brown 11 years ago in order to appear financially responsible. However, the greatest political benefit of PFI is that it enables ministers to announce magnificent 'investments' without immediately having to land us taxpayers with a huge and possibly indigestible bill for the corresponding massive costs. Moreover, the Byzantine complexity of PFI means that it remains largely incomprehensible to most taxpayers, to journalists looking for more interesting, 'easier' stories and to the majority of Members of Parliament. It thus escapes serious scrutiny, except by a few rabid PFI-phobics whom nobody listens to anyway.

Infrastructure valued at £57 billion has now been built under PFI, but not yet paid for, with plenty more to come. Suspect public finances will be shored up in the short term with a promised £36 billion sell-off of public assets, much of which will be rented back under PFI deals, while a further £45 billion worth of new schools are promised through PFIs. However, even these figures vastly understate the commitments of our future taxes to pay for PFI. Just on deals already signed, over the next 25 years taxpayers will have to pay out around £180 billion.[11]

Such costs can soon translate into a devastating effect on public services. We have started to see the effects in healthcare. The NHS is committed to over £50 billion of PFI costs already, a figure expected to rise to £90 billion when contracts due to be signed up to 2013 come on stream.[12] The lesson that PFI does not work is still some way from being learnt. A stifled National Audit Office report on PFI hospitals revealed poor design, fewer beds, dangerous over-occupancy and poorer cleaning.[13] A report into the unchecked C Diff outbreak at Maidstone and Tunbridge Wells NHS Trust that killed around 90 found that hospital managers were distracted from running the hospital because they were busy pushing through a horrendously complex PFI contract. Managers were described as being 'preoccupied with finances, and had a demanding agenda for reconfiguration and private finance initiative, all of which consumed much management time and effort'.[14]

The financial impacts have been equally stark. Over the next few years the NHS will be paying over £1 billion a year to PFI companies. The average NHS Trust with a PFI scheme had a 4.4 per cent shortfall in income in 2005–6, many times the national average.[15] Most were cutting services and slashing jobs to cope. Of 12 bankrupt acute hospital trusts that had to be bailed out as they simply could not borrow any more, eight had large PFI schemes – several times the ratio across all trusts.[16] The PFI monster, imposing contractual demands that take priority over core services, requires that services are adapted to fit it rather than the other way round. A 2007 report for the NHS in South London revealed that PFI debts at the Queen Elizabeth, Woolwich and Bromley hospitals, totalling £152 million, were forcing service cuts at a completely different hospital which was not saddled with PFI. To try to justify the huge PFI costs, the NHS had to move patients (and thus income) into the PFI white elephants, so feeding the PFI beast took priority over the health needs of Londoners. Most PFI deals have resulted in eye-watering profits for the companies involved – returns of 60 per cent to 80 per cent are not uncommon. One critic of NHS PFI projects explained:

> If taxpayers want to know why the NHS is in financial crisis, despite the government's extra funding, they should look at the sums that the private consortia and their shareholders are bleeding out of the private finance initiative.[17]

The waste and confusion of PFI could be put down to the need to massage Government figures: possibly the worst case of the presentational tail wagging the policy dog. By 2006 ministers almost admitted as much. Training for all the armed forces is currently being privatized because a relatively small amount of investment (£750 million) in facilities is required. To do this through the tried and tested method of owning the buildings, the Defence Minister claimed, 'is not affordable' simply because it would go on the books. The result is not only ultimately greater costs and a further drain on defence budgets, but a £19 billion deal under which private companies, many foreign, will train the British armed forces.[18]

The true nature of many PFI deals is not yet apparent as only a fraction of those signed are actually fully operating. One huge deal where we have seen the truth behind the Government's claims of better value for the taxpayer is the 30-year, £2 billion London Underground upgrade, handed over to the Metronet consortium. To his credit, Ken Livingstone, the Mayor of

London, fought hard to prevent the Treasury foisting this disaster on London. The fight between the Mayor and the Treasury went to court in 2001 and the Mayor lost. In 2003, Metronet were given the contract. By 2006, Metronet were struggling due to poor management, poor project planning and low productivity. Meanwhile, London's long-suffering Underground users had to put up with a massive rise in signal failures, delays and weekend maintenance closures.[19] In 2007, Metronet crashed into administration, leaving taxpayers to pick up the bill. Having forced Transport for London to accept their PFI contract in 2001, the Treasury was remarkably elusive when the whole thing ended in tears.

The lengths to which the Government will go to secure 'off balance sheet' investment are sometimes shocking. Long-term ownership of crucial infrastructure has to be passed out of public control, scuppering services when the PFI deals come to an end. The largest garrison in the UK, under construction in Colchester, involved giving PFI companies a 150-year lease on the land. The PFI contract, however, ends in 35 years, leaving the army with nowhere for the troops. A hospital PFI gave the land on which a hospital was built to a PFI company for 120 years. Similarly, at the end of the 27-year 'future strategic air tanker' PFI contract for in-flight jet refuelling aeroplanes, the aircraft will be owned by the PFI companies – just so the £13 billion commitment to the deal can stay off the Government's books. One MoD official said of the alternative of simply owning the planes: 'The Government can't afford it from an accounting point of view. They normally would.'[20]

This air tanker deal, already ten years in the making but still not expected to produce anything before 2011, provided a rare admission of the true nature of PFI from within the industry. Appearing before a committee of MPs, a businessman from EADS, the European company behind it, was asked whether PFI had proved 'expensive in terms of money or in terms of time?' His blunt answer was 'all things'. For similar equipment in another country not using PFI, he said, 'In three years, we went from the proposal to seeing the contract: a similar aircraft; a similar type of product'. When asked for his opinion on whether the British taxpayer would be overpaying by tens or hundreds of millions due to PFI, the candid businessman commented, 'It is good business for banks and lawyers, that is for sure'.[21]

## THE ECONOMIC GENIUS?

Naturally, the Government claims that it has been hugely successful in managing our economy:

> The UK economy is currently experiencing its longest unbroken expansion on record, with GDP how having grown for 58 consecutive quarters. Over the past 10 years, the Government's macro-economic framework has delivered more stability in terms of GDP growth and inflation rates than in any decade since the war. This historically low volatility puts the UK in a strong position to respond to the global economic challenges of the next decade.[22]

Predictably, the Conservatives disagree and also try to claim credit for the impressive performance of the UK economy that we have seen since the sleaze-ridden, obsessively infighting Tories were deservedly booted out in 1997. The former Chancellor Kenneth Clarke wrote:

> I passed on to Brown the strongest economy and the soundest public finances for a generation. Brown will pass on the bills of an unreformed public sector, a growing pension crisis and an increasing tax burden, which is undermining the strong economy he inherited. It remains an iron law of politics that the job of Conservative governments is to clear up the mess left by Labour governments.[23]

## They Cannot Both Be Right

Before examining these two conflicting opinions, we need to trawl through a few figures to get some facts about what is really happening with the UK economy. The headline figures are undeniably impressive. The UK economy has grown ever since New Labour took power. Moreover, it has grown faster and more consistently than our main European competitors. Inflation has been at a historical low, around 2.5 million more people are in work and the number of claimants of unemployment benefit has virtually halved from around 1,619,000 in May 1997 to 855,300 – less than a third of the utterly shameful level of over three million that it reached for four years under the Tories. In addition, the Government has (thanks largely to the PFI accounting wheeze) kept to its so-called 'prudent golden rule' that public-sector borrowing should not exceed 40 per cent of GDP.

Those who are either critical or envious of this Government's economic achievements like to say that the Government has benefited from a benign world economic situation – the growth of the Chinese economy has pushed down the price of manufactured goods, the increase in offshoring many service activities (call centres and IT systems development) to countries like India and Malaysia has dramatically decreased their costs and the absence of any major Middle East wars, apart from the ones that we started, has kept the price of oil relatively stable. While it is true that the Government has been lucky, previous governments of both main parties have managed to turn certain economic victory into spectacular economic defeat by using the economy to fight ideological battles rather than doing what was best for the country. The Tories, for example, probably got great satisfaction and cracked open a few bottles of champers when they crushed the mineworkers and virtually shut down our coal industry. This short-sighted and overtly political gesture pushed up unemployment and created quite unnecessary economic misery for hundreds of thousands of families who were thrown on to the scrapheap to satisfy ideological, rather than economic, goals.

What has been strikingly different about this Government is that it has managed the economy using pragmatism as well as political ideology. To get elected, New Labour had to turn its back on the Old Labour tendency to increase spending on public services and instead commit to meeting the Tories' policy of a two-year freeze on public spending. To generate economic growth at a time when our manufacturing industry was shrinking to invisibility, the Government had to cosy up to the City of London, limit regulation of financial services and allow the wealthy the freedom to pursue whatever tax avoidance schemes their accountants could think up. To provide a source of cheap labour to the growing service sector without pushing up wage inflation, it decided to open the door to almost unlimited immigration and pretended not to see the millions who streamed through. It is probably this readiness to substantially dilute politics with pragmatism which distinguishes this Government from any other and has allowed it to benefit from a helpful world economic situation. In its 1997 manifesto New Labour explained how it was turning its back on the old Left versus Right struggle: 'New Labour is a party of ideas and ideals, but not of outdated ideology. What counts is what works.' This Government has understood that non-intervention, rather than the constant meddling of previous governments, is the best way of ensuring economic progress. So while the Government can justifiably bask in its almost unparalleled economic achievements, the Tories have fulminated impotently and rather unattractively in the wasteland of their decade-long banishment from power.

## The Devils at the Door

However, behind the Government's undoubtedly effective, light-touch economic management lurk some unpleasant realities which may yet come to rain on New Labour's economic parade.

The Public Sector Borrowing Requirement (PSBR), having fallen impressively from 42.5 per cent in 1997 to 31.6 per cent in 2001, as the economy expanded rapidly, is now heading inexorably upwards to 38.2 per cent in 2007–8 (see Figure 25).[24] The Government then expects it to flatten and conveniently stabilize at just below the all-important 40 per cent level – the so-called 'golden rule' level. However, the trend suggests that borrowing will shoot effortlessly through the magical 40 per cent ceiling unless the Government 'refines' or 'improves' the figures, in which case borrowing will be at whatever level the Treasury and the helpful statisticians at the Office for National Statistics may choose.

More threatening than the rise in the PSBR, however, is the UK's balance of payments situation which has deteriorated significantly (maybe even disastrously) almost every year under New Labour, going from a small surplus of £1.8 billion in 1997 to a massive deficit of £48.4 billion in 2006 (see Figure 26).[25]

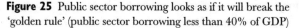

**Figure 25** Public sector borrowing looks as if it will break the 'golden rule' (public sector borrowing less than 40% of GDP)

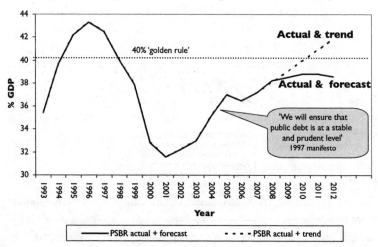

Particularly worrying is the precipitous decline in the amount of manufactured goods that we export compared to the amount we import. In its 1997 election manifesto, New Labour promised to boost growth in British industry, but the balance of trade deficit on goods has increased almost seven-fold from £12.3 billion in 1997 to £83.6 billion in 2006 – we have become addicted to buying in much more than we can make and sell. For the moment, our exports of services are helping to partially shield us from the rapid decline of our manufacturing industry. However, we will be extremely vulnerable to an economic crisis if our exports of services fail to grow fast enough to support our ever-increasing appetite for purchasing things made in other countries whose governments have actually supported their manufacturing base rather than just promising to do it.

Our employment figures look rosy, with employment increasing from 72.7 per cent in 1997 to 74.5 per cent in 2007, allowing the Government to claim that it has created over 2.5 million new

**Figure 26** The overall balance of trade deficit, and deficit in goods, have dramatically worsened under New Labour

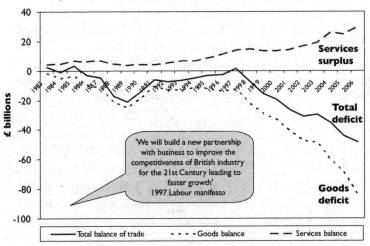

jobs, that 'employment in the UK is at its highest level since comparable figures began in 1971', and that the UK has the highest rate of employment of the industrialized countries.[26] Unfortunately, the majority of these new jobs do not seem to have gone to UK citizens as, since 1997, around two million National Insurance numbers have been issued to foreigners. In addition, more than 600,000 of these new jobs were in the public sector and most of these were in unnecessary extra administration, so they contribute little to nothing to our national wealth. Besides, the Government has already begun cutting some of the public-sector jobs it has created (handing out hundreds of millions of pounds of our money in redundancy payments) in the NHS, HMRC and many other departments in order to try to get public spending under control. What is not shown in either the figures for employment or unemployment claimants is a growing army of close to eight million people of working age who are 'economically inactive'. Of these, over 5.5 million are not even looking for a job. Since 1997 the number of people claiming unemployment benefit has reduced by almost 700,000. However, at the same time there are over 600,000 more people who are economically inactive and are not looking for a job, and of these over 400,000 are men (see Figure 27). This is in spite of New Labour's 1997 pledge: 'We will get the unemployed from welfare to work'.

This mass of people who have been left by the wayside as the economy has prospered is absorbing huge amounts of money in benefits and other support, and represents a potentially enormous financial and social burden should economic growth slow or even stop altogether.

However, it is perhaps the growing levels of household and personal debt (see Chapter 7, Figure 15) that most worry economists. Over the last 40 to 50 years the percentage of our income that we saved after paying taxes and housing costs averaged around 8 per cent. When this Government came to power the level of savings was 9.5 per cent. By 2004 this had fallen to just 3.7 per cent. After the banks tightened their control of people in

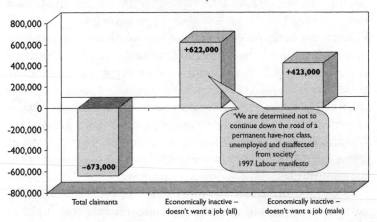

**Figure 27** Since 1997 unemployment has fallen, but economic inactivity has risen

debt, the savings ratio rose to over 5 per cent in 2005 and 2006. At the beginning of 2007 several economists predicted that people had become more sensible about their spending and that the level of household savings would rise to over 6 per cent.[27] Instead, we went on an unprecedented spending spree as we loaded up with large flatscreen televisions and game consoles and took ever more expensive holidays, so that in the first part of 2007 savings levels collapsed to a historic low of just 2.1 per cent. The amount we owe at the extortionate interest rates charged by credit cards companies has gone up from £18 billion in 1997 to £55 billion in 2007. This has created massive profits for the banks (on which, as we have seen, little tax is paid), but it has meant that British people now owe an average of £3,170 on credit cards, compared to £1,588 in Europe.[28] Within these figures are signs that younger people are failing to control their spending. An estimated 108,000 of 18-to-24-year-olds have credit card debts of more than £5,000.[29]

Even though the economy is still growing, some people are suffering as a result of taking on levels of borrowing which they cannot afford to service. Individual Voluntary Arrangements

(IVAs) – a form of personal bankruptcy – increased by over 50 per cent from 2005 to 2006 and these are expected to pass 100,000 in 2007. Most companies specializing in organizing IVAs are showing record growth and profits. There are also signs that some families are struggling to keep up their mortgage payments. About 280,000 mortgages are one month or more in arrears and although repossessions are still low they are increasing, with the number of Mortgage Possession Actions going up by 17 per cent in the last year. We are not yet in a crisis. The level of debt banks are writing off is increasing, but each year the main banks still manage to announce record profits, so most of us are still relatively solvent.

In Gordon Brown's first budget he promised, 'I will not allow house prices to get out of control and put at risk the sustainability of recovery'.[30] Since then we have seen the fastest growth in house prices in living memory and Mr Brown of course no longer mentions this pledge. For those of us fortunate enough to be on the property ladder, rising house prices have created a feeling of greater wealth and this has made us more prone to spend with abandon rather than save. Much of our economic growth has thus been fuelled by the rapidly increasing value of our homes and not by our overall economic success in world trade. If the house price bubble eventually bursts, or even if house prices just stagnate, we could see some awfully empty shopping centres and high streets as people stop spending and recession replaces growth.

Only a fool or an economist would try to predict the future. What is clear is that we have experienced almost unmatched economic growth and prosperity under New Labour. However, much of this is built on the shifting sands of unprecedented levels of debt rather than on our competitive performance in selling our products in world markets. We are in a precarious position, vulnerable to any economic shocks.

One danger is runaway inflation. We have had the benefit of the Chinese and Indian economic miracles in terms of lower prices in our shops, but as hundreds of millions of consumers in these huge countries now begin to spend the money they are getting from us on televisions, cars, fridges, better homes and all the other things we take for granted, their massive demand for raw materials and food is pushing up prices around the world. This means that imported inflation will probably increase. If the Bank of England then uses interest rate rises to try to control this imported inflation, many more people are going to drown in debt, consumer spending will collapse and we could enter a recessionary spiral.

Another risk is of the collapse of a few financial institutions. To support our financial services industry, the Government has adopted a hands-off approach to regulation by taking this away from the Bank of England and giving it to the anaemically ineffective Financial Services Authority (FSA). As the Northern Rock débâcle showed, the FSA seems to have been asleep. It did not notice that Northern Rock's rapid growth in mortgage lending was way in excess of its growth in savers' deposits and so seemed to be defying normal economic gravity. Even after the Government took billions of our money to bail out Northern Rock and after house prices appeared to be falling, almost all Northern Rock's top management were still in place and the company was still being allowed to give loans six times applicants' salaries and worth 117 per cent of a property's value.[31] Still the FSA slept on unperturbed. We have no idea how many other financial institutions have similarly had their kimonos wide open, and which could be in for a big shock were the economic winds to turn slightly chilly. There is a limit to the number of banks we taxpayers can afford to bail out to make up for the FSA's decade of supine inactivity. Incidentally, the person at the Bank of England responsible for financial stability during the Northern Rock crisis was our old friend Sir John Gieve, formerly boss of the Home Office at the time of the Blunkett nanny visa scandal, the release of foreign prisoners scandal and the failure of the Home Office to produce reliable financial accounts.[32]

The Chairman of the Treasury Select Committee, investigating the Northern Rock fiasco, accused Sir John of being 'asleep in the back shop while there was a mugging out front' and told him, 'frankly, I do not think you are doing your job'. Sir John countered that it was 'not my job to get involved with talking with risk managers from individual banks'.[33]

A third potential threat to our economic well-being comes from the further rises in taxation that will be needed to pay for the coming multi-billion-pound rise in the costs of public-sector pensions, the £180 billion of PFI bills that will have to be paid and continuing increases in social security benefits as economic prosperity still fails to reach millions of people. When we elected this Government no less than three times, most of us were prepared to pay higher taxes in return for the promise of improved public services and economic growth that would put more people into work. The Government kept half of its promise by giving us huge increases in taxes, but it has largely failed in the other half, namely improving public services and getting more people into work. Faced with failing schools, downgraded hospitals and rising social disorder, there may be a limit to our willingness to pay ever more for ever less.

We are a much less cohesive society than we were when this Government first took power. Moreover, around half the households in the UK have savings of less than £1,500 and so would be particularly at risk were the economy to turn sour. If we do get into a recession and a serious number of jobs are lost, things could begin to get quite messy.

# PART 4

## CARRY ON SQUANDERING

2012 Olympics ...... £14,000,000,000

EU superstate ....... £29,700,000,000

Two more years... £497,400,000,000

Total ................... £541,100,000,000

# CHAPTER 14

# OLYMPIC GOLD-DUST

Just before being chosen as Prime Minister in 2007, Gordon Brown was keen to assure the public that any government led by him could be trusted:

> One of my first acts as Prime Minister would be to restore power to Parliament in order to rebuild trust in the British people in our democracy. Government must be more open and more accountable to Parliament.[1]

As Chancellor, Gordon Brown was responsible for agreeing how much of taxpayers' money should be spent on the 2012 Olympics and as Prime Minister he will be responsible for ensuring that all money used for the Olympics is well spent. So the 2012 Games provide a good opportunity to test whether our new Prime Minister can really be trusted to spend our money wisely, and how open and accountable his Government will actually be.

Some people reading newspaper headlines such as 'Olympic budget trebles to £9.3 billion'[2] and 'London Olympics budget could pass £10 billion',[3] and observing the various shenanigans that have gone on surrounding the cost of staging the London Olympics, may have the impression that this is yet another big government project spiralling hopelessly out of control – a bit like a couple of Millennium Domes, a few Wembley Stadiums and the NHS IT system all being thrown together in one huge mess of confusion, chaos and gut-busting profits for all the private companies lucky enough to get a piece of the action. However, those responsible for bringing us the Games deny that there is a problem. The Secretary of State at the Department for Culture, Media and Sport (DCMS), Tessa Jowell, claims that the organizers have everything under control: 'we are determined to keep an iron grip on costs'.[4] Meanwhile, Lord Coe, Chairman of the London Organising Committee of the Olympic Games and Paralympics (LOCOG), showed his confidence when he said:

> The core costs of the London Olympic Games have varied very little. The costs of the actual Olympic venues themselves are much as they ever were: a little higher but by no means out of control.[5]

Yet a member of the Public Accounts Committee (PAC) described the project as 'the most catastrophic piece of financial mismanagement in the history of the world'.[6] Clearly, there are rather different and conflicting views about whether the Games are on course to be an impressive example of Mr Brown's careful financial stewardship and a cause for national pride or an expensive shambles that will take years to live down and even longer to pay off. One way of gaining some clarity about what is really happening with the 2012 Games is to go back a few years to see how the UK won the Games and what promises have been made, kept and broken since the Government first mooted the idea of bidding for the Olympics.

## THE SUCCESSFUL BID

Between January 2002 and May 2003 some initial work by consultants was commissioned by the Government, the Greater London Authority and the British Olympic Association to investigate the feasibility of bidding for the Games. In May 2003 the

Government announced that together with the Mayor of London it would support a bid to hold the Games in London at an estimated cost to the taxpayer of £2.375 billion.[7] Following this, five groups of specialist consultants were employed by the DCMS to help prepare the UK's bid. These included PwC (PricewaterhouseCoopers – an accountancy and management consultancy) and Partnerships UK (specializing in raising private-sector money for public-sector projects). As a result of this work, in November 2004 the UK proposed London as a Candidate City on the basis that we could hold the 2012 Olympics for a total cost of £4.036 billion – just under £3 billion for the Games themselves and about £1 billion more for improving the local infrastructure such as transport and power supply. This cost would be split between taxpayers, the National Lottery and the private sector (Figure 28).

Reassuringly, PwC also carried out a probability analysis which concluded that there was an 80 per cent chance that the

**Figure 28** At the time of the original bid, taxpayers were going to pay about £1.8 billion

| **Cost of the Games** | |
|---|---|
| | **£bn** |
| 'Core' Games | 2.992 |
| Infrastructure | 1.044 |
| **Total cost** | **4.036** |
| | |
| **Who pays for the Games?** | |
| | **£bn** |
| National Lottery | 1.500 |
| Taxpayer | 1.798 |
| Private sector | 0.738 |
| **Total funding** | **4.036** |

final costs would be within plus or minus 10 per cent of the estimates, though the company did warn that there were many uncertainties which needed to be examined further and that there were significant costs that were outside its terms of reference.

At the time, those involved seemed quite satisfied with the results of their work. The DCMS said that these cost figures had been 'carefully constructed' and 'based on thorough estimates'.[8] The International Olympic Committee Evaluation Committee appeared impressed, calling the London bid 'well supported and documented'.[9]

Based on this bid, on 6 July 2005 London was chosen as the host city to the great delight of all those involved, including the then Prime Minister Tony Blair who had actively campaigned to help the UK win the Games. Confusingly, just over a year later, when costs seemed to start doubling and then trebling, one of the bosses of the Olympic Delivery Authority claimed that the original bid was no more than 'a concept developed in a matter of months'.[10]

## DOUBTS ARISE

Once the UK had won the Games, work started in earnest on planning the great event. More consultants were employed to review the figures and assumptions made by the five consultancies that had helped prepare the bid. As Tessa Jowell explained, 'we are conducting a fundamental review of the costs that were carefully constructed as part of the original bid.'[11] Almost immediately, there were worrying rumours – security costs of many hundreds of millions of pounds had not been included, neither had hundreds of millions more in VAT, the costs of clearing and decontaminating the land and significant construction costs. Moreover, the amount expected to come from the private sector had apparently been over-estimated, leaving a bigger bill for the taxpayer. Faced with a barrage of questions about how high the eventual bill would be, the Olympocrats went strangely silent, claiming that it was far too early to give a final budget estimate. So, we taxpayers were left rather in the dark by those whose generous salaries and pensions we paid, feeling that the cost was moving relentlessly upwards but not knowing how much we would finally have to stump up for the Olympocrats to fulfil their Olympic dreams.

In the meantime, there were apparently ructions within the ranks of those organizing the Olympics. Jack Lemley, an American multi-millionaire who had been part-time head of the Olympic Delivery Authority on a salary of £611,000 a year, received a payoff of £388,000 when he quit after serving only seven months of his four-year contract. Initially, he was reported to have left 'to spend more time on his construction business', but soon newspapers wrote that he was pushed to resign after disputes with Olympics Minister Tessa Jowell.[12] It was later reported that Mr Lemley was less than complimentary about the whole enterprise. It was claimed that he had said in an interview that 'the costs are going to go up on an exponential basis', that 'it was so political that I think there is going to be a huge difficulty in the completion both in terms of time and money' and that he did not want to stay in the job as it would ruin his reputation for 'being able to deliver projects on time and on budget'.[13]

Pressure to come clean on the figures seemed to reach a crescendo by 5 March 2007 when the PAC, responsible for ensuring taxpayers' money is well spent, questioned the 2012 bosses about progress and costs. Anyone who has a feeling that the Government and its Olympocrats have been less than forthcoming with the truth about the costs of the Olympics might find the following extracts from the PAC hearing quite instructive. Here, the supposedly powerful PAC seemed to be having some difficulty in getting a commitment from Jonathan Stephens, the Permanent Secretary at the DCMS, as to when a final budget for the Games would be available:

| Question 10 Chairman: | When can you provide to Parliament something approaching a view of a final budget? Do you not owe us that? When will you be doing it? |
| Jonathan Stephens: | The Government want to provide a final budget. |
| Question 11 Chairman: | When? |
| Jonathan Stephens: | Soon, but I do not have a date. |
| Question 12 Chairman: | Will it be in weeks, days, months or years? |
| Jonathan Stephens: | All I can say is that it will be soon. |
| Question 13 Chairman: | What does that mean? |
| Jonathan Stephens: | It means soon. |

This difficulty did not seem to be resolved over 100 questions further on in the hearing:

| Question 139 Mr Wright: | The DCMS Committee … noted that 'there remains a lack of clarity about the expenditure of such a significant sum and we recommend that the Government issue a detailed breakdown as to how the figure was reached and how it is to be spent.' Has that been done yet? |
| Jonathan Stephens: | And this is what will feature in the comprehensive budget, when we will set out the breakdown of that and other key figures. |
| Question 140 Mr Wright: | Could you remind me of when that will be? |
| Jonathan Stephens: | Soon. |
| Question 141 Mr Wright: | Right, we are back to 'soon'.[14] |

awarded to London. The other strategy was to try and explain away the massive cost increases as being nothing to do with the Games. This could be done in two ways. Firstly, the Olympocrats claimed that what they called the 'core' cost of the Games had only gone up by a billion or two and therefore there had only been a small increase in cost. This explanation chose to consider the massive £2.747 billion contingency as not being part of the 'core' costs of the Games. Incidentally, this contingency alone was higher than the £2.375 billion that was the basis of the Government agreeing to support a bid in the first place. The other explanation was to insist that the cost increases were due to the 'increasing ambition' for the regeneration of the area, in particular providing more homes and improved transport. However, this seems to be contradicted by the fact that the infrastructure costs only went up by £629 million – a small proportion of the overall increase of £5.289 billion from the original £4.036 billion to £9.325 billion. We can confidently assume that both strategies – heaping scorn on critics and trying to explain away cost increases as not really being cost increases – will be repeated many times up until, during and long after the Games. However, the bottom line for us taxpayers is that when the bid was submitted to the International Olympics Committee, we were expected to cough up only £1.798 billion, yet by 15 March 2007 our part of the enterprise had risen almost four times to £7.150 billion. Whatever obtuse and barely credible explanations the Olympocrats managed to pull out of a hat, we would be paying an awful lot more for the 2012 extravaganza than we had originally been led to believe. Incidentally, Gordon Brown, Chancellor at the time, who would have had to agree the new budget with the Culture Secretary, was not in the House of Commons when the Culture Secretary announced the huge increase in the cost of staging the Olympics.

Although there now appeared to be a budget for the Games, there were several aspects of the Culture Secretary's announcement which were less than reassuring. This new figure of £9.325

billion was apparently not a final agreed budget; instead, it was called an 'outline budget providing a funding envelope and showing at a high level the main categories of expenditure and sources of income'.[16] It was, therefore, far from complete and would be subject to constant review, so the costs could (and definitely would) go even higher. Moreover, there were billions of pounds of Olympics costs that still were not included in the Government's new figures at all. For example, the £9.325 billion only covered the costs of building the Olympics facilities – it was 'assumed' that the £2 billion or so costs of actually holding the Games and Paralympics would be covered by sponsorship and ticket sales. Moreover, there was not a penny provided in this new budget for the almost £1 billion necessary to build the Olympic Village to house around 17,000 athletes because it was 'assumed' that this would be funded mostly by the private sector and by selling the houses after the Olympics. The costs of acquiring the land, over £1 billion, were not included either as these would be paid for by the London Development Agency (LDA), namely the taxpayer. Moreover, it was 'assumed' that after the Olympics some land would be sold again, making a profit for the LDA. Unfortunately, in 2008 the LDA admitted that it might have overvalued the land by about £1 billion, meaning that the anticipated profits might never actually materialize.[17] And costs of maintaining the Olympics venues and adapting them for public use after the Olympics were similarly left out of the budget as it was 'assumed' that our extremely well-paid Olympocrats would find somebody else willing to cover these costs.

A key feature of any Olympic bid is that the government of the winning country must provide a guarantee that taxpayers will cover all costs of the Games. The total cost of the London Games will not be the £9.325 billion announced on 15 March 2007, but rather closer to £14 billion (Figure 30). The Olympocrats know this, but apparently they do not feel it is worthwhile sharing this information with us. What none of us will know until after the event is how much of this £14 billion we taxpayers will have to

**Figure 30** There are more than £4.3 billion of extra costs over and above the 15 March 2007 (£9.325 billion) 'budget'

|  | **£bn** |
|---|---|
| Budget cost | 9.325 |
| LOCOG* | 2.000 |
| Olympic Village* | 1.000 |
| LDA land buying* | 1.300 |
| Adapting venues | not estimated |
| **Total** | **13.625** |

*Estimates based on National Audit Office report

pay. Probably, it will end up even higher than our Olympocrats would like us to think.

## AREAS FOR CONCERN

Around £14 billion is quite a lot of money for a few weeks of minority interest sports and the construction of five sporting venues in a run-down part of London, appropriately close to that other monument to governmental waste and incompetence – the Millennium Dome. However, there are further strong indicators that the cost of the Games may go even higher still. In addition to the inexorably rising official budget, there are at least three issues that should concern us taxpayers: overcharging by suppliers, rising construction costs and the complex, possibly unworkable organization that is supposedly managing the Olympics.

### Overcharging by Suppliers

If you want to build a new extension on your house, you will generally get a reasonable price if you are in a strong bargaining position. For example, this might mean that you ask several builders to bid for the work, you tell them that you need it done for well under £20,000 pounds, you are flexible about when it needs to be completed and you tell them that if you cannot get it done for the right price, then you are not going to go ahead at all. However, if you only ask for bids from a couple of builders who know each other well, who are aware that you must build it by a fixed date and who know that although you would like it done for under £20,000, you actually have £40,000 available (the contingency fund) and also that you have a multi-millionaire uncle who will guarantee to pay whatever it costs if the final bill is above even that (i.e. the taxpayers' guarantee), then you clearly have a weak bargaining position.

Unfortunately for us taxpayers, the Olympics organizers had a remarkably weak bargaining position from the very start – there are very few companies with the size and experience to provide the venues, the small group of viable firms know each other well and it will be a national humiliation if everything is not ready and working by a fixed date. Moreover, all the companies are aware that, although the Government would like the cost to be as low as possible, there is an inviting extra £2.747 billion contingency fund of our cash available should the builders like to get their hands on it. Even worse for us taxpayers, the builders also know that if they manage to siphon off all the contingency fund, the taxpayer has been committed by our Government to providing a blank cheque to cover any further cost increases, however high these may go.

Generally in life, when handed a blank cheque most people, and especially most companies, will fill it in with the biggest number they think they can get away with. This situation does not bode well for the Government's claims that it will 'keep an iron grip on costs'. Even the normally docile National Audit Office (NAO) could not avoid mentioning that builders might take the Olympics organizers right royally to the cleaners, though as usual the NAO showed its long-refined skill in understatement:

Public knowledge of the scale of the contingency provision, the fact that the Government has underwritten the Olympic programme, together with the high public profile of the Games and the immovable deadline may influence the pricing strategies of suppliers.[18]

## Rising Construction Costs

At the same time as the Olympics are being prepared, the Government has at least two other major construction projects on the go. An estimated £45 billion is to be spent on the 'Building Schools for the Future' programme to rebuild all the country's secondary schools and an additional £8 billion is going on building 210,000 affordable homes to try to alleviate the housing crisis. In addition, there will be billions more invested in new PFI hospitals, roads and prisons. All these projects will put massive pressure on construction companies, there will be shortages of building materials and skilled labour and inevitably building costs will shoot up. This situation is further exacerbated by the current rapid economic growth in China and India which is causing worldwide shortages and therefore price increases of basic building materials like steel and aluminium. The Olympics budget has 'assumed' building costs will go up by 5–6 per cent a year.[19] Probably, the increase will be much greater.

By the end of 2007, construction companies had so much other work that many were not even bothering to bid for the Olympics contracts and there was only one bid each for the Olympic stadium and the aquatic centre. The chief executive of the Construction Federation said, 'There are plenty of opportunities in the marketplace, allowing suppliers to choose the best opportunities'. He also explained that construction companies were wary of becoming involved in something that could turn out to be a disaster: 'It is also highly exposed and if things went badly wrong a contractor could damage its reputation irretrievably'.[20]

This lack of competition will inevitably weaken the organizers' bargaining position and push up costs. The Olympocrats naturally denied there was any problem: 'Although we are working to a challenging timetable in a highly competitive market, we are successfully procuring high-quality contractors to help deliver the London 2012 venues and infrastructure'.

## The Many-headed Monster

We all know that we are most efficient when working for one single boss who takes responsibility for results; that working for two bosses can cause difficulties; and that working for three bosses simultaneously usually leads to conflict, confusion and a lack of clarity about who, if anybody, is responsible for anything. The lesson we have learnt over many thousands of years is that the simpler an organization's structure, the more likely it is to achieve its goals. Unfortunately, it is not obvious that this lesson has been learnt by the Olympocrats.

As required by the International Olympic Committee, there are two main organizations charged with the Olympics. There is the Olympics Delivery Authority (ODA) which is responsible for providing all the sporting venues, transport and the Olympic Village; and there is the LOCOG which must run the actual Olympic Games and subsequent Paralympics. This two-headed beast should be manageable, although there is some lack of clarity about which of these two bodies is responsible for equipping all the buildings where the sporting events will take place. Apparently, this will be decided between the two bodies on a case-by-case basis through close cooperation and negotiation.

However, there are several other official bodies involved. These include the DCMS which is responsible to the Government for staging a successful Games; the London Development Agency which has bought the land for the Games and which is also responsible for ensuring the Games give sustainable regeneration to the area around the Olympics Park; the

Mayor of London who will be providing some of the funding for the Games; the National Lottery which will be contributing over £2 billion; and the British Olympic Association which will be choosing and fielding the British team. In order to help all these diverse organizations with different interests to work together effectively, the Government has set up a new body: the Olympic Board. This consists of the Secretary of State for Culture, Media and Sport (now the Olympics Minister), the Mayor of London, the chair of the British Olympic Association and the chair of LOCOG. Curiously, at the time of writing, the chair of the ODA, the organization that would be spending most of the £9 billion, was allowed to attend meetings of the Olympic Board, but not allowed to vote at those meetings. To help it keep control of what was happening, the Olympic Board also had an Olympic Programme Support Unit.

It is theoretically possible that all these different groups will work harmoniously and professionally together to bring us a great Games at a value-for-money price. It is also possible that the involvement of so many varied groups, all with different priorities and different agendas, will just lead to five years of squabbling, slow decision-making, expensive compromises and ever-increasing costs. The chief executive of the Construction Industry Council expressed his members' worries about the Olympics organization: 'The ODA has too many masters. These include the IOC, Ken Livingstone, the DCMS, the Treasury, Gordon Brown, the Olympic Board and the five London boroughs.' He was also concerned about the involvement of the DCMS:

> There are also a whole group of DCMS civil servants without any operational responsibility. They are only there to make sure other people are doing their jobs which can lead to complete inertia. There is no clear leadership at the top so no one makes decisions.[21]

The PAC was similarly worried about the difficulty in identifying anybody who was actually responsible for successfully delivering the Games. As one PAC member asked:

> Following on from what the chairman said at the beginning, there is no one person with overall responsibility. Is that in anticipation of failure or is it an insurance policy so that no one will carry the can?[22]

## PROGRESS SO FAR

The best way to judge any great project is on what is achieved rather than on the often inflated promises of what will be achieved, especially when those involved have huge vested interests in not rocking the boat in which they are comfortably sailing along on a sea of our money. Three key actions on the great voyage to the 2012 Games have so far been completed and the results confirm the worst fears of the Olympophobes, and could well give a few sleepless nights for even the most ardent Olympophiles.

Firstly, the ODA has proudly announced its 'success' in setting up the organization that will project-manage its part of the Games. A small detail that the ODA has tended to downplay is that the original budget in the bid was £16 million for programme delivery, yet by 2007 this had reached £570 million – over 35 times the original budget.[23]

Another 'success' has been that the London Development Agency has managed to purchase all the necessary land by the planned time. Mayor of London Ken Livingstone said:

> This is a truly fantastic achievement. With the world watching and many cynics predicting failure and that the 2012 Games would be jeopardised, the London Development

Agency worked professionally and steadily to assemble the land needed on time and on budget.[24]

Although the land was acquired on time, the original budget had predicted we would pay £478 million. Realizing that we wanted their land for our Games, the owners naturally pumped up the price. We were then told this would 'not exceed £650 million'.[25] The final figure is likely to be over £1 billion and probably nearer to £1.5 billion – over three times the original budget.[26]

The third achievement was producing the Olympic logo. 'Am I proud? You bet I'm proud,' Lord Coe, Chairman of LOCOG, declared.[27] However, some other people were not so impressed at what we taxpayers got for £400,000. Some compared it to the design used by the Nazi SS, probably one of the most hated symbols of the twentieth century. Others expressed concern that there had not been an open national competition and that the contract seemed to have been awarded to one company without first inviting bids and preliminary ideas from several design companies. The founder of the Design Museum described the new Olympics logo as 'a puerile mess, an artistic flop and a commercial scandal'; almost 50,000 people signed an online petition calling for the logo to be scrapped; and a film promoting the versatility of the new logo had to be withdrawn after triggering epileptic seizures in some viewers.[28]

## RAIDING THE LOTTERY

Another aspect of the 2012 Olympics that has worried some observers is the amount of National Lottery money that will be diverted from good causes to help feed the Olympocrats' severe attack of spendicitis. In the original bid, it was expected that the Lottery would provide £1.5 billion. In the March 2007 Games budget, this was raised by £675 million to £2.175 billion. Of this £2.175 billion, about £515 million (24 per cent) was expected to come from new Lottery games associated with the Olympics and the other £1.66 billion (76 per cent) would have to be taken from revenue that should have gone to good causes. This loss of over £300 million a year for the next five years is likely to cause quite a degree of stress to many deserving charities around the country. However, not only would this raid on Lottery funds affect charities, perversely it would also mean almost £125 million being taken away from the sporting bodies that would be expected to produce the British athletes to compete in the 2012 Games: Sport England would lose £99.9 million, the Sports Council for Wales £7.3 million, Sport Scotland £13.1 million and the Sports Council for Northern Ireland £4.1 million.[29] Fortunately, we need not worry that these budget cuts will adversely affect our chances of winning a few medals in 2012. The Olympocrats already have contingency plans in place and look as if they are trying to do a 'Zola Budd', the South African athlete who suddenly became British when her own nation was barred from competing. They are reportedly busy scouring the world for any athletes with the slightest connection with the UK who could be given a 'passport of convenience' on condition that they will compete for the UK, even if they have already represented their real country at previous international events. An Afghan wrestler, an American basketball player and a Jamaican high-jumper are thought to be the first targets of this somewhat suspect recruitment effort.[30]

In recognition of the National Lottery's contribution to the Games, the Olympocrats proposed to share with the Lottery some of the profits generated from selling land after the Olympics. These arrangements were set out in a memorandum of understanding between the Government and the Mayor of London.[31] However, this arrangement is not legally binding and the London Development Agency, which had bought the land at a much higher price than originally planned, has first call on any profits. So the Lottery may have to wait some time before seeing any money ever entering its bank account.

## WINNERS AND LOSERS

The initial budget for the 2004 Athens Olympics was £840 million. By the time of the Games, this had increased by more than a factor of five to £4.4 billion. Much of the increase came in the last couple of years before the Games started as the Greeks threw money at them in order to avoid the national humiliation of not having the venues ready on time. The 2000 Sydney Games more than doubled from AU$3 billion to AU$6.6 billion. A report by the Auditor-General of New South Wales found that costs such as infrastructure, facilities and security had not been included in the original bid – a conclusion that might sound familiar to any British Olympophobes concerned about the cost of our 2012 adventure. The Auditor-General also criticized the excessive secrecy which surrounded both the bid and the build-up to the Sydney Games: 'One of the issues which has provided a backdrop to this audit is the unnecessary secrecy which has been associated with the preparations for the Sydney 2000 Games'.[32] The most recent Games, the 2008 Beijing Olympics, will cost about £22 billion. Our 2012 Olympocrats claim that London and Beijing are not comparable as the Beijing Games include building 14 new venues (London will only need five), a new airport, new roads and a new rail system. While this is true, it is also the case that construction costs in China are probably less than a tenth of similar costs in the UK. Moreover, the Chinese Government can just appropriate the land and materials it needs without having to spend billions buying them.

A common feature of the Olympic Games seems to be that the decision to bid for them is political rather than economic – governments see winning the Games as giving them electoral or other kinds of advantage. This means that governments will always hugely underestimate the costs of the Games at the time of the bid in order to get press and public support, in the full knowledge that once the Games are 'won', it is too late to turn back, however high the final, real cost. In this respect, the British

Government seems to have been true to type and to have been more economic with the truth about the real cost than it has been with our money. Naturally, the Government disputes this: 'The Government has been open and transparent about the cost of the Olympics'.[33]

There will be many winners and losers in the 2012 Olympics. The way things look at the moment, the real winners will be the three main groups of Olympic cheerleaders – the Olympocrats with their big salaries and generous expense accounts; the consultancies and construction companies who are being handed blank cheques with our signatures on them; and 'friendly' journalists who will be wined and dined and get buckets of free tickets to the best events that they can sell off on eBay in return for writing a steady stream of 'good news' stories about the impending débâcle. The losers are likely to be the British athletes whose funding is being cut to pay for the Olympics and British taxpayers who will have to foot almost all the £14 billion or so bill for the whole sorry mess.

In 1970, Denver was awarded the 1976 Winter Olympics. By 1972 the estimated costs had trebled (a smaller increase than we have already seen for 2012). As the US is a democracy, the people of Denver were allowed to vote on whether to continue with the Games. A 60 per cent majority voted against Denver's taxpayers footing the bill and so the Winter Games were handed back to the International Olympic Committee and held in Innsbruck instead – as Innsbruck had hosted the 1964 Winter Games, it already had much of the necessary infrastructure in place. Unfortunately, it seems that the UK is a bureaucracy, not a democracy, and so we will not be given any such choice.

However, the one question that nobody seems to be asking is 'Why hold the Olympics in London or anywhere else?' The Olympics started in Greece. In 2004, Athens did a quite creditable job with their Games, which they are still paying for. If the Olympics were only held in Athens in the future, the Greeks would find some use for all the expensive facilities they have already built and many tens of billions of pounds could be saved. This money could then be employed for something useful like helping to develop agriculture to reduce food shortages and starvation in the Third World, rather than just enriching Olympocrats, construction companies, consultancies and thousands of other carpet-baggers who, encouraged by a Government hoping that the 'glory' of staging the Games will distract us from its mismanagement of our economy and our public services, are all out to plunder our taxes.

# CHAPTER 15

# THE EUROPEAN RIP-OFF

## STITCHED UP

Perhaps one of the most easily avoidable squanderings of our taxes came at the December 2005 meeting to agree the European Union (EU) budget for the seven years from 2007 to 2013. For months, the Prime Minister Tony Blair had been preparing his stance with tough talk of 'red lines' and the 'need for change'. Gordon Brown, Blair's Chancellor, even said he would not hesitate to use his veto to protect the UK's interests. Blair, supported by Gordon Brown back in London, marched into the meeting with a stern expression and an uncompromising stance. Later, he emerged having generously and humiliatingly agreed to give away a large part of our annual multi-billion-pound EU rebate in return for not a single meaningful concession from any of the other participants. This abject capitulation would raise the annual contribution of UK taxpayers into EU coffers from an average of about £3.3 billion between 1997 and 2006 up to around £5.6 billion per year over the next seven years – a stunningly magnanimous increase of about 70 per cent (see Figure 31).

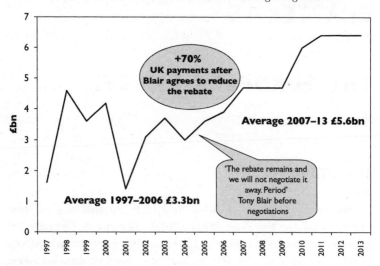

**Figure 31** Our net contributions to the EU will rise by 70 per cent due to Britain's cave-in at the 2005 EU budget negotiations

## THE ROAD TO RUIN

In June 2005 the UK helped block an EU Commission proposal that would have massively increased the EU's budget. Then in July the UK took over the rotating EU presidency and Blair delivered a real belter of a speech about how the EU faced a 'moment of decision' and needed to reform:

> This is not a time to accuse those who want Europe to change of betraying Europe. It is time to recognize that only by change will Europe recover its strength, its relevance, its idealism and therefore its support amongst the people.

Blair accused other European leaders of ignoring the messages sent by French and Dutch voters in rejecting the EU Constitution, and to drive his point home he evoked the biblical story of Jericho:

> It is time to give ourselves a reality check. To receive a wake-up call. The people are blowing the trumpets around the city walls. Are we listening? Have we the political will to go out and meet them so that they regard our leadership as part of the solution not the problem?[1]

With headlines like 'Blair squares up for a fight with Old Europe "weaklings"', and 'EU must reform or it will risk massive failure, Blair warns', several UK newspapers began to have excited visions of our supposedly tough Prime Minister taking his crusade for modernization into the heart of reactionary Old Europe.[2] Blair even won plaudits from other European leaders for his verbal pyrotechnics.

Blair's key demand was that the EU should reduce the more than 40 per cent of its budget that was spent through the Common Agricultural Policy (CAP) on the 5 per cent of its population working in agriculture, and instead should be investing more in industry and innovation to improve its international competitiveness and reduce unemployment. Before his speech, Blair made it clear to the House of Commons that the British rebate, negotiated by Margaret Thatcher, would be safe in his hands: 'The rebate remains and we will not negotiate it away. Period.'[3] Chancellor Gordon Brown was equally adamant about defending the British budget rebate: 'It is wholly justified. And if we did not get the result that we wanted we would not hesitate to use our veto.'[4] Both Blair and Brown had long disliked the CAP. In 2002 Blair said, 'The CAP is the wrong policy. It's anti free trade, it's a waste of money,' a view reiterated by Brown in 2005 when he talked of the need to 'urgently tackle the scandal and waste of the Common Agricultural Policy'.[5] In the 1997 Labour manifesto the party promised 'urgent reform of the Common Agricultural Policy' because 'it is costly, vulnerable to fraud and not geared to environmental protection'. However, in 2005 Blair did signal that he would be prepared to be flexible with the British rebate if CAP spending could be reduced:

The rebate remains because the reason for the rebate remains ... Of course if we get rid of the CAP and we change the reason why the rebate is there, then the case for the rebate changes.[6]

However, as soon as Blair had delivered his speech to mark the UK taking the six-month presidency, he disappeared back to London basking in the glory of his oratorical success and the real politics began. Brilliantly and cynically outmanoeuvring Blair, French President Jacques Chirac managed to take the other EU leaders' attention away from the huge €51 billion spent on CAP, of which over €10 billion went straight into the pockets of French farmers. Instead, Chirac managed to foment a growing movement to get rid of the British budget rebate, *le chèque britannique*, even though this only cost about €5 billion a year. One senior EU politician dismissively warned Blair that he could not just fly over, make speeches and leave:

We have lost the President of the Council. From what we hear he is the British Prime Minister Tony Blair, although nobody has seen or heard of him since the summer recess ended. One rhetorically brilliant speech without consequences or follow-ups is simply not enough to secure success ... The man himself is showing none of his promised European leadership.[7]

As for reforming CAP, the French President, who had been the French Farm Minister at the time the UK joined the EU, repeatedly made quite clear how unwilling he was to negotiate. In June 2005 he said, 'We cannot accept any reduction whatsoever of the direct aid to our farmers'.[8] Then in July he underlined his complete intransigence: 'I am not willing to make the slightest concession on the common agricultural policy ... The CAP is the future.'[9] And yet again in October the great man spoke out:

France has a clear position, which is that the Common Agricultural Policy must be respected in its entirety ... It is out of the question for us to take a step further.[10]

Unfortunately for us UK taxpayers, neither Blair nor the Rolls-Royce brains at the Foreign Office seemed to pick up on Chirac's less than subtle megaphone messages that, come hell or high water, he would not budge one millimetre on the issue of CAP reform. Nor did our leaders and diplomats notice either the growing European revolt against the UK's plans for EU budget reform or the increasing enthusiasm of other countries to get their hands on our rebate. By the time of the December 2005 budget negotiations, there were two clearly distinct groups facing each other – the UK versus the rest. The UK proposed a reduced seven-year EU budget of €849 billion; the others wanted an increase to €871 billion. One by one, the other leaders trooped in to Blair demanding a bit of the British rebate for themselves. A British official accused the other countries of 'bidding for a pot of money that was not anything like as big as the bids'.[11] The UK was criticized for its 'lack of solidarity' by those who most coveted our money. Leading the attack was of course Monsieur Chirac: 'The time has come for our British friends to understand that they must now make a gesture of solidarity'.[12]

By being all talk and no trousers, Blair had painted himself, and us, into a corner. Now he could either refuse to do a deal and face the humiliation of his six-month UK presidency ending in abject failure or else he could cave in and give further billions of pounds of our money away. Sure enough, he and his Chancellor crumbled and handed their European partners almost everything they wanted. The final EU budget was agreed at around €862 billion. Almost all of the difference between Blair's original €849 billion and the agreed €862 billion would come from our pockets through reducing the British rebate by about €1.4 billion a year. In return for accepting a large reduction in our rebate, Blair got a vague statement that the EU Commission would review its expenditure, including the CAP, at some point between 2007 and 2013. The Commission could then, if it wanted to, use this review to propose changes which could be introduced provided all countries agreed to such changes. However, as the French retained a veto to block any such changes, this review was worse than worthless.

Not only did Blair and Brown see their great plans for reforming EU finances ground gleefully and unceremoniously into the dust by Chirac and his mates, but they also had to face the additional indignity of large rises in precisely the areas of the EU expenditure that they had sought to reduce. The new agreed 2007–13 budget allowed an increase of 28 per cent in the EU's administration costs and the hated CAP would rise by over 10 per cent so that it would consume an even larger percentage of ever greater EU spending. France's President Chirac expressed satisfaction with the outcome of the 'negotiations' which resulted in France retaining the CAP, which so effortlessly poured our money into French pockets, while the UK ended up as the country that received significantly less EU money per head of population than any other European Union country (see Figure 32).

This is not meant as a criticism of the French. Instead, we should be applauding them and the Belgians, the Irish, the Portuguese and the Spanish. They have all learnt how to play the euro-game – give as little as possible to the EU and run off with as much as you can carry – and they all have been playing the game with skill, panache and consistency for several decades, usually at our expense. We should be lambasting our gutless politicians for allowing these other countries to so easily pillage our wealth. For example, when the EU changed the method of agricultural subsidies to give more money to countries with poor quality agricultural land, Luxembourg, a state lacking the troublesome terrain of either mountains or deserts, suddenly found that 98 per cent of its land was of 'poor quality'; Greece went for over 80 per cent; and even fertile Germany discovered that 50 per cent of its farms were on unproductive land. Not a

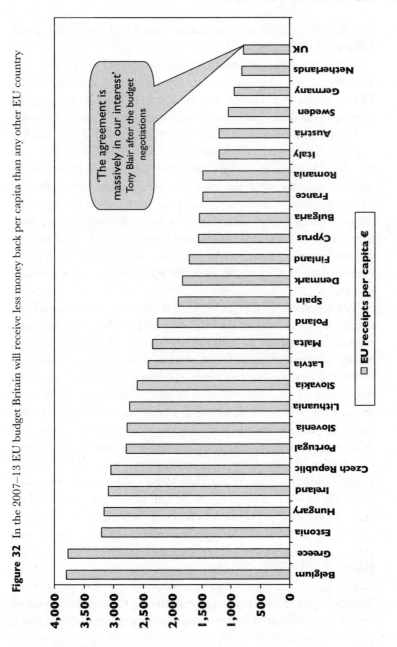

**Figure 32** In the 2007–13 EU budget Britain will receive less money back per capita than any other EU country

murmur of protest at such blatant fraud was heard from our MEPs or MPs.

Worse still, the 2005 budget rout of the UK should simply not have occurred. This was the first budget negotiating round for several new East European members – Poland, the Czech Republic, Estonia, Latvia – all of whom should have naturally sided with countries like the UK, Denmark, Holland and Sweden to break the Franco-German stranglehold on EU policy and spending. With these new potential allies, Blair and Brown had a historic opportunity to get some kind of balance and control of EU expenditure. Instead, through an extraordinary mixture of self-congratulatory hubris and bungling incompetence, they threw away this once-in-a-lifetime chance to ensure our money was well-spent. We will all be paying the price of their bottling-out for the next 20 to 30 years at a minimum, and probably longer.

Our spending of £4 billion to £6 billion a year on the EU is, of course, almost insignificant compared to the Government's annual expenditure of over £540 billion. However, whereas money invested in the UK for hospitals and schools should give us taxpayers something in return – better healthcare and teaching – money given to the EU can appear to end up going straight into the welcoming bank accounts of citizens of other EU countries, almost without any benefit for us. Moreover, even our small net contributions mount up quite quickly to substantial piles of cash. Since we joined the EU, we have paid over £90 billion to finance the well-being of our European cousins and under the 2007–13 budget another £39 billion or so will be similarly poured down the great black hole of EU finances.

## MERCI BEAUCOUP

The EU website informs us reassuringly that our money is being used for 'good, agreed purposes'. Moreover, the EU states that 'the EU budget is decided democratically' and subject to 'proper management and control'. How the EU uses our money is surprisingly simple for such a large organization. Just under half the money goes to the CAP, a little bit less goes on European regional aid projects and the rest gets put into foreign aid and administration (see Figure 33).

This bias towards supporting agriculture is a consequence of the conditions that existed in continental Europe at the start of the 1950s. Recovering from the Second World War and subsequent food shortages, the two key founder members of the EU, Germany and France, set up a system whereby Germany could have access to French markets for its industrial products without having to go to the bother of invading the country every 30 years or so. In return, Germany committed to subsidizing the modernization of French agriculture. The world has moved on since then, but the EU's approach to distributing its cash has not changed one iota. So, although just 5 per cent of the EU's population works in farming and just 1.6 per cent of the EU's economic output comes from agriculture, the CAP still comfortably absorbs almost half the EU's budget.

**Figure 33** Over 80 per cent of the EU budget is spent on agriculture and regional aid, which are both subject to massive fraud

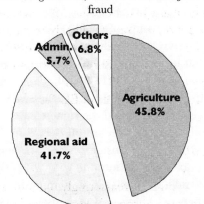

If the CAP genuinely benefited poorer farmers, then we might not have grounds to resent the more than €50 billion of EU taxes that gets showered on the agricultural sector every year. However, there are pretty clear indications that the way the CAP functions has fairly major negative consequences for at least three groups – many European farmers, all European consumers and, perhaps most seriously, hundreds of millions of the most impoverished people in the world's most deprived countries.

## Making the Rich Richer

Predictably, the big winners from the CAP are French farmers, hence the absolute refusal of French politicians to allow even the slightest tinkering with the CAP system. Although less than 10 per cent of EU farmers are in France, the mysterious alchemy of the CAP ensures that these farmers get around 25 per cent of all CAP money. More than 130,000 French farmers, compared to nearer 40,000 in each of Spain, Germany and the UK, get over €20,000 a year, with about 3,000 French farmers receiving more than €100,000 each in subsidies. Although France and its farmers constantly complain and protest about how difficult it is to make a living from farming, the average earnings of farmers in France are around 60 per cent higher than the overall average earnings of all French workers.

One of the supposed aims of the CAP was to preserve rural life by ensuring the survival of smaller farms, but most of the money gets siphoned off by the largest farms and the major agri-businesses who own the big beef, cereal, dairy and sugar beet acreages. About 80 per cent of the CAP's annual €50 billion goes to just 20 per cent of farms and the richest 2 per cent of farmers and agricultural companies cream off over a quarter of the EU farm budget. Several big businesses receive seriously healthy amounts of the taxes we pay into the CAP. In 2004, Tate & Lyle received €178 million, four Danish companies picked up over €200 million between them and three Belgian food companies managed to grab over €180 million.[13] Many of Europe's elite also seem to do very nicely each year out of the money that we taxpayers pour into the CAP. Albert, Prince of Monaco, reportedly pockets around €300,000 a year, several French politicians get over €100,000 each and numerous EU politicians also receive similar amounts.[14] In the UK, according to one newspaper, in just one year the Queen got about €800,000 from the CAP, the Prince of Wales over €300,000, the Duke of Westminster (worth £5 billion) over €500,000 and the Duke of Marlborough (worth £1 billion) over €500,000.[15] In fact, our money flows so generously to the already well-heeled that across Europe many businessmen and other speculators, with absolutely no connection to farming, are busily buying up land just for the EU subsidies of up to €16,000 an acre that they can then bank every year.[16] To qualify for payment, owners of land do not actually have to do anything that either looks like, sounds like or even smells like farming. One tax accountant, who owned a few acres and was thus eligible for CAP payments, criticized those cashing in on the EU's incontinence with our money: 'I would feel a bit of a fraud claiming this. It is for farmers, not for people like me. People are claiming money for really doing nothing on their land.'[17]

The CAP has become such a goldmine for the already wealthy that even some French farmers are becoming frustrated with the way it favours the rich. One French farmers' leader said, 'In France there is no transparency about aid because they know that if details of how the money is distributed were published tomorrow nobody would continue to pay for it'.[18]

## Milking Consumers

At first the CAP encouraged farmers to produce as much food as possible, so we taxpayers ended up paying billions to grow, store and later destroy butter and beef mountains while over half of the world's population did not have enough to eat. CAP also managed to burden us with a 17.8-billion-litre lake of extremely low-quality wine – apparently enough to give four bottles to everyone in the world.[19] Each year we pay for around 700 million bottles of French and Spanish wine to be turned into industrial alcohol, having already paid hundreds of millions to the growers to produce this wine that nobody ever wanted to buy in the first place. And now the EU plans to give grants of €2.4 billion of our taxes to wine-growers to encourage them to cultivate something else.

Faced with the PR disaster of this massive and costly waste, the EU did not consider reducing the amount paid to farmers. Instead, it just changed the way our money was handed out. The EU introduced what it called 'decoupling'. It partially broke the link between subsidies and the quantities produced, so farmers were now paid some of their EU money just for having farms, with no need to produce very much. This still did not make much of a hole in the embarrassing food surpluses, so the EU introduced 'set-aside', meaning that farmers were paid not to grow anything at all on parts of their land. Naturally, many farmers kept on growing as much as possible to get the maximum amount in subsidies while eagerly grabbing whatever extra cash they could by just 'setting aside' those bits of their land where it was almost impossible to grow anything anyway.

Unfortunately, at the same time as the EU bureaucrats used billions of our money to reduce the amount of crops grown, the EU has also insisted on greater use of biofuels (fuel made from crops). This rush to biofuels has predictably caused increased need for some of the very crops whose production the EU has used our money to reduce. This mind-boggling short-sightedness, coupled with rising demand for food from the growing economies of China and India, has led to worldwide shortages of some foods and major increases in prices for us consumers.

The CAP pushes up prices for consumers in another way: as imports of food into the EU are heavily taxed to protect European farmers, we end up paying often two to three times as much for imported food as we should. Three different bodies have all produced estimates of the real cost of the CAP to European taxpayers. The independent consumers' association, Which?, calculated that a family of four in Europe pays about £1,000 a year in higher food prices because of the way the CAP inflates the price of food. The World Bank put the cost of artificially high food prices in Europe at around $63 billion a year in addition to the $50 billion spent on the CAP. And in its 2004 budget report, the Treasury came up with similar figures to the World Bank and also highlighted how unnecessarily high food prices are particularly onerous for poorer families:

> The Common Agricultural Policy is estimated to cost EU taxpayers and consumers around $100 billion a year through subsidies and high food prices. The poorest, who spend the greatest proportion of their income on food, are hit hardest by an implicit tax on food of around 26 percent.[20]

## Impoverishing the Impoverished

As we are reasonably wealthy in Europe, we can perhaps afford the absurdity of wasting over €50 billion a year on the lavish subsidies to farmers and about another €50 billion on the unnecessarily high food prices to consumers that result from the CAP. After all, the CAP only costs us about €250 per person per year. The CAP's most pernicious effects are actually most painfully felt in the poorest countries of the Third World, far away from our comfortable lives.

Agriculture accounts for less than 2 per cent of Europe's economic output. However, for many poorer countries agriculture makes up 80–90 per cent of their wealth, so the only way these countries can drag themselves out of poverty is through being able to sell their agricultural produce on world markets. Oxfam have estimated that if Africa could increase its share of world trade by just 1 per cent, it would earn enough to lift 128 million people out of extreme poverty, providing the money was not just siphoned off into offshore bank accounts by the continent's many kleptocratic leaders.[21] However, the CAP prevents these poorest countries trading their way out of poverty in three ways. Firstly, subsidies to European farmers still encourage them to over-produce things like cotton, sugar, wheat and tobacco, thus stifling demand for imports from the Third World. Secondly, high import duties put on products from poorer countries often make them uncompetitive compared to subsidized food produced in Europe, thus preventing Third World farmers from exporting to Europe. Then thirdly, the EU pays European farmers billions in subsidies to export their excess production so they can dump it into Third World markets at less than it costs local subsistence farmers to produce.

The effect across the Third World has been devastating. Import duties and €700 million of subsidies given to Greek and Spanish cotton producers prevent countries like Chad, Mali and Togo from selling their crops to Europe. The CAP also gives European producers (mostly large corporations) of expensive beet sugar over €700 million a year of our money, while imposing import tariffs of over 200 per cent on the less expensive cane sugar to protect uneconomic European sugar businesses. This makes it almost impossible for countries like Mozambique to export to Europe. It also leads to over-production, which has consequently resulted in the dumping of five million tons of excess European sugar on world markets, driving down the prices that poorer countries can get. The situation is similar with milk, beef and many other agricultural products. After the Asian tsunami, an EU politician asked the Thai Government how the EU could help rebuild the Thai fishing industry. He was told that Thailand did not need any EU money; all it wanted was a reduction in tariffs imposed on Thai fish sold to the EU. However, this would have been opposed by French and Spanish fishermen and so Thailand ended up getting nothing. Even more ludicrously, because we cause so much misery in the Third World through protecting our farmers, we are faced with the additional costs of mass economic migration from poorer countries whose development we prevent, and we have to give them more in aid to try to limit the starvation and disease that result from their inability to earn money from trade. It has been estimated that for every dollar we give poorer countries in aid, we take away two dollars because of the CAP's unfair trading.[22]

Our politicians are so generous with our money that they spend about €2 per day in subsidies for every cow in Europe, when more than half of Africa's population has to live on less than €1 a day. One UK diplomat called the CAP 'the most stupid, immoral state-subsidized policy in human history, Communism aside'.[23] He accused it of farm subsidies which 'bloat rich French landowners and pump up food prices in Europe causing African poverty'. When these comments were made public, the Foreign Office said they were meant as a joke. Sadly, there are millions of people in poorer countries who cannot appreciate the funny side of the absurdly wasteful and damaging CAP.

Both Blair and Brown have talked tough on the damage the CAP causes. Blair said, 'We need more open trade and opening up of markets in general and an end to trade-distorting subsidies which are the greatest problem that developing countries face'.[24] Gordon Brown was equally unequivocal in his condemnation of the CAP: 'If we are to make poverty history ... let us seek to make the excesses of the CAP history'.[25] However, when push came to shove and Chirac refused to budge on reforming the CAP, both our two great leaders decided to cave in completely and sacrifice the welfare of millions of Third World poor in order to save face by creating a completely unconvincing semblance of European unity. This capitulation will cost UK taxpayers billions that perhaps we can afford, but it will cost the poor billions that they do not have and never will have. As the EU politicians and bureaucrats crowd into expensive Brussels restaurants to toast their success in maintaining the status quo on the CAP, hundreds of thousands will die in the Third World because, while we go to concerts to 'make poverty history', we allow billions of pounds of our taxes to be used to prevent the poor from trading their way out of poverty.

## ANYTHING GOES

The EU has probably deservedly become synonymous with waste, fraud and corruption. Vast amounts are squandered on worthless and unnecessary projects. Many of these are so-called 'prestige projects' designed to prove, usually unsuccessfully, that the EU is the technological equal of the US. There was the Eurofighter, produced almost a decade late and costing several times that of an equivalent US-made fighter. There was also Galileo – the European equivalent of the US satellite-based GPS system. After ten years, around £2.5 billion had already been committed. In 2007 the consortium of European (mainly French) aerospace companies created to run Galileo collapsed in acrimony. Another £4–£5 billion will now be needed to rescue the project, possibly by taking it into public ownership. Naturally, the French want our taxes increased to pay for this white elephant which has always been more an expression of Gallic vanity than a realistic commercial proposition. If Galileo is ever completed, it will not be operational till 2012 and it was probably totally unnecessary in the first place as the US system works perfectly well. It is more than likely that France will succeed in pressurizing our lily-livered leaders to keep funding this technical and commercial disaster in the interests of 'European solidarity'. Billions more are wasted on various European, often French-inspired, attempts to set up a rival military force to NATO. Yet every time the Euro-army is sent into 'action', as is happening in Afghanistan, it often appears that its soldiers seem to hide away in the safety of their barracks where they can march around in their smart new uniforms while British, American and Canadian forces have to go out and risk their lives in real fighting.

The EU policy that most clearly shows its utter contempt for its citizens and their money is probably its capitulation to the French demand that the EU Parliament should meet in Strasbourg for four days every month. To satisfy French economic interests, 12 times a year 732 MEPs, over 2,000 staff and numerous hangers-on travel a couple of hundred miles from Brussels to Strasbourg, accompanied by a fleet of lorries carrying documents and luggage. This ludicrous movement of people and equipment for no useful purpose wastes both a huge amount of time and more than £120 million a year – about 15 per cent of the EU's total budget. For over a decade the EU has been discussing stopping this massive and easily avoidable squandering of our money, but so far no action has been taken as it is expected the French would veto any proposal to change this arrangement. To add insult to injury, in 2006 it was revealed that for more than a quarter of a century the Strasbourg city authorities had been creaming off extra money for themselves by secretly inflating the rent paid for the parliamentary buildings by several million euros a year. When the EU finally and belatedly did demand to see what was happening to the money handed over to the French city, the city authorities just refused to cooperate and denied the EU access to their internal budget documents.[26]

Another avid devourer of EU cash is the €35 billion plus annual regional development fund. A recent audit of over €2 billion worth of projects in Bulgaria and Romania found that more than half the money had been wasted through mismanagement and fraud. Previous similar studies in Greece and Italy have come up with comparable results. According to the EU's own admission there are at least 12,000 cases each year of fraud against EU funds – in reality the figure is probably much higher. The difficulty in uncovering the true extent of the theft of our money is that most of it takes place not in Brussels itself, but in member countries. Each country is reluctant to admit that its citizens have been stealing EU cash as this would reflect badly on that country and also reduce the amount of EU money going to that country. For the last 12 years the European Court of Auditors has refused to sign off the EU Commission's accounts because it could not be confident as to how more than 60 per cent of the EU's budget had been spent. In some years the amount that could not be reliably traced reached 93 per cent, so every year probably in excess of €70 billion of European taxpayers' money disappears somewhere without anyone being able to say for certain what it has been used for. If any commercial company acted in this way, its directors would go to prison. In the US they would go to prison for a very long time. However, in the EU it seems anything goes.

## THE 'OH LAUGH'

The EU has its own investigative body, OLAF (Office européen de lutte anti-fraude – pronounced 'Oh laugh'), which is charged with investigating and prosecuting the fraudulent use of EU funds. OLAF professes to be the dutiful guardian of our money:

> The European Institutions have a duty to guarantee, with regard to the taxpayer, the best use of their money and in particular to fight as effectively as possible against fraud. In order to intensify this action, the Community Institutions established the European Anti-Fraud Office (known by its French acronym – OLAF) in 1999.[27]

However, OLAF seems to have just two skills – the ability not to investigate anything and, when forced by blatant fraud to actually do something, the tendency to delay and cover up so that nothing ever happens to those who steal hundreds of millions of our hard-earned cash. When senior EU officials were implicated in defrauding us of tens of millions of euros through corruptly awarding security contracts, it took OLAF about four years to investigate and then hand the matter over to the Belgian police, who then did next to nothing.

When officials in the Commission's humanitarian aid office pocketed about € 2.4 million, OLAF helpfully informed the company implicated in the scam that it was intending to raid its offices. This allowed the company's owners time to hide incriminating documents in plastic sacks outside the building's doors. After the predictably fruitless raid, an EU official collected the sacks and they have not been seen since. Three years after OLAF launched an investigation into an Italian businessman suspected of bribing EU officials, he was still being awarded lucrative EU contracts. Meanwhile, most of those involved in the 2003 Eurostat corruption affair, described by investigators as the tip of 'a vast enterprise of looting', were just transferred to other posts within the EU, with their salaries and pensions intact.[28]

Of around 3,000 cases handled by OLAF over six years, just 37 resulted in convictions.[29] In almost all instances those convicted were 'outsiders' – business people who had bribed EU officials or simply stolen large wads of EU money: EU employees who take bribes and steal money are almost never sanctioned. One EU employee who did have his contract cancelled after being implicated in a multi-million-euro fraud was even given a severance grant of over € 100,000. Many other EU employees involved in fraud are never prosecuted because they do not exist: a common administrative scam is to claim salaries and expenses for fictitious employees – what the Eurocrats call 'ghost employees'. Usually, the Eurocrats get away with this as, firstly, nobody checks and, secondly, even if they were found to be defrauding EU funds, nothing would happen to them.

However, while being remarkably forgiving with those who steal immense amounts of our money, the EU has been brutally efficient in dealing with those who have dared to reveal the enormous scale of EU waste and corruption. There was Paul van

Buitenen, widely credited with exposing the top-level corruption that brought down the EU Commission led by Jacques Santer in 1999. Van Buitenen was moved to a minor job in Luxembourg but continued his fight to expose EU corruption. In 2001 he sent Lord Kinnock, the EU commissioner responsible for controlling mismanagement and corruption, a 35-page dossier, backed by 5,000 pages of documents, alleging that many old fraud cases had been abandoned and also exposing new scandals:

> I saw the same people responsible for all these abuses still there in the commission, or even promoted. I read articles saying that Kinnock was pushing through all these reforms, when I knew it was not really happening. So I just had to react.[30]

A year later, van Buitenen resigned, apparently in disappointment at the lack of action.

There was also Marta Andreasen. She was made the EU's Chief Accountant after the Santer scandal. She was reportedly appalled by what she found and was suspended in 2002 when she refused to sign off the accounts because she claimed that a lack of control of the EU's 200,000 accounts in 45 banks worldwide left EU funds 'massively open to fraud'.[31] Following a 28-month suspension on full pay, she was sacked in 2004 for breach of trust and disloyalty. However, she was unrepentant:

> I have acted really in the interests of the public … I do not withdraw the claims that I have made and I am not sorry for the actions that I have taken.[32]

Three years after losing her job, Andreasen's case against the EU for unfair dismissal had still not been heard.

Many of Marta Andreasen's criticisms seemed to be confirmed by Jules Muis, brought in from the World Bank in 2001 to serve as Director General of the EU's internal audit service. He described her as a 'focused and determined professional who was asking the right questions' and stated that he believed her charges of fraud to be 'factually substantive and correct'.[33] This did not prevent Andreasen being fired by Lord Kinnock's office. Muis also characterized the EU's accounting system as 'chronically sordid'.[34]

## GETTING BETTER?

Over the last few years, we have heard much less about waste and corruption in the EU. This is partly because the EU is so closely associated with profligacy and fraud that new revelations are no longer seen as 'news' by much of the media. It is also linked to the fact that EU-friendly media (television, magazines and newspapers) get millions in grants from the EU for propagating positive stories about it and so are often unwilling to bite the hand that feeds them.

Whether the dearth of corruption stories is also due to the EU actually cleaning up its act is less clear. In 2006, Jules Muis wrote in evidence to the House of Lords about why the EU accounts had not been signed off for the previous 11 years:

> feeble leadership ... reactionary defensive management ... feeble checks and balances ... sordid lack of leadership ... too much muddling through ... unnecessary denial for too long ... too much posturing ... a pretty dysfunctional Audit Progress Committee.[35]

The EU constantly claims that it has made huge advances in improving its financial management. However, when Muis was asked by the Lords whether the EU accounts now met 'good contemporary standards', he replied:

> I will answer through the silence of others. The Accountant so far has never signed off on the system. The internal auditors of the Directorates General have never signed off for

the adequacy of the systems as a whole. The Chief Internal Auditor has never signed off the accounts as a whole. The Audit Progress Committee, the Audit Committee itself, has exempted itself from responsibility for the accounts. You are asking me whether I would substitute for the wisdom of all these people who have gone for the exits so far; and I will not do that. I will follow their wise advice. At this moment there is simply no basis to give positive assurance on your question.[36]

The bottom line for us taxpayers is that most of the money we pay into the EU is being either wasted or stolen. Our MEPs will not do anything because they all have comfortable, well-rewarded seats on the gravy train and most also have their snouts deep in the euro-trough. As for our MPs, even though they are fully aware of what is happening, they have shown time and again that they do not have the *cojones* to do anything about the full-scale recidivist plundering of the billions of our money that they give to Europe. Anyway, many of them are probably looking forward to the day that their bosses will reward their years of loyal service with a lucrative sinecure in Brussels.

There was a time when we could hit back in a very limited way against members of the rapacious euro-elite by voting against their plans to increase their own power over us. However, to avoid the inconvenience of asking for our approval, they have now decided to move ahead with the creation of their European superstate without consulting us any further. By doing this they have written themselves an almost unlimited number of blank cheques with our signatures on them so they can continue to spend, waste and steal our money as they wish without any proper accountability or control.

# CHAPTER 16

# NO WAY BACK?

## FROM SPEND TO SPIN

In 1997, Blair and his ministers probably genuinely believed that they could make major improvements in our public services by increasing public-sector investment and modernizing management methods. However, Blair was a lawyer with no real managerial experience. Moreover, very few of his ministers had ever held a job outside the narrow world of politics. To assist them, the Government brought in an army of advisers, self-proclaimed experts and private-sector consultants all eager to encourage naive ministers' grand visions of 'transforming public services' in return for being given huge power and vast amounts of our money. Under the spell of their new management gurus, New Labour ministers unleashed a flood of initiatives, a blizzard of targets and a tsunami of our money to turn their good intentions into reality. However, when public services such as the NHS and schools proved more difficult to change than the Government had at first imagined, our leaders were unable to admit openly to us that there were problems and that some reforms would take longer than expected. Instead, they increasingly fell back on spin and PR in order to claim results that were not actually there. Eventually, ministers found it was much easier just to spend and spin rather than actually do the tougher job of bringing about real improvements in public services.

This abdication of responsibility by the Government has led to a decade of abject mismanagement – the numbers of unnecessary deaths in our hospitals have soared; our poorly equipped and inadequately supported soldiers are being killed and maimed; private-sector pensions have been decimated; our police hide behind their paperwork in their fortress-like HQs; our schools flip-flop aimlessly from one fashionable initiative to another; the ranks of the unemployable and economically inactive swell by the day; the EU has become a thieves' paradise; and our politicians stuff their pockets with our money while doing little to nothing for those they are supposed to represent. This Government has squandered not only more than £1 trillion of our money, but also a once-in-a-lifetime opportunity to use the benefits of a decade of economic prosperity to invest in bringing about radical change in public services. So far we have not really begun to feel the results of this historic waste of our money. However, as economic growth slows, as we have to pay for PFI projects and as the public-sector pensions bomb hits us, there will probably be real reductions in the money available for frontline public services and we will face years of punitively higher taxes accompanied by exceedingly painful service cutbacks.

## THE DEATH OF DEMOCRACY

While the waste of so much money is disappointing, we are a rich country and can afford this profligacy. Potentially more harmful than squandering so much money is the way this Government has transferred power away from elected politicians to an unelected and largely unaccountable administrative elite. The ever-growing armies of bureaucrats, quangocrats, Eurocrats and Olympocrats have awarded themselves massive salaries and pensions as they increasingly expand their empires, safe in the knowledge that mistakes are never admitted, incompetence is never punished, dishonesty is always covered up and once you have joined the club of the new power elite, you will always be well looked after thanks to its unlimited access to our money and its obsession with protecting its own members.

We consumers have partied our way through the last ten years on borrowed money. We have been distracted by our new gadgets – the internet, iPods, digital widescreen televisions, snazzy all-singing all-dancing mobile phones. We have vegetated in front of worthless, dumbed-down reality shows and started to believe that the highest pinnacle of human achievement is to become a celebrity regardless of skill, talent or hard work. And while we have indulged ourselves, we have allowed a political coup where democracy has been usurped by bureaucracy. When our leaders sign up to the EU Constitution-by-another-name, that coup will be complete. Then politics and politicians will have become just an expensive but meaningless sideshow, a verbose and occasionally entertaining talking-shop, because all the key decisions over our lives will be made in administrative offices by the ever-increasing multitude of ever more highly paid public-sectorcrats. Moreover, because there is no longer any account-ability or control, this new elite will be free to tax us as much as it likes while spending, wasting and stealing our money without any need to fear any adverse consequences from its mismanagement, bungling and thieving. All in all, this is a pretty sad epitaph to the hopes we once all had in 1997.

## MANAGEMENT – LESSON I

The classic dilemma in managing any large organization is how to achieve the right balance between centralized control and decentralized decision-making. Centralized control has the advantage of ensuring that chosen policies are carried out consistently, while decentralization allows organizations the flexibility to react to local conditions and to adapt their products and services to local needs. If you are running a worldwide chain of completely standardized burger restaurants, car factories or supermarkets, then you will need a highly centralized control system with clear targets and goals to provide the same service and quality levels in all your many locations. However, if you are managing a complex organization, like a health service or the police, delivering a wide variety of services to many different sections of the population, you should be aiming at a more subtle combination of centrally-defined overall goals, balanced by the freedom to adapt to changing local needs. As the Soviet Union and all other similar centrally-controlled economies have found, when you try to run a complex structure using simplistic, inflexible targets, things never turn out as intended and then the bureaucrats at all levels cook up whatever fantasy figures are necessary to prove that all is well in the best of all possible worlds. The key to successfully leading a complex, decentralized organization is not in imposing clever initiatives and heaps of targets, but rather in creating a consistent managerial culture that encourages the promotion of the most competent, rather than of the most compliant, and rewards people for putting the organization's clients before their own personal short-term interests. Very few large organizations achieve this.

This Government has approached reforming the public sector with the fundamental misconception that only a small clique of insiders knows what is best for our public services and that anyone who disagrees with this group either does not understand the 'vision' or else is 'resistant to change'. Ministers have been encouraged in this fallacy by their business 'friends', advisers and computer systems suppliers whose goal has been to maximize their profits from a credulous New Labour's supposed 'transformation' of public services. This has meant that change has mostly been driven by setting rigid, centrally-decided targets, constructing huge inflexible computer systems and bringing in the supposed magic of private-sector management skills through around £180 billion worth of PFI schemes. This centralizing approach has not delivered the intended improvements.

Instead, it has only led to a massive gulf between ordinary people and the ruling bureaucratic elite, and reinforced an administrative culture where almost unbelievable levels of poor decision-making, failing grandiose projects, serial inefficiency and almost criminal waste are covered up by the constant creation of 'good news'.

## FIGHTING BACK?

In its managerial naivety and impatience to cause change, New Labour has created a myopic, lumbering, bureaucratic monster which is feeding a vast army of self-serving parasites. Moreover, by politicizing public services, the Government has replaced a public service ethos with a 'fill-your-boots' culture which looks after its own and is indifferent to, and even contemptuous of, those it is meant to serve. If New Labour was running a private-sector organization, then the whole enterprise would have long since collapsed into bankruptcy, abandoned by its customers and destroyed by its own financial mismanagement. However, most of us are captive customers of this Government's experiment in increasing taxes to fund its failing, centrally controlled public-sector reforms – only a few hundred thousand people each year can pack their bags and move abroad to avoid the effects of this Government's mistakes.

It is theoretically possible to halt this Government's disastrous and wasteful bureaucratization of Britain, but this would require a strong leader with at least some basic understanding of organizational behaviour and managerial practice. There are a number of actions that need to be taken to reverse the flow of power to the new profligate, rapacious, bureaucratic elites:

### Restoring a public-sector service ethos
It is now clear that the Government's experiment in hugely increasing managerial salaries in the public sector supposedly

in order to bring in higher quality people from the private sector has failed. Instead of leading to improved services, it has just contributed to the creation of a new pampered, self-serving bureaucratic elite, many members of which could never get jobs in the private sector anyway. We need to reverse this trend by limiting public-sector managerial salaries and reducing administration costs. People should be attracted to working in the public sector because they want to make a contribution to the lives of others, rather than because they see the public sector as an easy way to earn a large salary and get a generous pension. The Government should impose a three-year hiring freeze on administrative positions in the public sector, a four-year salary freeze on all public-sector managerial staff earning between £50,000 and £80,000 and a five-year salary freeze on public-sector managers earning over £80,000.

## Limiting public-sector pensions

We need to reduce the burden on taxpayers from the exponential increase in the cost of providing public-sector pensions. It is morally unacceptable that we will be seeing cuts in public services for the needy to pay for the pensions of the UK's wealthiest pensioners. The Government should aim to make the pensions of all public-sector employees earning over £50,000 self-financing. This could be done by imposing a special pensions tax of say an additional 20 per cent (above the current 40 per cent income tax level) on all public-sector earnings over £50,000, and paying the tax revenues into a fund to be invested in Government securities and used to pay the pensions of higher-paid public-sector managers and quangocrats.

Public-sector managers would certainly protest against the two proposals above – but were most public-sector managers and quangocrats earning over £50,000 a year to go on strike, it is not certain this would cause any major disruption to our lives.

## Lighting the bonfire

The Government must halt the spread of unaccountable and wasteful quangos. It should completely scrap at least 100 quangos and free up their employees to find more productive and fulfilling jobs elsewhere rather than just hiding them somewhere else. In addition, the Government should reduce the budgets of all remaining administrative and regulatory quangos by 5 per cent a year for the next six years. This would give quangos time to reorganize so that they only deliver the services that are absolutely necessary rather than indulging in a vast range of wasteful activities, which are not essential and which are often undertaken simply to justify their own existence and expanding budgets.

## Restoring accountability

The Government needs to rebuild the discredited National Audit Office (NAO) under competent, independent management to do the job that it is paid to do. All new heads of the new NAO should be hired from the private sector so that they are actually motivated to reduce public spending and do not have loyalties to protect other public-sector department bosses, colleagues and friends. NAO top bosses should never be allowed to serve for more than five years to avoid their becoming too close to the people whose spending they are supposed to be controlling. Moreover, there should be a contractual obligation on all public-sector department heads that their departments implement and prove they have implemented within a reasonable time all the recommendations made by the NAO and Public Accounts Committee. Failure to implement these recommendations should lead to disciplinary action, and repeated failure should result in dismissal without severance pay. However, the best people to ensure that public-sector managers do not waste our money are frontline workers. The Government should introduce a whistleblowers' act which guarantees to pay frontline public-sector workers a percentage (say 5 per cent) of any savings achieved if they report examples of waste to a reorganized, effective NAO. Accompanying this should be disciplinary action, including dismissal without severance pay, against any public-sector managers shown to have repeatedly wasted public money. The Government can use the US's False Claims Act as a model for this new legislation.[1]

### Scrapping a few white elephants

The Government should call a halt to some of the most conspicuous examples of waste. The £5 billion plus ID Cards programme should be abandoned – the technology doesn't work and rather than reducing identity fraud, it will actually make it easier for anybody who manages to overcome the system's security. If, in a few years, another country successfully develops an effective identity cards system, then the UK could adopt that system at a much lower cost than if the UK tries to develop its own system.

The NHS computer system project should be stopped immediately, its proposed centralized database of our medical records should be dropped, the project's management replaced and the NHS's IT systems budget reduced to, say, £3 billion. The new management should then come up with proposals as to how this £3 billion can best be used for the benefit of patients rather than bureaucrats and computer companies.

All work on the 2012 Olympics should be halted, the organizations managing the Games disbanded and the Games handed back to the IOC because it is now clear that a mixture of incompetence, arrogance and greed from those bringing us the Games means that the UK cannot stage the Games at a justifiable cost. Hopefully, the Games can then be held in Athens both in 2012 and in the future. Even if we have to pay the IOC a few billion in compensation, this will still save taxpayers in the UK at least £10 billion and many tens of billions more for taxpayers in other countries whose governments will no longer be able to squander their money on the increasingly worthless Olympic dream.

## Reducing the cost of politicians

The UK has 646 MPs in Westminster, 129 MSPs, 60 Welsh Assembly members, 108 Members of the Legislative Assembly in Northern Ireland (MLAs) and 78 MEPs – 1,021 politicians to represent the interests of less than 70 million people. This gives us one politician for about every 68,000 citizens. There are also hundreds more politicians in the House of Lords and thousands upon thousands in local government. In the US, with 435 Members of Congress, there is a Member of Congress for every 680,000 citizens. There is no reason why we should not at least halve the number of UK-based politicians (MPs, MSPs, members of the Welsh Assembly and MLAs) to reflect the continuing and accelerating transfer of political power to the EU. This would save many hundreds of millions every year in reduced salaries, expenses and administration costs.

## Returning power to the people

Before this Government came to power, there was a clear ideological difference between the main UK political parties. So there was a real choice for the electorate at elections. Now that the three main parties all have very similar ideologies and policies, the electorate has virtually no power to influence the way it is governed. While we should still retain general elections, the only way to truly restore some form of democracy is to make increased use of referendums on key legislative proposals, so that we move towards voting more on policies than on parties – ID Cards, the EU Constitution-by-another-name, deciding the right level of immigration, halving the number of politicians, abandoning the 2012 Olympics, making the pensions of public-sector managers self-financing – all these would make quite suitable subjects for national referendums. Though, as the gulf between Britain's ruling elite and its ordinary citizens grows ever wider, our leaders are likely to find an increasing divergence between the views of ordinary people and the financial interests of the politicians and bureaucrats who rule us.

## Calling a halt to the EU rip-off

The Government should refuse to make any more contributions to the EU budget until independent British auditors have given a clean bill of health to both the EU accounts and the processes by which EU money is spent. Moreover, the UK should make it a condition of our continued payments that all cases of fraud are prosecuted, and EU employees found guilty of fraud should be fired without severance pay and should also lose all their pension rights. Any EU official or politician obstructing a fraud investigation should also be thrown out without severance pay. Those countries which profit most from EU waste and fraud would protest most loudly. On the other hand, such a decisive political stand would also gain support from those countries which each year see their billions being squandered and stolen. It is time to clean out the EU's Augean Stables and UK politicians should show some backbone by taking a lead in starting the process.

However, such actions would require the political/bureaucratic establishment putting the well-being of ordinary people above its own narrow, self-serving interests. Unfortunately, this does seem somewhat unlikely.

# NOTES TO CHAPTERS

## 2  THE NHS CAN DAMAGE YOUR HEALTH

1  Patient Safety Report, NHS website, 2007
2  Calculation done by the author comparing mortality rates in the UK with those in other EU countries
3  British Medical Journal 327:1129
4  Office for National Statistics
5  *Daily Mail*, 22 February 2007
6  Press Association, 22 February 2007
7  Figures from the Office for National Statistics
8  *Daily Mail*, 22 February 2007
9  BBC News, 6 May 2004
10  *The Times*, 10 December 2004
11  *The Times*, 10 December 2004
12  Anna Walker, Chief Executive, Healthcare Commission
13  *Annual Report and Accounts 2006–07*, Monitor
14  *NPSA, Annual Report and Accounts 2006–7*
15  Public Accounts Commission, 2006 Session
16  BBC News website, 5 July 2006
17  Labour Party manifesto, 1997 General Election
18  Queen's Speech transcript, October 2007
19  *Daily Telegraph*, 24 April 2007
20  *The Times*, 7 August 2006
21  Email to Amanda Steane, 2007
22  Email to Amanda Steane, 2007
23  *The Times*, 26 December 2007
24  *Daily Telegraph*, 5 January 2008
25  Email to Amanda Steane, 2007

26 *The Times*, 1 May 2007

27 *Daily Telegraph*, 9 February 2007

28 *Daily Telegraph*, 9 February 2007

29 *Accountancy Age*, 29 September 2006

30 *The Times*, 8 June 2006

31 *Daily Mail*, 20 October 2007

32 *Daily Telegraph*, 2 February 2007

33 *The Times*, 17 February 2007

34 *Daily Telegraph*, 13 July 2007

35 *Daily Telegraph*, 12 October 2007

36 See *Plundering the Public Sector,* David Craig with Richard Brooks, Constable (London), pp. 183–226, for a fuller account of this catastrophe

37 *EHInsider*, November 2007

38 House of Lords Committee on Science and Technology, 13 March 2003

39 Healthcare Computing conference, Harrogate, March 2003

40 Public Accounts Committee meeting, 26 June 2006

41 Channel 4 News, 3 May 2006

42 *Plundering the Public Sector*, pp. 183–226

43 www.silicon.com, 30 October 2006

44 *The Times*, 19 February 2007

## 3  LAW AND DISORDER

1 *Home Affairs Committee Report*, 2007, pp. 6–7

2 Home Affairs Committee Oral Evidence, Question 5

3 *Home Affairs Committee Report*, 2007, p. 8

4 Home Affairs Committee Oral Evidence, Question 10

5 Home Affairs Committee Oral Evidence, Question 10

6 Government News Network, 25 January 2007

7 Letter from the PM to John Reid, 15 May 2006

8 Government News Network, 25 January 2007

9 *Daily Telegraph*, 26 August 2007

10 Home Office Press Office, 26 January 2006

11 Ibid.

12 *Independent*, 28 November 2007

13 *Home Affairs Committee Report*, 2007, p. 14

14 *Ten Years of Criminal Justice under Labour*, Centre for Crime and Justice Studies, King's College London, 2007, p. 32

15 *Sunday Times*, 26 December 2006

16 *BCS 2006/7*, Table 2.10
17 *Sunday Times*, 19 August 2007
18 *Daily Mail*, 2 August 2007
19 Tony McNulty, Home Affairs Committee Oral Evidence, Question 75
20 *Daily Mail*, 1 October 2007
21 *Daily Mail*, 19 August 2007
22 Home Office press release, 27 March 2007
23 Home Affairs Committee Oral Evidence, Question 47
24 Home Affairs Committee Oral Evidence, Question 49
25 Home Affairs Committee Oral Evidence, Question 52
26 *Ten years of criminal justice under Labour*, p. 23
27 *Home Affairs Committee Report*, 2007, p. 12
28 Home Office study, 1999, www.crimeinfo.org.uk
29 *Daily Mail*, 17 August 2007
30 *The Times*, 14 August 2007
31 Home Office submission to HAC funding enquiry, 2007
32 *Daily Telegraph*, 2 April 2007
33 *Daily Telegraph*, 2 April 2007
34 Home Affairs Committee Oral Evidence, Question 9
35 Home Affairs Committee Oral Evidence, Question 47
36 *Home Affairs Committee Report*, 2007, p. 8
37 *Delivering a Step Change in Police Productivity*, HM Treasury, 2006, pp. 1–2
38 *Sunday Times*, 26 August 2007
39 *Daily Telegraph*, 2 April 2007
40 Home Affairs Committee Oral Evidence, Question 36

## 4  A MILITARY DISASTER

1 *Sunday Times*, 18 November 2007
2 *MoD Annual Report and Accounts 2006–7*, p. 23
3 *The Times*, 13 August 2007
4 Defence Communications Strategy, 27 February 2007
5 MoD Prnewswire, 19 June 1997
6 HM Treasury PFI Projects database, September 2007
7 *Metro*, 7 January 2007
8 BBC News website, 1 August 2007
9 *Metro*, 7 January 2007
10 www.ogc.gov.uk/news, 5 April 2006
11 BBC News website, 1 August 2007

12 *PAC MoD Major Projects Report*, 2004–5

13 Press Association, 24 November 2006

14 *PAC MoD Major Projects Report*, January 2007, Uncorrected Oral Evidence, Questions 77–8

15 *The Times*, 29 November 2007

16 Press Association, 24 November 2006

17 *Lions, Donkeys and Dinosaurs*, Lewis Page, Heinneman (London), 2006

18 *Plundering the Public Sector,* p. 63

19 *PAC MoD Major Projects Report*, January 2007, Uncorrected Oral Evidence, Question 6

20 Press Association, 30 November 2007

21 MoD Prnewswire, 19 June 1997

22 *MoD Annual Report and Accounts 2006–7*, p. 204

23 *MoD Annual Report and Accounts 2006–7*, p. 208

24 *Lions, Donkeys and Dinosaurs*, Chapter 9

25 *MoD Annual Report and Accounts 2006–7*, p. 14

26 *Lions, Donkeys and Dinosaurs*, p. 228

27 Quoted in *Better Government* by the Taxpayers' Alliance, January 2007

28 *Sunday Times*, 18 November 2007

29 *Plundering the Public Sector*, pp. 61–62

30 *Daily Telegraph*, 20 July 2007

31 *Independent*, 15 September 2007

32 *Daily Telegraph*, 8 October 2006

33 *Daily Telegraph*, 18 June 2007

34 *Herald*, 1 August 2007

35 *Cost Effective Defence*, Lewis Page, Economic Research Council, p. 32

36 *The Times*, 21 August 2007

37 *The Times*, 24 November 2007

38 Defence Communications Strategy, 27 February 2007

39 *Daily Telegraph*, 17 November 2007

# 5  EDUCATION AND IGNORANCE

1 Labour Party manifesto, General Election, 1997

2 *The Times*, 5 September 2007

3 *The Times*, 5 September 2007

4 *Daily Telegraph*, 17 August 2007

5 *The Times*, 16 August 2007

6 *Daily Telegraph*, 16 August 2007

7  *The Times*, 17 August 2007

8  *Independent*, 29 November 2007

9  *Daily Telegraph*, 11 October 2007

10  *Daily Mail*, 31 August 2007

11  *Department for Education and Skills, Department Report*, 2007

12  *Daily Mail*, 12 August 2007

13  *Daily Telegraph*, 10 November 2007

14  *Daily Telegraph*, 23 August 2007

15  *Daily Telegraph*, 6 August 2007

16  *The Times*, 29 August 2007

17  *The Times*, 27 August 2007

18  *Daily Telegraph*, 8 October 2007

19  *Department for Education and Skills, Department Report*, 2007

20  Budget Speech, July 1997

21  *Welfare isn't Working*, Reform, May 2007

22  *Department for Education and Skills, Department Report*, 2007

23  *Daily Telegraph*, 11 April 2007

24  *Department for Education and Skills, Department Report*, 2007

## 6  THE HOME OFFICE – HOUSE OF HORROR

1  Home Office website, 2007

2  'Capability Review of the Home Office'

3  Home Affairs Committee, Q 866, 23 May 2006

4  Public Accounts Committee, Home Office Resource Accounts, Questions
   50–8

5  PAC Home Office Resource Accounts, 2004–5, Questions 84–5

6  PAC Home Office Resource Accounts, 2004–5, Questions 86–8

7  *The Times*, 21 July 2006

8  The level of failed applications was based on a theoretical figure which was
   deliberately lowered to allow the IND to achieve the tipping point

9  *Returning failed asylum applicants*, Home Affairs Committee, p. 3

10  *Home Office Statistical Bulletin*, 22 May 2007

11  *The Times*, 17 May 2006

12  www.migrationwatchuk.org, briefing papers

13  *Daily Mail*, 6 January 2008

14  *Daily Mail*, 30 October 2007

15  *Daily Mail*, 21 August 2007

16  *Guardian*, 10 September 2007

17 'Staff in Post' reports, Probation Service, 2000–7
18 'New Labour because Britain deserves better', General Election manifesto, 1997
19 *Home Office Targets Autumn Performance Report*, 2006
20 *Strengthening powers to tackle anti-social behaviour*, Home Office, p. 19
21 'The war on youth', *New Statesman*, 16 October 2006
22 Home Office Offender Management Caseload Statistics, 2007
23 NOMS website, 2007
24 *Hansard*, House of Commons written answers, 9 January 2007
25 *Home Office Research Study 208*
26 *Strategy Unit Drugs Report*, Prime Minister's Strategy Unit, 2003
27 PAC Home Office Resource Accounts 2004–5, Question 21
28 *Plundering the Public Sector*, pp. 194–5

# 7  TAX BECOMES MORE TAXING

1 *The Blue Book*, ASHE and the Adam Smith Institute, 2007 edition
2 Adam Smith Institute website
3 *Daily Mail*, 20 November 2006
4 *The Times*, 26 February 2007
5 HMRC Corporation Tax, 2007
6 *Financial Times*, 11 October 2006
7 Department for Education and Skills
8 Student Loans Company

# 8  THE GREAT PENSIONS ROBBERY

1 *Daily Telegraph*, 22 January 2006, 28 January 2007 and 10 August 2007
2 *Daily Mail*, 3 November 2006
3 Figures based on 'Public sector pensions', Scrutiny Unit Briefing Note, May 2007
4 Cabinet Office Civil Superannuation Resource Accounts and *Daily Telegraph*, 28 February 2007
5 'Contributions to private pension schemes', Office for National Statistics
6 *ABCmoney*, 18 August 2007
7 *Sunday Telegraph*, 3 September 2006
8 *Sunday Times*, 2 December 2007

9 *Interactive Investor*, 8 November 2004
10 *Daily Express*, 8 March 2006
11 Cabinet Office Civil Superannuation Resource Accounts
12 *Plundering the Public Sector*
13 *Daily Mail*, 12 November 2007
14 'Occupational Provision in the Public Sector', Pensions Policy Institute
15 BBC News, 26 September 2007
16 *The Times*, 8 August 2007
17 *Daily Telegraph*, 13 January 2007
18 *Daily Telegraph*, 17 March 2007
19 *Daily Mail*, 30 August 2007
20 *Daily Telegraph*, 17 September 2007
21 *Guardian*, 10 June 2007
22 *Guardian*, 10 June 2007
23 *Daily Telegraph*, 31 March 2007
24 *Scotsman*, 1 April 2007
25 Ibid.
26 *Daily Telegraph*, 31 March 2007
27 Ibid.

## 9  GIVING IT ALL AWAY

1 'Public Expenditure Statistical Analyses 2007', HM Treasury
2 DWP website
3 DWP website
4 *Annual Report and Accounts*, HM Treasury, foreword by the Chancellor
5 *Annual Report and Accounts*, HM Treasury, p. 58
6 Department for Work and Pensions Resource Accounts, 2004–5
7 Department for Work and Pensions Resource Accounts, 2003–4
8 Press Association, 25 July 2007
9 For a fuller description of the chaos, see *Plundering the Public Sector*, pp. 8–11
10 PAC Report, Oral Evidence, 23 October 2006, Question 108
11 *Daily Mail*, 21 November 2007
12 For a fuller description, see *Plundering the Public Sector*, pp. 6–7
13 *Daily Mail*, 25 July 2006
14 *Sunday Times*, 2 December 2007
15 *Dealing with the complexity of the benefit system*, National Audit Office, p. 11
16 Press Association, 3 December 2007
17 DWP website

18  Office for National Statistics Time Series data

19  *A New Deal for Welfare*, Department for Work and Pensions, January 2006

20  *Helping people from workless households into work*, National Audit Office, p. 24

21  *Sunday Times*, 15 July 2007

22  *Helping people from workless households into work*, National Audit Office, p. 13

23  Ibid p. 12

24  *Daily Telegraph*, 20 August 2007

25  *Helping people from workless households into work*, National Audit Office, p. 20

26  Ibid p. 41

27  *Daily Mail*, 1 August 2007

28  *Helping people from workless households into work*, National Audit Office, p. 21

29  *Welfare isn't Working*, Reform, May 2007

30  *HM Treasury Annual Report and Accounts 2006–7*, p. 57

31  BBC News, 27 March 2007

32  *Chicken and Egg: Child Poverty and Educational Inequalities* by Donald Hirsch, Child Poverty Action Group (London), 2007

33  BBC News, 27 March 2007

34  *HM Treasury Annual Report and Accounts 2006–7*, p. 57

35  BBC News, 27 March 2007

36  BBC News, 21 March 2007

37  *Sunday Times*, 26 August 2007

38  Institute for Fiscal Studies, quoted on www.cpag.org, 12 September 2007

39  Department for Work and Pensions, quoted on www.cpag.org, 13 September 2007

40  *HM Treasury Annual Report and Accounts 2006–7*, p. 58

41  DWP website

42  'Income Related Benefits Estimates of Take-up', DWP

43  Research for Help the Aged carried out by the Institute for Fiscal Studies, July 2007

44  London School of Economics, November 2007

45  *Tackling pensioner poverty*, PAC, p. 3

46  Help the Aged, 28 November 2007

47  Capital Economics research for the *Daily Telegraph*, 13 August 2007

48  The Age and Employment Network

# 10   A PROFUSION OF PLUNDERING POLITICIANS

1  Scottish Parliament website, FAQs

2  BBC News website, 8 June 2006

3  Scottish Parliament Accounts, 2005–6
4  *Guardian*, 1 July 2003
5  *Guardian*, 13 December 2001
6  *Guardian*, 1 July 2003
7  *Who really governs Britain?*, the Bow Group 2001 and *The Times*, 9 June 2007
8  *The Times*, 19 October 2007
9  *House of Commons Annual Reports*
10  *House of Commons Annual Report 2006–7*, p. 7
11  April 2007 to April 2008, www.civilservice.gov.uk
12  BBC Social Affairs Unit, October 2007
13  *Daily Telegraph*, 21 February 2005
14  *Daily Telegraph*, 13 April 2005
15  www.andrewduffmep.org.uk/news/000162
16  *Personnel Today*, 31 August 2005
17  Transport for London Accounts
18  Greater London Authority 2007

# 11  WELCOME TO QUANGOLAND

1  Parliamentary research paper, 2005
2  BBC Politics, 8 August 1997
3  Speech by the Shadow Chancellor Gordon Brown, 12 January 1995
4  Sixth Report, Select Committee on Public Administration
5  Parliamentary research paper, 2005
6  *The Essential Guide to British Quangos*, Efficiency in Government Unit (London), 2005
7  *Sunday Telegraph*, 19 August 2007
8  *Daily Mail*, 19 August 2007
9  Government list of NDPBs as quoted on www.conservatives.com, 23 August 2007
10  *Scotsman*, 14 January 2006
11  *Scotsman*, 26 September 2007
12  Ibid.
13  *Scotsman*, 29 October 2007
14  Ibid.
15  BBC Politics, 8 August 1997
16  *Guardian*, 16 July 2004
17  Economic Research Council, 2007
18  Economic Research Council, 2007

19 *Millennium Commission Annual Report and Accounts*
20 *The Essential Guide to British Quangos*
21 *The Times*, 3 September 2006
22 Coal Authority website
23 *Coal Authority Annual Reports*
24 *Daily Telegraph*, 24 August 2007
25 Food Standards Agency website
26 *Sunday Times*, 25 November 2007


## 12   REGULATORS WITHOUT REGULATION

1 BBC News, 15 June 2006
2 Ofwat website
3 'Employment and profit margins in UK water companies', PSIRU, 1999
4 Ofwat website
5 *Daily Mail*, 21 June 2006
6 *Guardian*, 5 July 2006
7 *Guardian*, 17 October 2006
8 *Daily Mail*, 29 June 2006
9 'Ofwat – Meeting the demand for water', PAC, Questions 45–9
10 Ibid Questions 45–51
11 Ibid Question 158
12 www.edie.net, 10 May 2007
13 Press Association, 14 November 2007
14 *Guardian*, 14 November 2007
15 Ofgem's website
16 *Ofgem Annual Report, 2001–2*, p. 62
17 Energywatch website
18 *Energywatch Annual Report 2006–7*, p. 6
19 *Evening Standard*, 31 May 2007
20 *Daily Mail*, 11 April 2007
21 www.thisismoney.com, 1 May 2007
22 www.fool.co.uk/news/money-saving-tips
23 *Evening Standard*, 17 May 2007
24 Energywatch, 2 August 2007
25 *Daily Telegraph*, 2 January 2008
26 *Sunday Times*, 13 January 2008
27 Ibid.
28 Contact author for source

29 NAO Resource Accounts
30 For a fuller discussion of the NAO's limitations, see *Plundering the Public Sector*, pp. 71–80
31 *Private Eye*, No. 1198, 23 Nov–6 Dec 2007
32 NAO report on Financial Services Authority, 2007
33 *Daily Mail*, 5 January 2008

# 13   NOT A NATIONAL TREASURE

1 *HM Treasury Annual Report and Accounts 2006–7*, p. 13
2 Ibid p.91
3 Treasury press release, 7 May 1999
4 *The Times*, 15 April 2007
5 Ibid.
6 www.marketoracle.co.uk/Article670.html
7 *The Times*, 15 April 2007
8 Ibid.
9 Ibid.
10 'Review of the sale of part of the UK gold reserves', HM Treasury, paragraph 5.5
11 HM Treasury website
12 *Private Finance, Public Deficits*, Mark Hellowell and Allyson Pollock, Edinburgh University, 2007
13 *Private Eye*, No. 1187
14 *Private Eye*, No. 1196
15 *Private Finance, Public Deficits*
16 *Private Eye*, No. 1185
17 *Guardian*, 10 May 2006
18 *Private Eye*, No. 1170
19 *Plundering the Public Sector*, p. 131
20 *The Business*, 10 October 2007
21 House of Commons Defence Committee, 'Strategic Lift' Session, 2006–7
22 Budget, 2007, p. 3
23 *Guardian*, 25 April 2005
24 Office for National Statistics
25 Ibid.
26 *HM Treasury Annual Report and Accounts*, 2006–7
27 *Independent*, 10 January 2007
28 www.moneyweek.com, 3 January 2007

29 *Independent*, 28 September 2006
30 *The Times*, 17 September 2007
31 *Sunday Times*, 23 September 2007
32 www.bankofengland.co.uk/about/people
33 *Guardian*, 25 September 2007


## 14 OLYMPIC GOLD-DUST

1 www.blairwatch.co.uk
2 *Daily Telegraph*, 17 March 2007
3 *Daily Telegraph*, 20 July 2007
4 *London Paper*, 20 July 2007
5 *The Times*, 20 July 2007
6 *Sunday Times*, 2 December 2007
7 *The budget for the London 2012 Olympics*, National Audit Office report, p. 13
8 Public Accounts Committee report, 2006–7 session
9 *Hansard*, October 2005
10 *Daily Mail*, 20 November 2006
11 *Daily Mail*, 20 November 2006
12 *London Paper*, 20 July 2007
13 Transcript of *Idaho Statesman* interview, October 2006
14 Public Accounts Committee, Uncorrected Oral Evidence, 5 March 2007
15 *Daily Mail*, 20 November 2006
16 *The budget for the London 2012 Olympics*, p. 27
17 *The Times*, 15 January 2008
18 *The budget for the London 2012 Olympics*, p. 27
19 Ibid p. 21
20 *The Times*, 14 November 2007
21 *The Times*, 14 November 2007
22 National Audit Office
23 *The budget for the London 2012 Olympics*, p. 6
24 Press Association, 24 July 2007
25 *The budget for the London 2012 Olympics*, p.25
26 *Daily Mail*, 20 November 2006, and PAC Uncorrected Oral Evidence,
   5 March 2007
27 *The Times*, 27 July 2007
28 *Sunday Times*, 1 July 2007
29 *The budget for the London 2012 Olympics*, p. 34
30 *The Times*, 26 August 2006

31 *The budget for the London 2012 Olympics*, p. 25
32 *Auditor-General Report*, New South Wales, 2002
33 *Daily Telegraph*, 7 September 2007

## 15  THE EUROPEAN RIP-OFF

1 *The Times*, 24 June 2005
2 *The Times*, 11 June 2005 and 24 June 2005
3 Parliament, 9 June 2005
4 *The Times*, 23 May 2005
5 *The Times*, 21 May 2002, and UPI, 7 January 2005
6 *Open Europe* briefing note, Autumn 2005
7 'The UK presidency of the EU', *Open Europe* briefing note, 2005
8 *The Times*, 11 June 2005
9 Speech, 14 July 2005
10 *Daily Telegraph*, 29 October 2005
11 *Independent*, 16 December 2005
12 *The Times*, 11 June 2005
13 *The Times*, 14 December 2005
14 *The Times*, 14 December 2005
15 *Metro*, 7 November 2005, and *Independent*, 9 November 2007
16 *Sunday Times*, 29 July 2007
17 *Sunday Times*, 29 July 2007
18 *The Times*, 14 December 2005
19 *The Times*, 23 June 2006
20 'EU budget/rebate briefing', *Open Europe*, 2005
21 *The Times*, 23 May 2005
22 *The Times*, 22 June 2005
23 *Metro*, 12 December 2005
24 *Financial Times*, 30 June 2005
25 Labour Party Conference, 2005
26 *The Times*, 26 April 2006
27 OLAF website, 2008
28 'City Comment', *Daily Telegraph*, 15 March 2005
29 'File on 4', BBC Radio Four, 2005
30 *Daily Telegraph*, 26 August 2002
31 *Observer*, 31 October 2004
32 Ibid.
33 *Sunday Telegraph*, 20 March 2005, and *Accountancy Age*, 27 November 2003

34 'City Comment', *Daily Telegraph*, 15 March 2005
35 Minutes of Evidence, 18 July 2006
36 House of Lords Examination of Witness, 18 July 2006

## 16   NO WAY BACK?

1 *Plundering the Public Sector*, pp. 243–4